The
Enneagram
and
Spiritual
Direction

The Enneagram and Spiritual Direction

Nine Paths to Spiritual Guidance

JAMES EMPEREUR

continuum
NEW YORK • LONDON

2007

The Continuum International Publishing Group Inc
80 Maiden Lane, New York, NY 10038

Copyright © 1997 by James Empereur

Printed in Great Britain by Biddles Ltd, King's Lynn, Norfolk

---

Library of Congress Cataloging-in-Publication Data

Empereur, James L.
   The enneagram and spiritual direction : nine paths to spiritual
guidance / James Empereur.
     p.   cm.
   ISBN 0-8264-1059-6
   1. Spiritual direction. 2. Enneagram. 3. Empereur, James L.
I. Title.
BV5053.E47 1997
253.5′3–dc21   97–26193

With Gratitude to
Mario De Paoli, M.D.

Contents

Introduction

The subject of this book is the use of the enneagram in the ministry of Christian spiritual direction. Its primary audience is those engaged in spiritual direction as directors and as directees. Its wider audience is those Christians who pursue the spiritual life with some distinct intentionality and who, knowing the system of the enneagram, wish to enhance their spiritual lives through that system. An even wider audience includes those, Christian or not, who wish to deepen their spiritual lives and their knowledge of the enneagram.

This is not an introduction to the enneagram. In my view, there is no need for such a book, given the published material that is now available. Books that could be used for introductory purposes are noted in chapter 1. There is also a bibliography of selected books for those with particular interests in the enneagram system. Those searching the market for new books on the enneagram are seeking publications that will deepen their use of the enneagram in some way. This is certainly true regarding the area of spirituality, but it is equally true of business, psychology, and research. Indeed, it seems that authors now are vying to give their own distinct approach to the enneagram.

This is not an introduction to spiritual direction. Again, there is now a wealth of material available for that purpose. Chapter 2 discusses some of this material. For those who are in need of understanding what spiritual direction is, what its history is, how it has functioned in the past, and what its general contours are, there is much that can be recommended. But as in the case of the enneagram, what is needed in the area of spiritual direction are studies that are noted for their specificity and depth. This desire is understandable since in the past there was considerable repetition among the authors. Like the enneagram, spiritual direction is an old and living tradition. Both in the past were primarily oral. Now we use the printed word and other forms of modern communication to pass along a tradition. This makes the knowledge of the enneagram and spiritual direction more universally available, but it also challenges the communicators to move to various levels of profundity in their work. The foundational studies have already been done.

However, those who do spiritual work with others, whether in the Christian tradition or not, will find in this volume, hopefully, much that will be of interest to them. It should serve as a way of expanding their horizons in an area where they are already functioning.

Finally, it will become evident to the reader early in the book that the subject matter is not confined to the narrow limits of a specific form of spiritual direction, but that there is much about spirituality here. I deal with the issue of the meaning of spirituality in chapter 2 and point to some areas that need reflection at this time. Even those who have relatively little acquaintance with the enneagram can find help from examining the variety of spiritualities that are at least implied in the application of the nine spaces of the enneagram to spiritual direction.

Chapter 1 presents the state of enneagram studies today. It reviews some of the pertinent literature and is thus a synthetic view of what has been achieved up to this time. It also contains some particular qualifications I wish to make that may be departures from some of the better known studies. Chapter 2 does basically the same thing for spiritual direction. It reviews some of the published material in the hope of communicating a bird's eye view of the phenomenon. It also contains some of my presuppositions regarding the practice of spiritual direction and spirituality in general. The nine remaining chapters deal with the nine enneagram points, detailing some of the issues that can arise in spiritual direction and how they might be addressed, this being done in terms of some of the stages of human growth.

One problem today's writer on the enneagram must confront has to do with proper attribution. When I began my enneagram work with Bob Ochs, S.J., in the early 1970s, there was no published material. There were some class notes reproduced in many forms, collated by others, added to by many, which made for a true hodgepodge of materials. I suspect that one of the reasons some of the students of the enneagram moved to publication was to clean up the mess of notes of divergent reliability. When copyrighted material began to appear, attribution became an issue.

Recently, this matter has been raised in the public forum and in fact has even reached the courts. Hopefully, the matter is now resolved, but this has made authors careful about attribution. As should be obvious from the previous remarks, proper attribution is not easy. First, we are dealing with an oral tradition. Then we have claims made by some of the early enneagram people about origins of the material that are probably impossible to substantiate. The early articulations of the system were not copyrighted. What belongs to whom is not easy to determine. And, perhaps, most of the central insights and thrusts of the system belong to no one, at least, no one living.

This is not to deny that there are those who have made distinctive contributions to the enneagram. I will be acknowledging my own debt to Helen Palmer in the course of the pages that follow. I try to indicate where I think other authors have made an original contribution. Like so many others in enneagram work, I have profited from the work of Don Riso, Patrick O'Leary, Maria Beesing, Richard Rohr, Suzanne Zuercher, and others. I acknowledge my own dependence on their writings, although it is not always easy to say what in their writings is distinctly their own. I have attempted to find a balance in giving proper attribution. Where I have failed, I will surely rectify the situation when it is called to my attention.

In some instances full attribution would not be appropriate, as in the case of Mario De Paoli, to whom this book is dedicated. It will become clear that, like Helen Palmer, Elizabeth Liebert has played an important part in the shaping of this book. A special note of thanks to Mike Moyhanan, S.J., for his usual creative suggestions for a title for this book. I want to thank Shane Martin, S.J., Maurice Monette, and Arturo Pérez for the reflections they gave me during the course of writing this book. And I wish to thank in a special way all the enneagram students I have had for many years.

Chapter 1

The Value of the Enneagram in Spiritual Growth

The Importance of the Enneagram Today

The enneagram, a system of human development that is based on nine personality types, has achieved such public recognition and acceptance in some of the helping professions that its value in several different areas is now established. This is true although as of yet there is no complete scientific grounding for the system. The nine spaces of the enneagram correlate well with the personality categories used by the psychological professions,[1] but there is still much regarding the enneagram that seems to be a matter more of art than of science. Even the origin of the system is obscure. When I first learned the system from one of its earliest promoters, Robert Ochs, S.J., it was taken for granted that the enneagram was of Sufi origin.[2] There was a later qualification that it arose more from an occultist setting. In recent years conflicts over the ownership of the enneagram, and especially claims made by Oscar Ichazo, have muddied the waters concerning the true origin of the system.[3]

But the value of the system does not depend on its origin. The source of the enneagram is people's experience, and it has proven itself through self-verification. We have the testimony of those who have now worked with the system for several years; we have the witness of those who have found that the enneagram helped them to clarify their lives, their relationships with others, and their religious faith. This verification has been strengthened by the various ways in which the enneagram has been appropriated by the different, but recognized, fields of learning. This journey of gradual acceptance reached a high point at the First International Enneagram Conference at Stanford University in California in August 1994.

The Stanford Conference brought together the leading contributors to and writers about the system. It was a kind of "ecumenical" gathering since there were enneagram teachers of differing points of view, some of them not easily reconcilable. Present were most of the names with which students of the enneagram are quite familiar, such as Helen Palmer, Claudio Naranjo (via video), Ted Dobson, Kathy Hurley, Andreas Ebert, Patrick O'Leary, Don Riso, Richard Rohr, and many others. Then there were the larger number of presenters who were less well known but who often made substantial and quite creative contributions. A listing of the tracks will give a sense of the comprehensiveness of this conference: Assessment/Research/History; Business; Education; Experiential Practices; Spirituality; and Therapy/Medicine. Daily meditations kept a very important aspect of the system in focus, that is, its spiritual dimension. Surely, the enneagram has come of age, and now it is a matter of finding ways to give a larger audience access to it as well as deepening our understanding of it so that we can go beyond the mechanics of the system itself.

Such deepening is the great challenge that lies ahead of the system. Can it be removed from the superficial treatment it has received from so many who have turned it into a parlor game or who feel qualified to give workshops on it after having done only a workshop or two themselves? My own belief is that if the enneagram remains primarily a tool used by business and the secular helping professions, which will treat it only as one of many personality typing approaches, it will level off at some kind of general acceptance that will not plumb the depths of the system and will thus not give it a central place in human development. For this reason I believe that the enneagram must stay in contact with the best of the religious traditions today, especially those traditions that honor the practice of spiritual guidance.

Enneagram Literature

It would be impossible to do an evaluation of all that has now been published on the enneagram. Nor is that the intention of this section. Here it is important to note those authors whose work is helpful for an application of the system to the practice of spiritual direction. When I began my journey with the enneagram, there were, as noted earlier, no published books available. There were handwritten and typed notes of various kinds, many of which had their origin with Robert Ochs, S.J. But once Ochs passed the system among many Jesuit communities, books began to appear such as *The Enneagram: A Journey of Self Discovery.*[4]

As will become increasingly clear, I have found the work of Helen Palmer the most helpful in relating the enneagram to spiritual direction. Her first book, *The Enneagram,* and her more recent one, *The Enneagram in Love and Work,*[5] are recognized as among the very best of the published materials. Palmer has found the system a useful device for developing her theory of attentional styles and the practice of intuition. My own work with Palmer in regard to the enneagram has been helpful, but my work with her in the areas of intuitive training has been invaluable for integrating the enneagram in the practice of spiritual direction. Her workshops on intuitive training have been very significant for my own work in spiritual direction.

I am indebted to all the authors on the enneagram in some way. The work of Richard Rohr and Andreas Ebert[6] is especially clear and seems to have much of the strong experiential basis characteristic of Palmer's oral tradition. Don Richard Riso is one of the most published authors in this field. He has published a number of books and has developed a definite following among enneagram advocates. His publications are noted for their psychological sensitivity and attempts to schematize the application of the system by the use of the categories of healthy, average, and unhealthy.[7] Kathy Hurley and Ted Dobson are two very familiar people on the enneagram scene and workshop circuit. They have done much to explore the three centers, which they call Intellectual, Relational, and Creative. One center is preferred; another is relied upon; and a third is repressed. Their work is meant to show how to recover what is hidden in the repressed center.[8] We are all indebted in some way to the work of Claudio Naranjo, who brought the enneagram to the United States and has done much to perceive its possibilities for moving beyond mere personality typing. While he approaches his work as a psychiatrist and as one who works with therapists, he opens up psychology to the spiritual.[9] The work of Margaret Frings Keyes on synthesizing the enneagram with the Jungian concept of the shadow and modern psychology is a significant contribution in deepening this dimension of enneagram studies. Her imaginative writing style makes her work available to a wider audience.[10] We are now in the era when the students of the main enneagram teachers are publishing. One example is Karen Webb, who follows the Palmer oral tradition. She has written an accessible introduction to the system.[11] One can only write on typology so long, and then it becomes repetitious. And so authors are trying to give their own special twist to the enneagram. One of these twists is the emphasis on spirituality.

The American, almost infallible, sign of the enneagram's popularity is the presence of newsletters of differing types. The *Enneagram Educator* and the *Enneagram Monthly*[12] both pass along timely information, whether through probing articles on present enneagram research or announcements and teaching schedules of the various enneagram experts. *NinePoints* is the name of the official newsletter of the International Enneagram Association.[13] It encourages dialogue between differing schools of thought.

The Enneagram and Christian Spirituality

The word "spirituality" has become so all-meaningful today that it means nothing. The word "spiritual" is applied to everything from interpreting one's dreams to a quiet walk in the garden. It now refers to anything that cannot be reduced to a muscle spasm. A glance at the books in the self-help section of most bookstores will confirm this. We see this in the cross-disciplinary fields. One example would be that of spirituality and the arts. This is a wonderful field of study and a natural one. However, the fine arts are spoken about in terms of their spiritual dimension in such a vague way that one can only conclude that all good art is spiritual. Perhaps that is true, but then there is little need to study any connection if art and the spiritual simply equal good art. Since we usually do not consider bad art as really artistic, we are caught in a redundancy: all art is spiritual.

At the Stanford Conference those workshops listed under "Spiritual" seemed to have only one common denominator: working with the inner life. Some were explicitly Christian in their content. Christian spirituality obviously deals with the inner world of the person committed to Christ. However, psychology, at least many of its different varieties, claims to work with the inner life also. So what is the meaning of "spiritual" here? I am not claiming that the Judeo-Christian tradition has a monopoly on spirituality. My point is that when a distinct field such as the fine arts or the system of the enneagram is put in conversation with spirituality, the latter needs to be sufficiently distinct in order that the conversation be conducted from the same levels.[14] There is, fortunately, a growing body of literature that treats the enneagram in specifically Christian terms. I refer to *An Enneagram Guide: A Spirituality of Love and Broken-ness,*[15] by Eilis Bergin and Eddie Fitzgerald; *Nine Faces of God,*[16] by Peter Hannan, S.J.; *Conversion and the Enneagram,*[17] by Bernard Tickerhoof, T.O.R.; and *Soul Stuff,*[18] by Carol Ann Gotch and David Walsh.

Three authors who have been especially helpful in the specific area of Christian spirituality are Barbara Metz, S.N.D. de N., and John Burchill, O.P., in their volume, *The Enneagram and Prayer,*[19] and Suzanne Zuercher, O.S.B., in her two volumes *Enneagram Spiritual-ity* and *Enneagram Companions.*[20] Metz and Burchill deal explicitly with prayer in terms of the three centers. They have devoted chapters to head-centered prayer: focused meditation; heart-centered prayer: expressive prayer; and gut-centered prayer: quiet prayer. They have a number of appendices that deal with individual's particular avoid-ance, the emotion least controlled, and praying with scripture. This last section is an invaluable resource when working with people who wish to use the enneagram explicitly in their spiritual journeys. Zuercher in her works articulates what she calls a contemplative approach to the enneagram. Unlike those who follow the more psychological approach or what I shall call the more generalized spiritual approach, Zuercher does not recommend the method of moving away from one's compulsions in the direction of integration (according to the usual arrow theory). For her this does not facili-tate the development of the individual in a transformative process. Her intention is to develop "a description of Christian maturity that depends on an attitude of contemplation rather than one that empha-sizes character-building. This latter approach perpetuates the work of the ego, which I call the first task of life."[21] For her the spiritual life of contemplation is on a level deeper than ego-development. It is obvious that this approach to the enneagram contains important components for integrating the system with Christian spiritual direc-tion. I know of no other author who has applied the enneagram to spiritual direction as explicitly as Zuercher. Most recently she has published a book on Thomas Merton as a Four, *Merton: An Enne-agram Profile.*[22] Apart from the merits of this book itself, this is a fruitful approach in connecting the enneagram and Christian spiri-tuality. So much of the literature of Christian spirituality has been in terms of the biographical. This moves spirituality away from the generalized into the concreteness of actual spiritual people, the only place where spirituality can be found.

The Importance of the Styles of Attention

Helen Palmer[23] has stated on a number of occasions that her original interest in the enneagram had a great deal to do with the fact that it provided her with a grid on which to place her work on styles of attention that are part of her intuitive work. Likewise, I have found the importance of styles of attention in the work of spiritual direction. Most importantly, for people using the enneagram in spiritual direction, or in fact, for those who simply wish to find their correct space,[24] knowledge of how one pays attention is indispensable. I have found no test or inventory guide that works conclusively in helping people type themselves. For me the two most effective ways to do so are listening to healthy types, such as when they speak about themselves on panels (Palmer's oral tradition), and through meditation. In both cases, especially the latter, one's style of paying attention will be salient.[25]

This emphasis on attention leads Palmer to see the enneagram as a tool of compassion, a map of experience. Because the system of the enneagram is filled with people's experience, it is a phenomenological tool. It is a tool to be used, but it does not give us the total reality. It does provide food for further work, whether in therapy or spiritual direction.

Those acquainted with the system will recognize immediately that it is a slanted style of attention developed early in life that creates mental preoccupations, described as the fixations (e.g., One = resentment, Eight = vengeance, Five = stinginess), and emotional preoccupations, described as the passions (e.g., Two = pride; Four = envy; Six = fear). All enneagram practitioners advise dealing with these preoccupations in some way in order to bring about personal and emotional health, to become redeemed, to become more spiritual, to be a self-appropriated individual, and the like. Because this is seen as such a central task, the enneagram often appears to the outsider as a kind of personality typing based on negative aspects of the individual. This, in fact, is the way that many have presented the system, and it is easy to understand since one's preoccupations are more obvious in an unhealthy state. The problem arises when this is considered the main contribution of the enneagram or the main part of the spiritual task.[26]

Spiritual direction will remain on a superficial level if it does not move beyond the arena of ego-clarification or if it is content to

deal with moving away from one fixation by compensaι.
strong aspects of one of the other spaces. It may well be
many, even those in direction, it will be necessary to begin therι.
that can only be a point of insertion. More is needed than behavioι.
modification. Discovering our own style of attention as different
from others and learning how to intervene so as not to be manipulated by it will soon open us up to the inner world where the life of
meditation and prayer takes place. But it may be necessary to assist
people first of all in recognizing how they pay attention. It is difficult
to know our true selves. We may think we are paying attention to
our interior lives, but in fact often we are not.

Palmer says there are six channels of perceptions according to
which our preoccupations are organized. There are four of the head,
one of the heart, and one of the body. Head channels are thought,
memory (the past), planning (the future), and guided images. The
heart channel is our feelings. The body channel is sensation. Guided
imagery makes use of all six channels, combining those of the head
with input from the heart and body. Our conscious life is controlled by these internal objects of attention. This state is what we
usually call being awake. But for Palmer it is really being asleep
because these internal thoughts, feelings, fantasies, and memories
stand in the way of true perception. This state is an obstacle to
the spiritual. It is slanted attention; it constitutes being controlled
by one's habitual preoccupations. To become preoccupied with one
or more of these ordinary forms of attention is to fall asleep.[27] The
enneagram is about being awakened from this slumber. It is about
becoming aware, having a wider and deeper range of perception. It
involves breaking out of the mental and emotional prison in which
we find ourselves so that a more expansive world of information appears. It involves becoming emotionally and mentally "ecumenical,"
that is, less biased, less slanted, less preoccupied by these channels
of attention.[28]

For Palmer, then, the point is to shift attention so that we can recognize the real situation so that the world of reality coming to us is
free of projections and is not filtered through our defensive preoccupations.[29] It should come as no surprise that often spiritual direction
may have to begin here before moving deeper. Shifting attention
helps us to discriminate between true impressions coming to us and
a projection and helps to get a sense of how styles of attention differ
from each other. This approach is so significant for spiritual direc-

tion because the process of self-discovery is not one of identification of external personality traits but one of knowing when perception is correct rather than being lead by habitual inner preoccupations.

Let me give a simple example of how I see the styles of attention operating in spiritual direction. One of the things I find in beginning direction with people is their difficulty, even inability, to distinguish their thoughts from their feelings. They will speak of thoughts in feeling terms and of feelings in abstract language. Helping them discover how they pay attention makes it possible for them to avoid projection, to be more sensitive to their thoughts and feelings, to not be narrowed by their biases, and to allow their imaginations to entertain possibilities. They become more able to distinguish thought from feeling. Often directees are able to make a long list of thoughts in abstract vocabulary, but their list of feeling words is quite short. It would be difficult to imagine that the process of becoming more fully human or of spiritual growth could move very far if this simple distinction is not possible for a directee. Here we have a good example of the simple therapeutic principle that growth takes place through clarification.[30] What is said about the directee also applies to the director. We help each other to become more awake.

Spiritual direction is very much about helping people to wake up in a certain context. Preliminary to much spiritual growth is the ability to know how and when the attention shifts among thought, memory, and planning and among fantasy, feeling, and sensation; also necessary is the knowledge of how to visit the other spaces on the enneagram besides one's own to experience other styles of attention.[31] This involves getting into another's world. For instance, I am a Six, with my own way of thinking, remembering, and planning, with my own ways of fantasizing, feeling, and sensing. I am not an Eight. How do I get into the world of the Eight? Not by reading books about it or even listening to Eights talk about it. I need to visit that space and live there for a while in order to discover how they think, remember, and plan, how they fantasize, feel, and sense. I cannot live in Eight, nor should I. But once I am acquainted with that world, I can then proceed to ask questions more pertinent to spiritual direction, such as: What is the nature of contact with God in that space? Or how do Fives fantasize about the historical Jesus? What does a Four remember about death?

We must enter the directee's world in order to deal with spiritual issues at any depth. Otherwise we will speak with trite language that applies to no one in particular. For instance, in the case of someone having difficulties in prayer, what good is it simply to suggest that they hand themselves over to God or abandon themselves to God's will or to suggest that good will come out of this experience? One approach is to deal with such an issue by asking the directee: Have you asked God about this? What does God tell you about this? Have you taken this to God? No doubt the directee has, but what does this mean? They may not be able to create an image of God that talks to them as does another person. Such an approach gets one involved in requiring the directee to respond to certain images of God, usually the director's. Imaging God is itself a serious issue in contemporary spirituality.

Working with others in spiritual direction involves learning how they pay attention and that often this will not be like the way that we pay attention. During the direction sessions the director needs to be able to visit the space of the directee by not only becoming an observer of the directee's style of attention but also becoming a participant-observer. We experience others as they experience themselves intellectually, emotionally, and bodily. Perhaps this is the most difficult part of spiritual direction. A helpful exercise in the training of spiritual directors is to have them visit all the spaces on the enneagram and sense which ones are comfortable for them and which ones are not. This means sensing what it is like being in another world. It is a form of inculturation where one enters a different culture and lives that life as fully as possible.

A skeletal description of the way each space pays attention would go something like this. Twos[32] have the natural ability to pick up other people's feelings. Their attention shifts from themselves and goes into the emotional world of others. It is outer-directed and focuses selectively. They leave their own inner world and go inside the other. They alter themselves to get a hold of the other's experience. They adjust themselves to other people. All this is a way of controlling the outside world.

The Threes' attention is focused on the feelings and expectations of the group and is prepared to act and change behavior accordingly. Their style is also outward-directed. It goes to what is to be accomplished. They pick up the sense of a group or of an action and so take on the feelings that are appropriate for what they discover outside. While Twos go for the feelings as a way of control, Threes go for the feelings of the task or group.

A Four's attention is directed to what is absent, what is not available, what is not in the pedestrian present. Fours attend to what is missing, what is unavailable. They move back and forth between the present and the absent, employing an external control directed not into the future but toward the absent. Twos augment feelings to make people more in need of their help while Fours augment feelings in terms of distance.

The Fives' retracted style is found not only in their observing others but in their watching themselves observing others. Fives are inner directed. Their real world is the mental one where there is a reduction in feeling and a going back and forth between specific concerns and more abstract ones. They watch themselves watching.

The Sixes' attention is focused on the possibly fearful, and so they scan the environment looking for the hidden sources of danger. The Sixes' attention is outward. Like Twos and Fours, Sixes augment their object of attention, but they do it by projection. Thus, they often take on a paranoid way of acting.

Sevens pay attention by not paying attention to anything very long and by creating a world of possibilities. This is what Palmer calls alternate thinking. One thing reminds them of something else, and that reminds them of something else again. They pay attention to multiple options by moving between present and future, between extremes, between relative values, and between the global and specific. Because their attention jumps, they can make unusual connections.

The Eights' attention is best described as a laser beam concentrating on one point or aspect of a thing or person. Theirs is a black-and-white world of narrow focus such that much of reality is denied. This style is also outward-directed. Eights put all their attention on the object and let the other parts fade away. There is an immediacy about this attentional style. That is because an internal control generates energy inside and then sends it out like a laser. This is not a diffused energy.

Nines are unable to focus their attention on anything without causing conflict with something else that commends itself to their attention. The image that is sometimes used is that of a wavering radio frequency. Conflict creates the need to diffuse the attention. The attention is outward and diffused toward the inessential things. Sevens settle for a moment; Nines never settle. It is like looking around in an open field in which there is no place to fix our gaze.

Finally, the Ones' attention is dominated by the inner judge. They automatically compare and contrast. Their back-and-forth movement is not between the absent and present (Fours), nor is it complicated by feelings (Fours), but it is between themselves and the outer world. Their view of the world is through the lens of their inner standard of evaluation.[33]

Certain Qualifications regarding the Enneagram

Anyone who is familiar with the literature on the enneagram today immediately recognizes that there is some difference of opinion regarding certain aspects of the system. The most obvious one is the nomenclature. It seems that each author is trying to come up with something more original if not more descriptive. Perhaps some day standardization will take place, if that is desirable. Three other areas about which there is some disagreement are the arrows, wings, and subtypes.

Arrows

The theory of the arrows is found in most of the books. If a person moves in the direction of the arrows, this is considered to be moving in the direction of compulsion and is unhealthy. Thus, if one is a Six, it would be unhealthy to move one's energy in the direction of Three, for that movement is with the arrows. To act against compulsion is to move against the arrows and so to move toward health. Thus if a person is a Seven he or she should move toward Five and not One.[34] Rohr (with Ebert) gives a clear statement of this theory:

> The direction of the arrows marks the path of regression and disintegration. In situations of stress, people searching for relief and consolation move with the arrow to another type on the Enneagram that is the stress point. At this point, however, they find only false consolation, which eventually is destructive. The paths opposite to the direction of the arrow show integration.[35]
>
> In times of positive life-feelings, after satisfying peak experiences, and on the way to spiritual maturity, we find true consolation with the positive qualities of the energy that we reach if we move against the direction of the arrows to our "consolation point."[36]

I find this theory of the arrows to smack of predetermination. First, the proponents of this theory choose the positive aspects of the point of "security," "consolation," "heart," or whatever name is current and encourage movement in that direction. They emphasize the negative aspects of the stress point and recommend moving away from it. Some authors seem to give the impression that these movements take place automatically. But what of free will? Why can I not move in the direction of the space of security and choose its negativity, and why can I not move in the direction of the stress point to utilize some of the positive qualities available to me? Palmer refers to this in her first book on the enneagram: "I have interviewed people who slide straight into the negative aspects of the security point when faced with a promising life situation; and I have also recorded many stories of those whose character has been formed by developing the best aspects of the action/stress point of their type."[37]

I prefer to understand the arrow theory as having to do with the way we choose to grow. That is, in times of stress, one can move toward one's stress point in order to gain certain energies to move forward while in times of relative calm, there are qualities in the security point that one can utilize to further one's journey. For instance, as a Six, if I have only two hours before my next class, which I have not yet prepared, it would make more sense to me to move to Three to pick up some of the efficiency in order to make some kind of adequate preparation. I doubt that my students over the past years would have appreciated it if I came in unprepared but announced to them that I had moved to my health space of Nine and was taking the matter in a nonchalant manner. Small consolation for those who are paying tuition!

My suspicion is that the usual arrow theory developed out of a basic principle found in a large part of Christian spirituality, a principle referred to by two Latin words, *agere contra,* which mean "to act against." The spiritual principle here is to act against one's passions, to move away from them. It is the opposite of the principle that leads us to move into our passions, move through them, and come out on the other side, using their energy to achieve health. I was taught the principle of *agere contra* in my days of Jesuit training, and I suspect that the Christians (especially the Jesuits) who were involved in enneagram work in the 1970s were influenced by that principle. In fairness it must be pointed out that Ignatius does not use *agere contra* in this sense. His rules for discernment urge acting not against one's passions but against desolation. This would be consistent with the importance that Ignatius placed on the passions and on the importance of the imagination in the *Spiritual Exercises.*[38]

Wings

The theory of the wings is found in most of the literature. A quote from Rohr's *Discovering the Enneagram* may be helpful:

> The entire circle that the Enneagram describes is a kind of gradual overlapping; each energy melds into the next. The Enneagram does not make jumps between the individual types. As a consequence, each number contains something of each of its neighboring numbers, which help to determine it and balance it.... While FIVEs are primarily determined by their own energies, blockages, and gifts, there are still two neighboring "theatres of war." The energies in the wings balance out the primary energy. There are, however, those who even say that the primary energy is formed by the tension from the wings! I have found this to be very true in several cases.[39]

Rohr goes on to say that the wing theory is important because if one remains in one's space only, one will find it more difficult to move toward integration. He believes that in the first half of life we stress and develop one of our wings while in the second half of life the task is to develop the other one. Quite possibly. Again, here I find Palmer helpful. In her discussion of the influence of the wings and how that differs between the core points of Three-Six-Nine and the other spaces, she says:

> The wings of any point are influential, however, because they give a flavor to that personality type. For example, in the anger group at the top of the Enneagram, a Nine, who will prefer to express anger indirectly and passively, will lean either to the Eight side (the Boss), making for a blunt and stubborn "don't push me" kind of passive anger, or to the One side (the Perfectionist), making for a nitpicking criticality, which will still be acted out in indirect ways.... For example, a fiveish Four would be a more withdrawn and private kind of Four, whereas a threeist Four would be a more flamboyant, dramatic Four, who maintains an active schedule, but still relates to the Four stance of melancholy, sadness, and loss. Each type is affected by

both of its wings, and although the flavor of one of the wings will predominate in the personality, it would be improper to discount the fact that the other exists as a potential.[40]

My work in spiritual direction confirms Palmer's approach. I have found helpful a simple example that she often gave in classes: the wings are like our elbows on which we are leaning; some times we lean on one, and sometimes on the other, and sometimes on both.

Subtypes

The subtypes, sometimes called instincts, are usually understood in terms of the gut or belly center. As Palmer puts it: "The operation of the belly center is largely unconscious, but can be recognized by the fact that we each have pressing concerns about issues that affect our physical survival (self-preservation), sexuality, and social life."[41] In Palmer's understanding there are three primary areas of relationships, and one of these has been damaged in some way. So to defend it, the person develops a mental preoccupation to protect it and to reduce the anxiety surrounding it. These three kinds of relationships are called (1) self-preservation or personal, that is, involving our relationship to our personal survival; (2) sexual or couple, that is, involving our intimate one-to-one relationships; and (3) social or community, that is, involving our relationships that relate to a group. We all possess all three areas, but one will predominate in our concerns. For Palmer the subtypes are ways the passions manifest themselves in these three areas.[42]

The subtypes are important in spiritual direction because they refer to the more instinctual body-based responses of the person. As in the other forms of human growth, spiritual direction needs to move in the direction of a more holistic person by emphasizing the body in particular, since it is the body that is usually the neglected dimension of the person. How we are bodily is how we are in the world. How we feel about our bodies (not necessarily an emotion) tells us a great deal about who we are. Our embodiment influences much about our lives: our point of view, our practical decisions, our biases, our movement toward growth. It is relatively easy to discover the fixations, which are mental, and the passions, which are emotional. But what is going on in the body is the least accessible to us. Sometimes we say: "I've got this feeling in my gut." But this is more a sensation than a feeling. What is the bodily experience that cannot be reduced to thought or feeling? I am convinced that it is in the area of our instinctual selves that we can make this discovery. In terms of spiritual direction I believe it is necessary to expand what is usually understood about the subtypes. Palmer's description is certainly valid, but it is perhaps more helpful at the earlier stages of growth and thus needs to be broadened because at the higher stages the spiritual life will be more fully Christian, more completely incarnational. And the simple fact is that people at lower levels are more reluctant to integrate the bodily, the physical, especially the sexual, than to integrate the more intellectual, emotional, and strictly spiritual dimensions of themselves. Responding instinctually, bodily, and spontaneously in a healthy way is probably the task of the more advanced stages.

I shall use myself to illustrate the qualification I wish to make. I am a Six. Like all Sixes, I possess the qualities of the social, self-preservation, and sexual subtypes. As a self-preservation Six, I create a warm environment to help me feel safe. As a sexual Six, I feel secure in my personal strengths and in the aesthetically pleasing aspects of my life. As a social Six, I create personal security by fulfilling my obligations, doing my duty. I am identified as a social Six. But why social and not self-preservation or sexual? Because while I try to be responsible, I do not enjoy it as much as when I create a warm environment or feel secure in my strengths and aesthetic interests. I do all three. I feel secure in all three. But one of them, the social, does not have the same sense of creating energy as do the other two. We can discover our bodily selves by experiencing the lack of comfortability found in that one subtype. It is the reason that we go by that subtype name.[43]

The Healthy and Holy Person in Terms of the Enneagram

I use the words "healthy" and "holy" as almost synonymous. But I do not wish to be reductionistic. Not everyone who is holy is healthy, and not everyone who is healthy is holy. But to a great extent I understand the growing toward health as in fact a growing in holiness. Not all would agree with that. There are those who would invoke the lives of saints in the Christian tradition as proof that health and holiness need not be coincident. It would very easy to list several canonized saints who would be considered psychologically unbalanced according to present health standards. And yet they are held up as models of sanctification and holiness of life. My point is that it is true certain saints may be holy and also psychologically disturbed, or at least, very eccentric, at the same time. But I maintain that said saints are not holy and unhealthy in the same dimensions of their lives. To be saints persons need not be 100 percent holy. Sainthood means that they may be held up for imitation. But they need not be models for others in *every* aspect of their lives.

Based on what I have stated above about the enneagram, my view of what constitutes health according to the system is somewhat different from some of the other authors. Often health on the enneagram is understood as developing one's own space more completely, such as becoming a better and better Two. The more usual recommendation is that one move away from disintegration (such as Fours moving away from the Two space) and move in the direction of integration (such as Fours moving toward the One space). Also, health according to some authors is developing the repressed center or the repressed wing. In other words, it is still very much a matter of ego-development in terms of achieving some kind of balance among all the variables.

While I would not deny that there is validity to these claims, I still find it too predetermined, still too focused on behavior, too much a question of seeking health according to certain rules of thumb. For me the truly healthy and holy person is not a Nine, for example, who has developed Nine by moving to Three and away from Six, has stopped repressing his or her preferred center,[44] and has integrated the repressed or weakened wing.

Rather I see healthy and holy persons as those who have integrated their own space into their lives by moving to both stress and security spaces, by picking up there whatever is useful for their growth at any moment of their personal journey, by drawing strength from both wings, by depending on the need at hand, as well as by being able to visit all the spaces on the enneagram as required or desired at any moment of their lives. Thus, healthy persons are those who move around the enneagram at choice. They always remain firmly based in their own space, where their principal energy is found. But they are not limited in their journey to leaning on either or both of their wings, nor are they required to move in one or other direction such as the 1–4–2–8–5–7 internal structure. Rather they can visit all the spaces at different times depending on their changing circumstances. An example might help.

I am firmly situated in the Six space but have lived a lot of my life depending on Four. I frequently visit the Four space either for consolation or for further strength and enrichment. It does not depend upon my being in stress or not. It is simply a good place to be many times. But Four is not connected with Six through the arrow or wing theories.[45] Again, I belong to a religious order, the Jesuits, whose founder was a One and whose official documents take on a strong One quality. All is done not for the glory of God but for the greater glory of God. One is not my natural home, but it is important to be able to visit that space at certain times, especially when I need to respond to certain specifically Jesuit situations. It is important to be able to visit that space when appropriate. I am not suggesting that there are not some spaces more or less difficult to visit, but I am saying that the spiritual task in terms of the enneagram is to grow to the point where one can visit all the spaces with some ease.

This approach explains better for me the application of the enneagram to Jesus Christ. Rather than seeing Christ as someone who simply has integrated all the spaces in his life completely,[46] Christ is one like us in all things who can move from his space (whatever that may be) and visit all the other spaces better than the rest of us can. This would be more acceptable to myself as a theologian as well as to many of my theological colleagues.

A significant area for becoming a healthy and holy person through the system is the relation of the enneagram to the body. The place of the body has become increasingly important in the helping professions. I refer to the body as more than a material reality. We cannot be reduced to our physical dimensions, and yet full embodiment is not possible unless we are in physical contact with the self. While there are bodily based practices connected with the system,[47] often the enneagram is not really embodied. But such bodily practices as rituals, chakra movements, massage, and various forms of touch as spiritual practices are necessary if we are to open up our personalities (in the positive sense of essence) but even more if we are really to touch God. That is why there is an increasing number of retreat houses that have a professional body person on their staff to offer massages to the retreatants. Also, the use of touch in spiritual direction can be very effective, although this is risky in a world where we are more sensitive to abuse as well as more litigious in inclination.

The purpose of these hands-on experiences is to set aside old ways of thinking and doing and enter into a new level of conscious-

ı as physical being. In many ways that is the purpose of
direction and the enneagram. The point is that it will be
.o profit fully from the enneagram's application to the spiri-
tuaı ı if a negative view of the body continues. The enneagram can
provide entrance points where we can specifically, according to our
space, find ways to care for and love our bodies. Ego-development
and interior attention are not enough for the healthy, holy person.
Bodily practices such as touch and massage can help us to clarify a
spiritual vision often clouded by the thoughts and images that are
projected from the unconscious depth. We live in the darkness cast
by this shadow. It is this shadow that prevents us from engaging another person fully. We cannot communicate with the transparency
and tranquillity with which we would like. The unhealed memories
of past failures render us impotent. Our failures become the failures
of others, and so we not only cannot appreciate the gifts of others
but also actually try to destroy or at least demean their achievements. What goes on in our streets in terms of violence and abuse is
a manifestation of the psychic debris that is found in our inner lives.

It is important to identify each space's particular issues in connection with the body is so that in spiritual direction both director
and directee may know what kind of hands-on experience is necessary for spiritual growth. It has been my experience in direction that
simple things like foot massage or hand reflexology or self-Breema
exercises[48] can be used to allow the body to feel. The actual feelings,
so often locked in various parts of the body, must be able to flow like
a stream from the top of the head to the soles of the feet and then
into the ground. The body then becomes alive and an instrument for
understanding the self. If it is true that the meaning of life is the
actual integration of the person in one's body, it is so because the
person is like an art object. The healthy, holy person is an integrated
whole; the integrated body is a source of pleasure and meaning, and
it is a sign of God's presence suffused throughout the world. In that
sense it has the character of sacramentality.

Chapter 2

Spiritual Direction

Spiritual Direction Today

The practice of spiritual direction in any religious tradition is as old as the tradition itself. It has been found in Christianity since its beginning. Its history demonstrates not only its vitality and importance for Christian living but also the varied ways in which it is imaged. For instance, in his well-received book *Soul Friend,* Kenneth Leech says that "the term 'spiritual direction' is usually applied to the cure of souls when it involves the specific needs of one individual. Max Thurian's definition is a useful starting point. 'Spiritual direction, or the cure of souls, is a seeking after the leading of the Holy Spirit in a given psychological and spiritual situation.' "[1] The image of direction here is that of seeker, on the part of both the director and the directee. This highlights one of the issues of contemporary spiritual direction, namely, what to call it. The title of director for many is too intrusive, too patriarchal, too hierarchical.

Leech opts for the name "soul friend" to describe the director, a friend of the soul and a guide on the way. He does not accept that spiritual direction can be reduced to conversation between friends where each speaks from ignorance or incompetence. For him the director is: (1) a person possessed by the Spirit, someone characterized by holiness of life and closeness to God; (2) a person of experience, someone who has already trod the spiritual path to a considerable degree, someone who has struggled with his/her own conflicts, darkness, and light; and (3) a person of learning, which does not mean a doctorate in Christian spirituality, but someone who knows the tradition, including some knowledge of scripture, is competent in one or other school of spirituality, and knows something about the various forms of prayer; (4) a person of discernment, a gift that has a certain intuitive quality about it, enabling the director to perceive the inner life of the directee; and (5) a person who gives way to the Holy Spirit, which quality in many ways makes Christian spiritual direction Christian — that is, all is done in the context of faith in the power of the Spirit of God to move the individual to deeper union with God. Direction then is a means and not an end. "The end is God, whose service is perfect freedom."[2]

One of the admirable things about Leech's book is that it pays attention to the findings of contemporary psychology and sociology. That is very characteristic of all of the writing on spiritual direction today. Such sensitivity has helped to overcome an excessive fideism in direction as well as a kind of religious voluntarism. It has also spurred the debate about the difference between therapy and spiritual direction. Leech devotes a chapter to distinguishing among direction, counseling, and therapy. As soon as the areas of the unconscious and sexuality are admitted into the arena of spiritual direction, such considerations cannot be avoided.[3]

The image of friend continues to dominate the writing on spiritual direction. The Episcopalian Alan Jones, in his *Exploring Spiritual Direction: An Essay of Christian Friendship*, writes about the need for companionship in our spiritual warfare, an image of the Christian journey.[4] The spiritual companion helps us to discern our own individual process in the midst of this greater religious drama. Since direction must take place in the real world of daily affairs, Jones sees the need for a spiritual friend "who both stimulates the imagination and also helps me gain a critical distance from the main currents and events of my life so that I can take a fresh look at where I am and where I am going."[5]

Jones, like many of the other practitioners of and authors on spiritual direction, finds a definite relationship between spiritual direction and the psychological sciences today. He sees that there is an alliance between spirituality and therapy, but he also is careful to distinguish the two. For him the difference between psychotherapy and direction lies in the fact that direction is "explicitly concerned with mutuality, grace, and worship." The person seeking direction must be relatively healthy. A closed person needs something else, namely, the skills of the therapist. Spiritual direction deals with the order of grace while, presumably, therapy does not. Finally, the context of direction is one of adoration; that is, it is liturgical worship of some sort. Jones sums up his position this way:

The therapist, the counselor, the psychiatrist can help us on our way. They can rescue us from particular blocks, get us back on our feet, can teach us to accept ourselves so that we can be on the move. But they cannot answer for us (nor would the best of them want to) those burning questions concerning the purpose and meaning for which we long. The spiritual guide cannot answer them either, but there is within the world of spiritual direction a conscious commitment to faith in God. The director and directee share in a community of faith with a common memory, a common hope, and a common longing.[6]

Tilden Edwards also employs the image of friend in his book *Spiritual Friend: Reclaiming the Gift of Spiritual Direction*. He sees spiritual direction as "one color on a many colored coat of resources. It is meant to be a part of the whole way of life, not an isolated resource."[7] The church has many forms of authentic guidance: the rites of reconciliation, the sacraments and liturgy, retreats, spiritual reading and scripture, devotions, and pastoral counseling. Edwards gives several reasons why there is a special need for a spiritual friend today: support in a time when a shared worldview has collapsed, the fact that education and the psychological helping professions are limited in their ability to deal with people's hunger for transcendence, the need to restore a balance to a social-activist emphasis, and a reawakening of an oral tradition of guidance that has been neglected in our dependence on books and scholarship.[8] Among the many helpful practical issues taken up by Edwards, his treatment of group spiritual direction is especially noteworthy. Group direction is important for many reasons: it fills the gap left by a shortage of qualified directors; it gives an alternative to the more nondialogical forms of preaching, teaching, and writing; and in many cases it is more beneficial for people.[9]

Not all who describe the passage to the fearful inner world use the language of friendship when speaking about spiritual direction. For instance, those who embrace Eastern Christianity would speak differently. Spiritual direction arose in the East and has long been part of its spirituality. In *Inner Way: Toward a Rebirth of Eastern Christian Spiritual Direction*,[10] Joseph Allen sees the ministry of spiritual direction in terms of the spiritual physician. He does a study of the "elders of the desert" in the tradition to discover the characteristics of spiritual direction, although he indicates that one cannot reduce contemporary spiritual direction to eldership. He also places this ministry in the context of the two other important ministries, that of liturgy and of reconciliation. It is a refreshing change of perspective from many in the Western tradition who tend to isolate spiritual direction as an individualized ministry, one that at times appears to distance itself from liturgy and the ministry of reconciliation of the church, if not the church itself. Although those who find the word "director" distasteful might agree with Allen that the purpose of spiritual direction is the same as that of the gospel ("to lead individuals deeper and deeper into the struggle for the Christian life, that is toward wholeness and healing"),[11] they would react less positively to imaging direction in the medical terms of a healer.

The importance of the Ignatian tradition and the *Spiritual Exercises* in the history of spiritual direction is well known. Space does not allow adequate comment here. A discussion of the *Exercises* could constitute a study in itself. Suffice it to say here that since Vatican II there has been a recovery of the authentic shape of Ignatian spirituality and the purpose of the *Exercises*. This recovery has been very closely associated with the individually directed retreat and with ways of "being in retreat" while still engaged in one's ordinary life activities. A good introductory book that makes the *Exercises* available to a large audience and is helpful for directors as well is William Barry's *Allowing the Creator to Deal with the Creature*.[12] One other book of a different order and purpose, more scholarly and less accessible, is Tad Dunne's *Spiritual Mentoring*. Its purpose is to guide people through their life decisions by means of the *Exercises*. It is a good book for spiritual directors because it deals with questions of human knowing and willing in contemporary terms. As Dunne puts it: "The reflections on life choices in the present work draw the reader's attention to the inner events of noticing, understanding, realizing, believing, and loving that shape a decision rather than on any doctrines in a person's religious tradition."[13] There is much in his hermeneutics of attention that would marry well with Helen Palmer's work on attention, which I described in the previous chapter.

The Ignatian tradition reaches wide. It plays a significant part in the movement called CLC (Christian Life Communities). CLC is a pivotal movement in the church; it involves mostly laypeople who seek to communicate the gospel by responding to human needs wherever they are found. They are a good example of living Ignatian spirituality precisely as a lay spirituality.[14]

The feminist perspective has had a very significant influence on spiritual direction. It has transformed the experience, changed the topics of discussion, and liberated much of the practice and teaching from long-held prejudices and closed points of view. As Kathleen Fischer says in *Women at the Well*,[15] feminism is another way of seeing. It presents a view of reality not colored by sexism. "Feminism is a vision of life emphasizing inclusion rather than exclusion, connectedness rather than separateness, and mutuality in relationships rather than dominance and submission."[16] What Fischer and those authors like her have done is to authenticate women's experience in the inner journey. And this is not only in terms of the persons seeking greater clarification about their spiritual lives but also in terms of those who do the actual assisting. The feminist emphasis affects not only the vocabulary and the ways of listening and knowing but the actual experience. Surely the experience has changed when now such a large percentage of recognized spiritual directors are women. Issues of power, violence, and abuse, which perhaps remained hidden in even the best of spiritual direction in the past, can now reach the light with greater clarity and with less trauma. The feminist perspective has initiated a revolutionary change in the way we understand our relationship with God, how we grow in the spiritual life, the meaning of discernment, and the place of Jesus in our salvation.

Why is it that so many Christians are seeking spiritual direction at the present time? They seek it both in a religious context and in other forms such as the various twelve step programs or New Age spirituality. Why is this so? Without being overly simplistic, I believe the main reason is the lack of a spiritual guide. Many of the spiritual guides of the past either no longer exist or have become ineffective. The history of the church and of the liturgy demonstrates the presence of various spiritual guides, although they are not always equated with a specific human being. For instance, the liturgy should really be the form of the church's spiritual direction. When the liturgical year is not treated literally as some kind of autobiography of Jesus Christ but is experienced symbolically as various ways of entering life in Christ past, present, and future, it provides a pattern and goal for life as well as a kind of discernment process. This symbolic pattern often functioned well in a world that was still sensitive to public feasts and celebrations and to such practices as *lectio divina,* a careful meditation on the scriptures.

As already noted, there have always been individuals who served as guides for others, but frequently this was limited to a few. What we need to note is that whenever there is a divorce between the symbolic world and the life of thought such as took place in the medieval university system and is taking place in our own time in its own way, more people will look for guidance on how to negotiate with their culture. When the culture no longer supports a religious world-view and the guidance of the liturgy is no longer meaningful, people will look for other supports. This is especially true in a pluralistic, more secular culture such as our own. It is not that pluralism is a twentieth-century phenomenon — indeed, even the post-Reformation world was more pluralistic than may appear to us. But pluralism *is* one of the main characteristics of postmodernity, and the danger is that such an environment may move spiritual guidance in an individualistic direction.

In the past Roman Catholics found some guidance in certain practices such as fasting and abstinence and certain devotional exercises because these created a kind of subculture that was supportive of their religious life as well as serving as signs of the converted life. They created a sense of belonging. In the absence of these, Catholics now turn to the individual spiritual director for the same kind of belonging. I believe many people come to direction as much for a human connection as they do for any particular kind of insight they are seeking.

In the past the sacramental system provided much of what spiritual direction does today. But for many this system has become confusing or has atrophied. The sacraments are not so clearly the identifying gestures of the church that they are supposed to be. In fact, one of the purposes of spiritual direction today is to reestablish the link between the inner life of Christians and the sacramental expression that can render their spirituality more public.

Spiritual Direction and Adult Development

There are many approaches to spiritual direction, and the above-mentioned books are but a fraction of the many books published in this area, each with its own take on what direction is and how it is to be done. There are also many ways to write a book on spiritual direction and the enneagram. I have chosen to do it in terms of adult development in spiritual direction. Many of the books on

direction refer to adult development in some form, some only implicitly, others more explicitly. In my opinion none does it like *Changing
Life Patterns: Adult Development in Spiritual Direction,* by Elizabeth Liebert, SNJM.[17] As I have indicated before, if the enneagram
and spiritual direction (or spirituality) are to be put into conversation, then the partners must be equally concrete. The enneagram —
with its nine spaces, its inner structure, and especially with the addition of the styles of attention — comes to the conversation in a very
distinct mode. The other partner must be more than a generalized
discussion of spiritual direction. The stages of adult development
give this latter partner the concreteness desired.

We begin with Liebert's understanding of spiritual direction:

> Spiritual direction particularizes spiritual guidance to each
> person's unique experiences, life circumstances, decisions and
> yearnings. Furthermore, spiritual direction always involves an
> explicit covenant to sensitize persons to God and encourage
> them to deepen this relationship in all its ramifications. Thus,
> spiritual direction is a more specific, individualized form of
> spiritual guidance.[18]

Again,

> Christian spiritual direction, then, is an interpersonal helping
> relationship, rooted in the church's ministry of pastoral care. In
> this relationship, one Christian assists another to discover and
> live out in the context of the Christian community his or her
> deepest values and life goals in response to God's initiative and
> biblical mandate.[19]

Moving from her synthesis of a variety of developmental theories and the structural developmental paradigm she has developed
(as distinct from a life-span paradigm), Liebert articulates and elabo-
rates three adult stages (which will more fully described below): the
Conformist, the Conscientious, and the Interindividual stages. It is
not quite this simple because there are other major moments[20] in
our development, such as the self-aware transition that takes place
before we are really at the Conscientious stage. The individualistic
transition occurs naturally on the way to the Interindividual stage.
Liebert also devotes a chapter to what she calls congregational spiritual guidance, a kind of group spiritual direction on a massive scale,
with which we will not be concerned here. Much more needs to be

said about this book, some of which will be done in the elaboration of the stages.

The Three Stages of Adult Development

Liebert's elaboration of the three stages of adult development[21] notes what she calls the four subdomains of each stage: the cognitive style, the conscious preoccupations, impulse control or character development, and interpersonal style. I follow that pattern below.

The Conformist Stage

This stage[22] is one that arises in adolescence but, in fact, may be permanent for many people, living there throughout their adult lives. Liebert's general description of this stage reminds one of the unhealthy Nine enneagram space:

> The unanimity characteristic of this stage suppresses the possibility of pluralism; groups appear to break up when something happens to upset the sense of communality shared by each member. Anger is particularly problematic for a Conformist person because expressing anger risks rending the interpersonal fabric which constitutes one's very self.[23]

This means that the central feature of this stage is that the self is constituted by the groups to which the Conformist belongs. Interpersonal relationships are defining for persons at this stage, whether they be with family, peers, one's ethnic group, or church. Persons at this level can also conform through activity that appears to be nonconformist or anticonformist. And while they can detect the differences between groups, they cannot make these distinctions among the individuals in the same group.

Cognitive Style. People primarily at the Conformist stage tend toward stereotypical thinking, using clichés and all-or-nothing statements. Their norms for judging are external to them, and their appeal is to the reality outside themselves. They view reality in black-and-white terms, simplistically holding that what is true in one concrete situation is true always and everywhere. Exceptions and extenuating circumstances are not readily admitted into their judgments. People at this stage do not know how to be inner-directed, and so the inner life is superficial. Not being practiced at introspection, they find it difficult to distinguish among their feeling states and have to struggle to differentiate feelings from thoughts. As a result their evaluations are on external behavior, reputation, social acceptance, and material things. It is an approach to life that often moves between sentimentality and unrealistic idealism because it is not based on the person's interiority.

The director working with persons at this stage needs to make use of the styles of attention to help the individuals to notice what is happening interiorly to them. From there the director can help them describe their inner movements and then incorporate their feelings into their prayer.[24] The process by which Conformists come to notice and describe their inner life will be very slow. Usually, they cannot describe their feelings in a nuanced way. The director should have them describe not only present feelings but also ones that they can remember from the past. The director may need to suggest words descriptive of feelings to the directees since their vocabulary of feeling words is limited. If they can be convinced that God is interested in their feelings and treasures them, they may be able to move those feelings to their prayer.

Working with people who remain at this stage for a long time will be challenging for any director. There may be no obvious change in their spiritual lives. Because they may not be able to shift from the externals of their lives or employ a variety of feelings in prayer, the use of the styles of attention may seem frustrating. Whether people at this stage will be able to identify themselves on the enneagram is a question. Certainly, as long as they attempt to do it in terms of external behavior, they may identify themselves incorrectly. But the ability to so identify themselves is a sign of movement into the next stage.

Conscious Preoccupation. Many of the characteristics of this subdomain make the Conformist seem like an unhealthy Three. Physical and social appearance is important for these people. They are aware of how others in the group see them. What they want for themselves is group identity and group values. They work for status symbols such as an office, a car, and professional diplomas. The bright side of this is that losing face among their peers or receiving criticism from them may propel the Conformists into spiritual direction. But it also means that spiritual direction will need to concentrate on external norms and concrete behavior. Prayer will focus on concrete styles such as the rosary, liturgy of the hours, and devotional reading. Prayer forms to be used are those expected by their group or church.

As individuals they readily form into groups, especially those engaging in similar behavior. The danger here, as Liebert sees it, is "misplaced concreteness." This means that they mistake nonessentials for essentials. What kind of silverware to use for a party may cause more discussion than the war in Bosnia, which indeed may never come up. They need to be encouraged to think for themselves, but this is more complicated at this stage because the issues of their group and certain prescriptions of the church will cloud matters for them. It is best to move them toward freedom in their personal search for God, that is, toward a point that does not necessarily carry a lot of church institutional questions.

Impulse Control. It would be easy to mistake a conservative or even a fundamentalist for someone at the Conformist stage because the latter readily obey the rules of the church, and they tend to think that all rules and regulations have the same value and binding force.[25] Rules are rules and are to be obeyed. Such obedience is a way of belonging. Because they have not learned to control their impulses interiorly, they need to follow the rules to do so. For that same reason they are concerned that others obey the rules also. Authority is important to them, and they need its approval or disapproval. They depend upon approval for advancement in their education and socialization. It seems clear that they continue to locate authority in the institution rather than taking it inside themselves. When life situations contradict their strong moral imperative, the director will best offer support by helping them to see the contradictions in their own firmly held, but biased, beliefs.

Not surprisingly, in spiritual direction the issue of "shoulds" arises. Conformists remind one of the unhealthy Eight and One because they are hard on themselves and can seem to be very judgmental of others. The director needs to stress the difference among various kinds of behavior and also challenge some of their personal judgments. Much of direction will be concerned with their denial of negative feelings, such as sexual or aggressive ones. They may deny their sexual attractions or that they get angry at God. Liebert cautions that this denial might look like psychological resistance, but it cannot simply be reduced to resistance. It can be a necessary part of the developmental stage of the Conformist. At the Conformist level all feelings are expressed vaguely and equally. Embarrassment or avoidance in the sexual or aggression areas may mean that sexuality or anger is their primary issue. It can also be that the person has an idealized view of God that will make these two areas negative for them. This is only exacerbated by "an exaggerated sense of sinfulness, badness or dirtiness with respect to sexuality or anger, or an inflated need to look good in the eyes of the spiritual director."[26] Spiritual direction can assure these persons that these feelings fall in the area of God's love and that pardon is always available. But at this level it seems that spiritual direction can only begin the process of addressing these concerns. Because shame is often the overriding response to any sin in these areas, the director should both clarify to the directee what is actually sinful here and also recommend participation in the sacrament of reconciliation. This can alleviate much of this shame.

Interpersonal Style. Conformists' style is clearly influenced by their desire to belong. They connect in trust and warmth with persons like themselves in parishes, religious communities or organizations, and at work. But here their connection is still on the conscious level. They are unaware of their unconscious motivations. Nor do they have a comprehensive social worldview. So they can be loving within their group but highly biased regarding other groups or people outside their ambit.

They understand their relationships in terms of action. That is, friends are people with whom you do things. The deeper feelings and motives that may be present are not accessible. And yet it is these relationships that constitute their identity.

Their view of God is very interpersonal also — that is, God is a person with whom they can have a deep relationship. God for them is concrete and anthropomorphic, but that does not exclude the possibility of God being a hierarch, a strict judge, or a demanding parent. They seek to do God's will, which is understood as involving a form of external behavior that can be sanctioned by clergy, spiritual directors, scripture, or what is religiously approved. Spiritual directors need to be more discerning here — they can easily yield to the temptation to become more directive because these people will respond to religious authority. The directors can collude with the directees and simply keep them at the level of conformity. Liebert's caution here is that directors cannot treat directees as if they have already attained the next stage of development.

In summary, the strength of this stage is its investment in persons and institutions outside the individual. Socialization takes place fairly easily. But this is also the weakness at this stage. Individuals can remain in the group, hidden as it were. They do not have their own identity, chosen and clearly appropriated by themselves. Like chameleons they take on many different identities depending on the group to which they belong. This pattern reminds one of the unhealthy Three.

In their favor, the Conformists are generous, helpful, and consistent. They further the goals of the group to which they belong. They can place their trust in God, and they will direct their prayer toward concrete actions. Their temptations are: impulsive behavior, limiting negative feelings, the literal interpretation of rules, prejudice against others, authoritarianism, harsh judgments on self and others, and shame for personal failures. These people can seem to be frustrating for directors because they do not seem to be able to take their lives in hand, to do the inner work that is necessary, or to pray affectively. As a result, the director could fall into the trap of taking on the role of the parent in the spiritual direction relationship.

Signs of Transition from the Conformist Stage. Apparently, there is no one time or sign of change taking place that clearly indicates transition from this stage. But it might be helpful to identify a congeries of signs: the realization that authorities disagree, an understanding that various groups demand contradictory commitments, or the realization of a failure to live up to an idealized goal. Another sign is that undesirable drives may break out.

The question for the directees is whether they will explore their unruly emotions and conflicts or whether they will regress to an earlier stage, a dualistic one. The challenge for the director is knowing what to support: the directees' previous position, their present confusion, or a possible new way of living.[27] The God issue must arise now in terms of the question: Who is the God of the directee's changing experience? The relationship between director and directee will change. In what direction does the director want to influence that change?

The Conscientious Stage

The Self-Aware Transition. The transition from the Conformist stage to self-awareness is normal, though it is hard to recognize development at this level. This is the usual kind of transition for young adults, although, according to Liebert, many older women begin spiritual direction at the time of this transition.[28] An increasing self-awareness helps in replacing group values with personal ones, which characterize this stage of consciousness. There is a gradual pulling away from the Conformist stage in that there is a greater emphasis on individual traits and roles. Rules now have exceptions. There is a greater awareness of the self in personal relationships. There is less tendency to stereotype people according to their roles or groups to which they belong. Here one finds more commitment, more dependence on oneself. In other words, the individuals are now more self-aware. More is included in their consciousness, and so ideals and models play a large role in their learning process. Mentors, whether an individual or a community, have significant influence on people at this level.

Many people settle at this level for long periods of time. Perhaps it is because at this stage they are learning how to introspect. Their strengths are personal vision, a deeper interest in all relationships, and greater flexibility regarding rules. There is more awareness of ultimacy in values and relationships but with less depth and vigor than will be possible later. People at this level are good, patient, and honest, and so the temptation is to stay here. Often some external change in their life, such as leaving home or going through a divorce, will cause them to move or at least want to move from this level. Such reasons will motivate them to seek spiritual direction, and the director's task will be to involve them in communities of persons who care about ultimate values.

Liebert notes that many women remain at this level for a long period of time. At this period of their lives they are claiming their inner voice and are trying many different ways to navigate through this transition. These women are a good example of what it means to move from one symbol system to another. As both men and women move from their past presuppositions, they are letting go of a lot and will feel empty and abandoned. They move into a time of ambiguity, liminality, and questioning. As they let go of a whole congeries of images of God they are in a space where they are not sure they believe in God at all. People lose their energy source as they move into this liminal world, a world no longer governed by past presuppositions. Writing about why this transition is especially a problem for women, Liebert says: "As a result of a variety of circumstances, they may develop an inner voice, but keep it to themselves because they fear that, if they say what they really feel, they may rupture the thread of communication binding their social world together."[29]

At the specifically Conscientious stage people possess all they need developmentally to enter into the spiritual direction process fruitfully.[30] This is the stage of self-appropriation, of our inner authority, of grasping our value system as our own. We *have* relationships and *are not* our relationships. The strength of this stage is that we can reflect critically on ourselves and the world. The limitation is that now everything is done in terms of a conscious mental process. This stage receives its name from the word "conscience," since here the adult conscience comes into its own. "These elements include long-term, self-evaluated goals and ideals, differentiated self-criticism, and a sense of responsibility for living up to goals."[31] The person is truly reflective and has a rich inner life.

Cognitive Style. Thinking here is more complex because these people can see themselves in context, for example, the context of community and society. They see consequences, alternatives, and contingencies. They have a wider range of emotions with more nuancing. They can perceive patterns and so can recognize personality traits. The differences they perceive in themselves they can now perceive in others. They are aware of the broader social context, although this may be rather abstract.

The downside of this is that these people can feel adrift. What was once simple and clear no longer is. Their own motivation is less certain, and the ground seems to be shifting beneath them because of the loss of a former frame of reference and of external certainties. In the face of confusions and uncertainties, these persons may try to retreat to a more simple life, although this will be difficult because they will have to defend themselves against their own inner life. Having accepted a relative (i.e., not absolutistic) worldview, they can no longer believe in a "simple, unquestioned sense." Even belief in God takes place in a more relative context. But their questions about the meaning of almost everything suggest the possibility that spiritual direction can be a powerful form of connection for them.

The temptations for religious persons are either to pass off all responsibility to God, in an unhealthy Nine fashion, or to use perfectionistic striving to protect themselves from the challenge of deeper values, as an unhealthy One would do. Because we have here the shifting of meaning systems, it is at this stage that we have our classic crisis of faith — because only here is it possible to be fully engaged by religious values and beliefs. Here are crises of all kinds: the rejection of images of God that are debilitating, the rebellion against

religious structures, the dismissal of patriarchy's claims, the questioning of a form of religious life or the understanding of the family. The
issue for the director is whether to promote or hold back the crisis.
Directees are vulnerable at this time. Directors may try to pass off
their own value systems to them because these directees may not be
ready to create their own spiritual identity. It is important that directors understand that movement to a new stage takes time and has
plateaus. It is at this stage that discernment becomes especially useful
and necessary. There is now an awareness of inner movements; the
person itself is claiming its meaning, and conscience is in evidence.
Moreover, discernment with someone is required because the self as
norm creates a blind spot: "I have prayed about it and I have decided." Here the director will have to challenge the directees since
their decisions have implications for other persons, and they cannot
act as if they are not part of a tradition.

Conscious Preoccupations. At this stage one is the author of one's
own destiny.[32] People here use internal standards to evaluate their
achievements. They have their obligations, ideals, traits, and achievements. Self-identity is central for a person at this stage. Time becomes
more meaningful for them. Spiritual direction is different here because these people have long-term goals and a sense of the self, and
so direction is about assisting people to discover and live out their
deepest values and goals.

This is also the stage of the demythologization of much that gave
meaning in the past. These people are now aware of their own motivations. What was formerly significant is no longer so. Directees
find life is more complicated — for example, some images of God
no longer work for them. They do not fit into things like they used
to. The movement from one symbol system to another that is part
of the self-aware level may be intensified here. For many, this is
the opportunity for opening up life, for growing up, for taking on
new responsibilities. It is at this time that individuals forge their
own unique style in response to life and their environment. This
uniqueness can be embraced before God if they choose to do so.

Impulse Control. Rules are grasped differently here. They are "internalized, self-evaluated and self-chosen."[33] Rules are not absolute;
there are exceptions. Standards of evaluation are inner moral ones.
The nature of guilt is different. For the Conformist, it is shame.
For the Conscientious, it is more a judgment[34] about certain actions
because motives are central in moral evaluation.

This stage of self-evaluation can cause a hypercritical stance toward oneself and others, including the director. Directees may be confused over what is right or wrong, but discernment can help them when done in the light of the place they have in community and their need for salvation. The directees here can review past assumptions that they could save themselves. Discernment is directed toward their greater reliance on God. At this time in direction the directee will most probably come to a fuller and more theologically accurate understanding of grace and of the fact that God saves us out of pure graciousness.

Interpersonal Style. Because relationships have become broadened and deepened, persons at this stage have greater capacity for intimacy and so for more intense relationships. They are more responsible and more communicative. Feelings are more easily differentiated. They can recognize their own strengths and weaknesses in relationships since the other persons act like mirrors. Being more objective about themselves means being more objective with others. This makes for the greater possibility of intimacy. But such a turn toward mutuality can cause a breakdown because many times other people do not act mutually. When these persons do not find themselves supported, they may say things like, "I can't grow in this situation," or, "There is no support for my inner life." They mean others should respond to their newly forged self-identity.[35] At the next stage these comments are more statements of fact and of their opportunity to move on with their lives.

At this stage, because there is a deepened sense of ideas and friendships, the person has more to give. The problem is that these persons care for everyone but themselves (the unhealthy Two) and so burn out. What care and concern mean must include the self. This care of self will make it possible to deepen their relationship with God at this time. It is now the God of the person, not that of the parents, church, or society. As a result prayer is more affective, although it may still be difficult to express sexual, aggressive, or angry feelings toward God. Directors should encourage an expression of a broad range of emotions toward God.[36]

In summary, the strengths of the Conscientious stage include an adult conscience; long-term, self-evaluated and self-chosen goals; reflexivity; and a developed and differentiated inner life. The limitations often present are problems dealing with a relativistic world, self-centered and subjective judgments about oneself, and excessive confidence in one's own assessments and reflections. The virtues, according to Liebert, are "inner moral standards, integrity, truthfulness, understanding, altruism, humor." The temptations are avoiding responsibility through alienation and cynicism, refusing to move toward self-appropriated standards, excluding ourselves from the scope of care, "getting sidetracked into a search for inner religious experience,"[37] and judging and controlling others by our own norms.

Spiritual direction is appropriate at this stage because of an awareness of the inner life, self-chosen standards and goals, and extended vision about goals and commitments. The adult moral conscience is present. Directors should not be disappointed that all their directees are not at this stage. Some will never be.

The Interindividual Stage

The Interindividual Transition. Liebert uses the term "Interindividual transition" to refer to the movement toward the Interindividual stage because "enhanced originality characterizes increasing developmental complexity."[38] We have here the characteristics of the Conscientious stage and the seeds of the Interindividual stage. Its characteristics include: a new toleration of self and others, an awareness of inner conflict, a toleration of paradox and contradiction, and a vivid portrayal of feelings and needs. Opposites may coexist at the same time: that is, there may be conflict between personal freedom and personal responsibility and more conceptual complexity. But as a result the person can grasp the difference between inner and outer realities and can come to have a true notion of development; further, the process becomes the natural way of being. Development becomes a way of life because of the better understanding of time. Here self-reflection moves more toward integration, toward finding causes and reasons for our experience, toward more understanding of ourselves in terms of relationships, and toward more awareness of psychological development.

The particular strengths of this transition include more ability to discriminate, especially between process and outcome between the inner and outer life, between how individual selves differ significantly, and regarding how we may be independent in many areas but emotionally dependent in others. There is more interest in the process of the spiritual journey. There is the recognition of many social problems, but the person may not yet be able to take any personal stand. People in the midst of this transition struggle with paradoxes, such as how to combine the pursuit of intimacy and achievement.

There are also limitations at this level, such as the inability to integrate personal and group needs, intimacy and achievement, and freedom and responsibility. Alternatives still seem to be along either/or lines.

The Interindividual Stage Itself. Probably few reach this stage before their midlife, although some in the college years do so. People move into this stage for many reasons, for example, disillusionment with life and having ideals collide with commitments. They now can see themselves as part of a larger world-context and can let others be individuals as such. Sometimes this stage is called autonomy, but the difficulty with the use of this word in the Western world is that it often refers to "an enclosed, isolated, nuclear self, completely unaffected by other persons and systems."[39] But that is not what it means to be at this stage because here the person is capable of deeper mutuality and equality. Because these persons let others be responsible for themselves, making their own mistakes, there is more intimacy and mutuality. They recognize that they are interdependent, and they have a broader view of life that allows them to enter into social justice issues.

Cognitive Style. As already noted, Interindividualists have the ability to deal with paradox and to perceive complex patterns in individuals and systems. They tolerate ambiguity. Two contradictory statements may both be true, or a statement may be true and not true at the same time. In other words, logic is not enough to explain things. They must pay attention to the context. The long-committed life makes it possible to think contextually. Discernment at this level is more complex. At this stage persons can understand such realities as social sin and sinful structures. Persons at this stage understand that they have the responsibility to work for change on both the personal and institutional levels.

Conscious Preoccupations. Clearly, the inner life deepens. Interindividualists express vivid feelings, both humorous and sorrowful. Sexual feelings naturally emerge within a mutual relationship. Development includes the whole person, both the physiological and psychological. Self-fulfillment is a conscious goal, but it is pursued within a social context. There is an expanded view of self-in-relationship. At this time of life when vision and action are brought together, commitments must be reexamined to be dropped or to be changed or to be reappropriated. Considerable discernment is called for here so that the director does not influence the persons one way or the other. At the Conscientious stage, they needed critical judgment to distinguish themselves from others. At this new stage, this critical distance needs to be relativized and seen anew. Union is now the goal.

Impulse Control. There is a mellow quality to this stage since the people know that there is more to life and spiritual growth than the dictates of conscience. They are realistic about themselves and so more compassionate and kind to themselves. They act morally from principles that flow from their desire to bring the inner and outer lives together. There is more toleration for inner ambiguities, and they have the capacity to see themselves in many different ways. Elements of the unconscious emerge at this stage through so-called negative feelings, which were not permitted to arise earlier. Often sexual feelings will reappear in interpersonal relationships.

A painful area of exploration may be the adjustment that needs to be made between their visions and self-ideals and the limitations of their life circumstances. They may be in a certain lifestyle and now their needs, which cannot be ignored, conflict with that lifestyle. Reintegration is called for here. They need to find a way of keeping their ideals alive but being realistic about it. For the Interindividual person there is always the need to reintegrate.

Interpersonal Style. As Interindividualists become more aware of their commitments and the legitimacy of other perspectives, there is the need to transcend the antithesis between groups and themselves and themselves and others. To move beyond these antitheses and to reconcile themselves with what is not possible to achieve is the work of the Integrated stage (see below). At the Interindividual stage, the whole matter of self-care is reframed. Now the self is included in any group for which one is caring. To take care of oneself is not considered a selfish act and a shirking of responsibility to others. It is living out of the insight that the self and the other are interdependent. We know ourselves as separate only insofar as we can distinguish ourselves from others. I am reminded here of Teilhard de Chardin's statement that "union differentiates."

God is experienced as other in a new way. Images of God that are based on images of the self no longer work very well. They may fall away. There is more darkness and obscurity present with increasing intimacy with God. John of the Cross's "dark night of the soul" represents the movement from the strong ego of the Conscientious to the more integrated ego of the Interindividual.[40]

Spiritual direction at this stage is different because the directees now assume more responsibility for their own path and spiritual life. At times the directee may surpass the director, who may not have attained this stage fully. Many directors will only be able to travel along with the directees as they make their own way. Such directees may still want someone to be with them, however.

In summary, the strengths of this level include: a vision and commitment beyond the self such that the self is part of the vision; a tolerance for the autonomy of others; and more reliance on the unconscious self and God. There are still weaknesses here: for instance, the self still remains divided, and one lives in structures and institutions that are at variance with one's goals and values.

The virtues of this stage are more intimacy with self, others, and God; a sense of co-creating with God; a commitment to social concerns that may move beyond one's own group, nation, religion, and so on; and more congruity between the inner and outer life and between moral principles and behavior. The temptations that beset those at this stage are refusing to go through the self-emptying process to accept the autonomy of others, neglecting to build relationships that are truly mutual and appropriately intimate, and avoiding confronting the sinful structures in which we live.

The Integrated Stage

This stage is rarely found,[41] although some enneagram experts talk as if we move from the Conformist directly to the Integrated stage. Others seem never to admit the possibility of this stage and for this reason continue to use the enneagram to deal with negativity. Liebert says that it is difficult to define this stage or describe it psychologically because it is one of highly nuanced spirituality and is complex in nature.[42] The struggles for personal identity bring together the various aspects of life. Intimacy and mutuality come together in the one personality, and that makes possible a broad range of social concerns. It may not be wise to try to describe the so-called ideal person who *may* be at the end of the process of integration. It is difficult to know exactly who is being depicted and how many people are being described when phrases such as "authentic self-transcendence," "being in touch with the very depths of themselves," or "living in deep harmony with all that is" are used. But we do know that these people's sense of community is more comprehensive and inclusive and their compassion is universal.[43] These people probably do not need spiritual direction or the enneagram.

Liebert ends her chapter 7 with some questions addressed to the various theories of personality development. For instance, these theories tend to postulate an ever-developing ego, stronger, more autonomous, more differentiated. Classical spirituality, however, speaks of self-emptying, self-denial, asceticism. Are these images or perspectives opposed? Her response is that we must have an integrated self to empty out and that we cannot begin already empty. The Conscientious stage sees things in terms of self-fulfillment, where the self is the norm of reality, but the Interindividual and Integrated stages see true fulfillment in handing ourselves over to a larger vision and purpose.

The director needs to be sensitive to the kind of death to self involved in each stage. The development of a bigger, stronger ego is neither the end product of the spiritual life nor the enemy of self-denial. We will see later how well this point accords with the approach to the enneagram applied here. Further, we need to remember that we cannot reduce God to a being who is available to each or any stage of development. God transcends all stages, and we have but a glimpse of the experience of God at any point in our life. And finally, directors should not force people into stages. People are not reducible to stages, no matter how adequate the stages may be articulated. Stages are helpful for grasping why a person sees something in a certain way. The same must be said about the spaces of the enneagram and the styles of attention.

Spiritual Direction as I See It

Before moving into a consideration of spiritual direction and each of the enneagram spaces, it is only proper that the reader have a sense of how I understand spiritual direction. First, let me state that I am in complete accord with Liebert's definition of spiritual direction given earlier in this chapter. In addition, this is my working definition of Christian spiritual direction: *The process in which a Christian accompanies others for an extended period of time for the purpose of clarifying the psychological and religious issues in the directees so that they may move toward deeper union with God and contribute to ministry within the Christian community.*

This definition implies that the method of the director is to follow the directees, not to be led by them. According to this definition the director does not intrude in the life of the directees by issuing instructions on how to live their lives or imposing on them methods of prayer or prescribed scriptural or other religious texts. Nor does the director remain nondirective, simply listening and "letting the Holy Spirit do the directing." I find that both the invasive and so-called nondirective approaches are cover-ups for incompetence or the director's desire to avoid dealing with painful human issues that they often characterize as not appropriate for spiritual direction.

Rather the director in the approach that I espouse is very much involved, asking clarifying questions, doing follow-up from previous sessions, and making concrete suggestions along the way. This approach is therapeutic because we are dealing with the human person, and spiritual growth cannot be so easily separated from psychological growth. And even at the higher levels of development there is still need for healing. It is Christian because a faith commitment is the presupposed environment, and the ultimate purpose is that the direction redounds to the benefit of the Christian community.

Some will still find this insufficiently Christian or spiritual. Usually they mean that spiritual direction should deal more with specifically spiritual issues and not so much with psychological and therapeutic ones. They think that the latter are more appropriate for pastoral counseling. This usually implies that a great deal of religious rather than therapeutic language will be used in spiritual direction. I do not agree with this approach. First, I do not find it that easy to compartmentalize humanity into two realms: the spiritual and the psychological. Second, as I have already noted, these directors have a tendency to ask directees such questions as: Have you asked God about this? or What does Jesus say about this? Directees who have had this experience have come to me confused. And rightly so, because God expects us to use ordinary human means to discover what it is God wants (if that is the right way to put it theologically). These means are psychological and therapeutic. The Holy Spirit may have intervened personally and directly at the time of the annunciation to the Virgin Mary in ways that bypass the human, but we cannot presume such activity in spiritual direction.

Often in the actual experience there is little distinction between psychological counseling and spiritual direction. Therapy too is an educative process where one can enhance one's spiritual life. It is not only intended for crisis resolution. Sometimes the differences between the two can be found only in whether one lies on a couch and the amount of the fee. One real difference is that spiritual direction must be concerned with the public arena, in particular the Christian community. Spiritual direction cannot be simply working on our own issues. It must move us into the larger areas of church life, such as matters of social justice. It must make us more aware of concerns larger than having been abused or rejected, not being able to pray, and the fear that God has abandoned us. Therapy can also move us into the public arena, but it need not.

Spiritual direction is one way the Christian is assisted to take the passageway of the paschal mystery. But this passageway is a public process. We are called out of being caught up in ourselves narcissistically. We are called out by love, love of others. The paschal mystery is not only about our own dying and rising with Christ but also about the liberation of other people. Transformation in Christ is not simply a personal matter. It refers to such things as the destruction of the ecological system, the maiming of the world around us. The interior life cannot remain interior only. It is my contention that the enneagram can help to make interiority more visible and accessible to directees themselves as well as to others.

Concluding Note

In the chapters that follow I shall apply the three levels of adult development to the individual spaces of the enneagram. This is meant to be a conversation between the two partners of the enneagram and adult development for the benefit of spiritual directors and directees and any others interested in spiritual growth. Much of the conversation is framed in terms of the enneagram and attentional styles as given by Helen Palmer[44] and the stages of growth as articulated by Elizabeth Liebert. Putting the two together is my own doing.[45] In the course of the conversation I have added a great deal of my own material arising from other sources and my own reflections. In that sense there are three persons involved in this conversation.

Chapter 3

The Space of Two

Twos enter spiritual direction in a variety of ways, depending on the level of their development. Usually their coming to spiritual direction has to do with things not working as positively as they would like. Frequently, feelings of resentment that they cannot explain are troubling them. They try to move away from their feelings with humor, compliments, and lots of talking. Most likely they feel that people do not pick up on their good intentions. They probably need some help in removing whatever masks of self-deception they are still wearing. Life may have become empty. They may feel lonely. They most probably feel unappreciated. They are experiencing some sense of lack or deficiency in their lives.[1]

Much in popular culture carries the feeling of Two. Many of the lyrics of the love songs of today communicate such ideas that if you are seeking love, the singer can offer more than anyone else. And if you need someone to lean on, you can lean on me. Many stock phrases contain this Two mentality when they put forth something as the honorable thing to do. One student of mine noted that the United Church of Christ has a bumper sticker that says:

> To Believe Is To Care
> To Care Is To Do

An anonymous poem catches the same quality:

> LOVE
> ever gives
> forgives
> outlives
> yet ever stands
> with open hands
> and while it lives
> it gives
> for this is

> love's prerogative
> to give
> and give
> and GIVE[2]

Direction with the Conformist Two

The director who is dealing with Twos at the Conformist stage will quickly perceive that their mentality is framed by the need for approval.[3] Their ego comes across clearly in terms of statements such as "I can help" or "I am needed," but there is general confusion regarding their self-imaging. The pride they take in being adaptable to others blinds them to their constant changing for others, and their need to be reassured on how helpful they are prevents self-knowledge and self-understanding. Since they look outside themselves for their self-definition, there appears to be little going on inside. This creates a bewilderment about who they really are. And since they are expert in picking up the feelings of others and have not developed the mechanism to distinguish their own feelings from those of others, this confusion is compounded. Added to this is the difficulty in following their logic since they are so programmed to get approval, usually indirectly, lest they reveal any need on their part to have their needs made known.

Conformists are persons whose self is constituted by the groups to which they belong. In the case of Twos this is complicated by the fact that they usually belong to many groups and usually are connected with a diverse number of individuals. People in some other spaces on the enneagram would tend to belong to fewer groups, and so it would be easier for the director to identify the kind of personality the directees are assuming through their group relationships. In the case of these Twos this will be very different since they change for every group and every individual. However, at later stages of development this ability to engage in multiple relationships with ease can be an asset to spiritual growth. They can have more and so richer relationships with God.

These Twos are at the beginning of the spiritual direction process. The director would do well to be slow to introduce subtle spiritual advice. It is not a good idea to recommend that they begin reading the mystics, unless, of course, they have such an inclination. An excellent therapeutic practice, good for all the spaces at this stage, is the facilitation of the directees' ability to distinguish their thoughts from their feelings. Strange as it may seem for Twos, they need to widen their vocabulary of feeling words. The first thing to do is to introduce some clarity in their cognitive process. At this level they are not fully able to feel shame over the fact that they help others often to satisfy their own needs, although that ability can have a beginning here. Many Twos at this stage present themselves as full of feeling, although they lack practice in articulating those feelings.

A special issue here is that Conformist persons tend to make their evaluations based on external criteria, and social behavior and fixated Twos tend to move all their energy outside and into other people. This constitutes a double jeopardy for these Twos, and so the director needs to urge them to discover how their attention works early in the process of spiritual direction. They need to feel something inside of themselves that is concrete and that can ground their attention inward. Prayer types that ask meditators to imagine certain feelings inside themselves are a good beginning. They may lead to the feeling of actual feelings that are clearly distinct from thoughts. In order for persons to intervene to break the cycle of their preoccupations, they need to have something with which to compare their usual way of attending. In the case of the Twos this will be the experience of something inside themselves. That way they can find their real inner emotions. It is these feelings and not the feelings of someone else that must be the basis of their spiritual growth. Often they find it difficult to make this distinction because they are so preoccupied with getting other people to accept their expression of their own needs. If their friends do not legitimate what they feel they need, they think there is something wrong with having such needs and so short-circuit their own feelings. For Twos who have difficulty feeling anything inside the director might suggest something concrete as a breakthrough. For instance, it may be that the directee has not had an effective connection with his/her mother. Perhaps, the mother is emotionally dead, and for a Two this can carry a tremendous feeling of loss and grief. This sadness that they feel inside may provide the opening.

Because Twos at this stage cannot recognize, or will not permit themselves to recognize, their unconscious needs, especially for attention and approval, they are concerned in direction with the matter of rejection. Some such experiences may have brought them to direction, and the director will soon sense the ways in which they try to avoid this rejection. Probably in the very first session, the Two directees will try to avoid anything that they think might cause rejection from the director. Since they are trapped by the attention that others give to them, they will alter for the director as much as they alter for anyone else. In the beginning directors will feel like they are being led through a maze as they try to follow these persons and their split attentional style. Some times they are focusing on their own feelings, sometimes on the feelings of others, sometimes on their attractions. Since they are blind to these needs and feelings, they find it difficult to be alone. Direction may be for them the one place where they are not alone and need not hide from their needs. A discerning director will sense when to support them in this and when to move them to solitude so that they can gradually recognize their needs on their own without any opportunity to change for others.

This overwhelming need for approval needs to be addressed early in direction. Their seeking of approval moves them in the direction of powerful and influential people, regardless of those persons' worldviews. The director should explore their motivation in this quest for approbation. The director could easily begin with their fidelity to the church, which could be for them one of the agencies of approval in their lives. One of my students had taught in a parochial school for five years. He was not an overtly religious person and was reserved about expressing his own religious commitments. But he found it difficult to be critical of the school administrators who promoted an outmoded form of devotion. He found it so much easier to be supportive of these same people in the other areas of their work.

Also, Twos are neighbors to Threes, and they can easily succumb to a world governed by external images. This will often involve them in a concern over things of very transient value such as fashion, what others in the office are doing for their vacations, and the like. In all this there is some kind of seeking for approval. For Christian Twos this can very easily take on the form of the practice of charitable works that baptizes their need to help others. It is also a source of great positive emotional feedback. This can also take the form of their being able to claim a number of good friendships that were the result of their own efforts. The attractiveness of their friends reflects back on them because they so closely identify with them.

The director's main contribution at this point may be patience as the directees slowly struggle to come to terms with the confusion brought about by their desire to be all things to all people. It may be that the director will first of all help Twos to see that they are confused. Once that process has begun, the director can assist them to feel the confusion, not something they usually do on their own at this point. But for Twos who are sincere about direction, the light will begin to dawn. Palmer's remarks are relevant here:

> Like an emotional athlete, Givers can be thinking, being, and feeling their relationship. The sense of the self invoked by the other becomes central. As Twos mature, they usually become more impatient with being central to so many. A confusion arises among the many selves. "Which one is me?" Recognizing a constant self is at the heart of the matter, because a self has definite needs.[4]

At the Conformist stage the way the Twos deal with their impulses manifests itself through some kind of control or manipulation. To the undiscerning person this control will not be obvious. They repress their own feelings in order to elicit love and approval from others. Their form of manipulation is indirect. They do not try to get you to obey them through command. Rather, they do it through giving, through making your agenda their own, through associating with authority figures, through masking their own uneasiness and ambiguity about sexuality under the guise of intimacy, especially external displays of affection. In the end, they have taken control of another's life, although neither party may have recognized what was going on. I vividly recall an experience with such a Two that I had years ago. Although I had met her only once before, when she entered my office she rushed toward me to embrace and kiss me. I was struck by the excess of energy involved. At that time I was not thinking in enneagram terms, but she, who is now a good friend, was, at that point of her life, more the Conformist Two.

Here the director can be of assistance by helping Twos recognize that when they think they are helping, they are actually invading. They need to know why they invade other peoples' lives. The director might well begin with the exploration of the place of negative feelings in their lives. This could open up for them some of their hidden needs. Unless that happens, the director will have little success with Twos. It is not too early to begin the exploration of the place of anger in the spiritual life of Twos. They are next to the gut center, where is there is a lot anger. One Two said that as a young person he was unaware of anger but that he now recognizes that he had transformed the anger coming from his neighbor, One, into a search for quality rather than quantity. He procrastinated a lot in order to feel prepared. He now wonders if that was a way of being angry. There is much that Twos are angry about: not getting the approval they think they deserve, not getting the emotional response they seek, and not being free. This latter concern is the most fruitful to explore in direction. What is real freedom for them? It is not the same as the kind of freedom they claim when they reject past relationships that they now consider oppressive. This is, of course, a form of freedom, but their real freedom has to take on the more positive form of self-appropriation. Although not much progress can be made in the integration of sexual feelings now, it is still appropriate to identify them as a way of feeling something interiorly, and so come to a stronger sense of the self.

The Twos' manipulative process gets its energy from their need to be number one in the life of someone. That explains their adeptness in altering their personalities, their ease in being supportive of others, and their natural movement toward other people. The director will usually find it easy to connect with Twos initially, since their energy is directed to making connections. They even pride themselves on whom they have for a director. The director needs to be aware that Twos find their identity in their relationships, including their relationship with the spiritual director. An unaware director can easily be manipulated here, believing that more is going on with the directee than really is. The contact may seem easy and warm, but it is also probably lacking in depth. Strong affective contact does not mean an exuberant embrace, as in the case of my Two friend coming into my office. It simply means that for Twos there is a lot of energy in their relationships, especially in their attractions. As Palmer notes, "to give is to get" is the guiding principle. Some Twos find themselves acting in a coquettish way, engaging in seductive behavior not so much for an erotic satisfaction but rather as a way of seeking affirmation. They need to know that they are desired and loved by someone who is desirable to them.

Usually Twos at the Conformist stage begin spiritual direction because they want to move, to change, because they have sensed some desire to be free. Of course, others come to direction because it can serve as a way of getting approval. But usually these persons come to direction because they want to break out of the prison of supporting others. They are tired of conforming to others.

There are numerous reasons why this process may begin for them. Often it will have something to do with solitude. When the director, as was suggested earlier, encourages them to take advantage of moments of solitude, it should be for a purpose. As I noted earlier, it is in these moments of solitude that Twos can engage in distinguishing thoughts from feelings. The director should give this task priority because the feelings of the Twos are their entrance points to their needs. If the director is with them in their solitude, then they are not completely alone and can feel supported in their attempt to break away from their dependency on others. In their aloneness they can recognize their manipulative tendencies. Hidden anger is lurking somewhere in the Twos at this stage, and it will benefit the spiritual direction if the director can help Twos discover it.

The main principle for the director working with the Conformist Twos is to help them shift their attention so they can look at the question: Who is the true self here? What remains the same amid all these changes? With that as the main principle, the main task for the director is to be with Twos in the self-aware transition to the next stage, the Conscientious one. The temptation will be to move Twos away from their preoccupation with group values toward more personal ones. However, what needs to be done at this period of transition is to move the Two away from the values of *the other* to more personal ones. Since this transition often begins when Twos realize that they have enslaved themselves to helping and now want to be free, they need to become aware of precisely which persons they are enslaved to. Being betrayed after all the good they have done often causes them to seek spiritual direction. But they have been betrayed by some one specific. Twos more than most other spaces on the enneagram need to know that they are not their relationships. It is precisely the negative experiences noted in a definite relationship that can help them to become more reflective. That is the moment when the director can assist them in their shift of attention. The point here is that all Conformists overidentify with groups. But Twos need to separate from individuals first. Once they can learn to intervene when they see their attention going out to some *person*, they can then learn how to do the same with attention going out to some *group*.

A form of prayer at this time that could move these Twos to healthier images of God is the kind that places the Two alone with God — just God and the directee are present, with no possibility of other referencing. Twos will not find out who they really are as long as they are looking to other humans for definition. They should be reacting to only one person, and that is God or Christ. I suspect that at this time even devotion to the saints could introduce the kind of split attention in their prayer that would distract them from finding the one (not several) true self in God.

Since Twos have lost their connection with the freedom that belongs to them as human beings, and so, therefore, the freedom that as Christians they possess in a life committed to Christ, the content of their prayers and meditations, their spiritual reading, and their spiritual practices need to emphasize the concrete experience of freedom. The director could suggest to them figures, whether historical or contemporary, who are models of freedom. They cannot become free if they do not know what freedom is. They can be greatly helped by meditating on the lives of those who achieved freedom by recognizing their way of keeping themselves dependent on others, who were not tricked by their hearts to stay connected to certain people, who learned to break out of the prison of their minds, and who found that in becoming free they did not lose the love of others but became more loving toward themselves. Twos find centering prayer helpful because it is so freeing for them. They discover that they do not have to *do anything*. I suggest the following meditation as a way of moving the directee to health and opening some areas that call for further growth:[5]

> *Quiet your whole person and pay attention to your breathing. Make sure you are inside. Locate some feeling or sensation but not something that is so powerful that it would distract you. Contact some ordinary feeling. Stay with it. Observe yourself feeling inside. Now watch to see if you enlarge the feeling to make it bigger. Are you associating some importance to the feeling? Had you thought of this before? Name some of the feelings that are emerging. Do you feel anxiety? Anger? Follow first the anxiety. Does it point to something that you really want but have not been able to pursue? Now follow the anger. Does it lead you to any repressed needs? Note where these two journeys take you.*

Direction with the Conscientious Two

On most levels, Conscientious Twos are more aware than Conformist Twos. The self-aware transitional period to this stage is a very significant one for direction since this is the time of liminality for the directees. They are moving away from all the presuppositions of the Conformist stage to accept the world in a more pluralistic way. They are living in between the structures of two levels of development. They are caught in the cracks of life. The Twos are becoming fully engaged in the process of deconstructing and reconstructing their self-identity. Focusing on the needs of others now is found to have many exceptions. They are less willing to put themselves in the category they have used in the past: the caring person for whom relationships are the most important thing. Most significantly they are entertaining doubts about their past ideal of what makes love to be real love. Love is not that which someone else needs to affirm in them. They are dipping their toes in the waters of true intimacy. They are beginning to look inside themselves. They are still aware of the feelings and emotions of others, but they now no longer feel the need to take them upon themselves. One Two said that he tries not to own the other's feelings but to let the owner of the feelings retain ownership. He can also better express his own feelings now because he does not have to distinguish them from those of others.

Since during this transitional time Twos are very much influenced by their mentors, the director needs to be aware of this and to be particularly sensitive to what is taking place. This means that the director must know what the directee is feeling. The director may be feeling something else. If the director feels happy and the directee feels sad, the directee, who can easily pick up the feelings of the director, may assume a happy feeling s/he does not actually have.

Conscientious Twos are more articulate about their questions such as: To what degree is the image of God as rescuer good for them? What really is God's will in a certain situation? Should they be helping religious and church structures given the deficiencies in such organizations? They are more at ease examining questions of faith. They still do not acknowledge all their needs, but they do claim their feelings of anger and anxiety about who they are. This provides an opening for the director to move them to greater depth. The directees still need support here because the temptation is to react to these feelings and go in the opposite direction of their Conformist stage and become totally independent. To the degree that they try to avoid the challenge of their own feelings, these Twos look like Ones with a stress on their perfectionistic wing. Twos need to move away from this tendency because it prevents them from becoming intimate with their emotional lives, a necessary part of their becoming free.

The director can accompany Twos as they deal with these faith questions, allowing them to ask them and to pursue them. But it would be well for the director to help Twos to see if there are any connections between these questions and the anger and anxiety they are beginning to admit on the conscious level. For instance, getting in touch with some of the anger and resentment in their lives will open up for these Twos some of the reasons that they do certain things and hold on to certain beliefs. It is not too early for the director to explore with them some of the motivations behind their commitment to certain doctrines, spiritual practices, or religious ideals. In fact, this should have begun at the Conformist stage. This connection between anger and religion showed itself in the case of a Two friend of mine as she became increasingly aware of her anger at the church for creating an atmosphere that produced severe scrupulosity in her mother. She suddenly became angry at me, to my confusion. Upon reflection she realized that her anger at the church was transferred to me because I am priest.

As would be expected at the Conscientious level, the Twos are much more cognizant of their preoccupations. They are claiming their self-identity. This means letting go of certain ideals, not their own usually, but the ideals of others that they have taken on and with which they have identified. The central concern in spiritual direction at this time is what these Twos really want. Since their rescuer/helper God no longer works for them, they cannot count on this image of God to supply their identity. As they pursue the path of self-identity, the director can help them see that they already have their own uniqueness, that they are persons with their own feelings and actions. This means intervening in their practice of altering for others, assuming the many selves that they can become. About the Twos' altering practice Palmer says this: "It's not a matter of faking it or putting on a mask; it feels more like getting along with people so that we all like one another."[6] For committed Christians, does that not sound like the promotion of Christian charity? It will be up to the director to help them distinguish this practice of switching to different selves from true Christian concern and love. Here the director will be dealing with a specific issue for these Christians who are pursuing the path of holiness and Christian charity as it has been understood by the tradition. While Christian spirituality is not based on some kind of narcissistic, masochistic theology of the suffering Jesus, neither is it a way of life that equates virtue with helping others feel good. Too often what comes under the aegis of Christian charity is only a thinly disguised invasion into personal privacy of others, an attitude of condescension, and an attempt (often unconscious) to take control of the life of the recipient of the giver's beneficence.

No longer do these Twos try to control their impulses through shame, through feeling bad when they are not preoccupied with everyone else's agenda. Now they are more able to distinguish when to offer their services and when not to do so. The director can be helpful in assisting them to reframe their questions and concerns in a larger context. The main thing the director wants the directees to avoid at the Conscientious level is going to the opposite extreme of what they were like at the Conformist level. Previously, they had been entirely too dependent on the approval of others. The solution is not to adopt a "pull oneself up by one's bootstraps" kind of spirituality. The virtuous action here is to let go of the feelings outside of themselves and to take on their own feelings.

The transition to health for Twos will involve the experience of anger. Realizing how much they have given away, now they want to claim their freedom. The temptation is to move too far away from their past habit of trying to please others. The anger they feel about having suppressed their own needs propels their flight to freedom. That certainly has been the case with the friend who projected her anger onto me. Also, in her struggle for freedom she may have moved away from a relationship too precipitously. The director is the moderating guide in the midst of this turmoil and the seemingly overwhelming cascade of feelings that come. It is important that the director affirm the directees at this time. However, this affirmation should be for those moments of breakthrough that these Twos have achieved. To affirm the Twos without discrimination might backfire. They may fall back into a tendency to want to help the director or to get the director's approval.

The director will notice that these Twos bring to direction concerns about personal relationships that now have a greater depth. This is simply because the relationships are now pursued with greater perception. While at the Conformist stage there was often a great display of closeness without the concomitant degree of intimacy, now the demonstration of intimacy is more closely matched by the intimacy in the inner world. The two come together because Twos can now identify with their own feelings. Rather than projecting their needs onto others, they can now understand the other person's reaction to them. They are gaining objectivity regarding their own feelings.

Such claiming of their own feelings will create problems for Twos in some of their relationships, and often this will be the material of spiritual direction because our human relationships often shape the way we relate to God. Often friends of Twos have become used to the Twos' past mode of proceeding and may not like a different kind of Two. It is very similar to the case in which one partner is in therapy and the other is not. As the partner in therapy grows, the other becomes increasingly threatened and confused because s/he cannot operate in the expected way. A certain kind of co-dependency has been interrupted. But some past relationships will remain for Twos, and these will be enriched by their growth process (and, hopefully, this will be the case for the other party too).

Change in the area of relationships is very significant for Twos for two reasons. First, when they move in an unhealthy direction, they often burn out on caring for others. This burnout may bring them to spiritual direction and will be the place where the director will start. Second, since they have defined themselves in terms of their relationships, when these change or cease, it causes a kind of identity crisis. This crisis will also be the subject matter of direction. However, the dynamics that caused the burnout or crisis must change if fruitful direction is to continue. The directee needs to accept that the relationships have changed.

What the director can hope for and what the directee is ready for is a more fully emotional experience of God. How to become intimate with God is a key issue at this time. One cannot become intimate with God unless one is intimate with oneself first. Intimacy with another will not substitute for this self-intimacy. Previously, the reigning image of God was of a being to whom Twos had to conform. Such a God will never warm the hearts of anyone. But as Twos continue to claim the full panoply of their feelings, they will have more ways of imaging and relating to God. They can have as many "Gods" as they have feelings. The most rewarding part of direction with Twos at this level is the way in which the director can assist them in naming all the "Gods" of their lives. One student of mine, a Two, suggested this meditation to gain access to these different "Gods":

I picture myself with a close friend. How do I look? What feelings am I having? Now I picture myself with a relative whom I love deeply. How do

*I look now? Is it different? What feelings am I having? Are they the same
or different than before? Now I see myself with a new acquaintance.
How do I look and what are my feelings? Now I picture myself with
God. How do I look and what are my feelings? I notice how my images
and feelings change in these relationships.*[7]

Two areas where newer images of God will most probably not be as
readily available are those that originate from sexual and aggressive
feelings. The director might more prudently wait until the directee
moves to the next level to explore these areas more fully. Initiatory
work here is appropriate, of course.

The arrow dynamic of the enneagram is, I believe, most helpful in
spiritual direction at the Conscientious level. At the previous stage,
the Conformist one, the arrow theory could too facilely be seen as
operating along the more deterministic lines by which it is usually
understood. That is, one moves in one direction and becomes more
fixated, or one moves in the opposite direction and feels more secure. This theory might give further nuance to the stress and security
aspect of the Twos' lives, but it is not that helpful in utilizing the
enneagram as a tool in spiritual direction. The reason is that at the
Conscientious level persons can more consciously choose to move in
one direction or the other and are more capable of picking up good
(or negative) energies from the various points. These energies can
assist them in their clarification process.

When the Twos feel secure and safe to claim their own needs, they
can profitably move to Four to ask about the depth and authenticity
of their feeling world. As Palmer puts it: "You form a relationship
with yourself. You befriend your own potentials and learn to honor
them with the same enthusiasm that you give to significants. A secure Two knows what others feel and can separate at will from their
emotions."[8] Many Twos find that when they move into Four in a
healthy way, their artistic side emerges. Although not naturally inclined to artistic endeavors, they can appreciate the beauty around
them. Moving in this direction stimulates their creativity and spirit
of youthfulness.

Twos at this point will be aware of how at times they take
on the anxiety, melancholy, and disorientation of Fours. It is usually scary and confusing for them to be there. They know there
is something right about being there, but it takes them a while to
settle down when they visit this space. The emotional landscape

of the Four is foreign to them, and so they do not feel comfortable there. Their feelings do not seem to be as clear as the feelings of those who actually come from the space of Four. This shows how the Twos and Fours differ, although preoccupation with feeling is something they have in common. Because Fours reflect upon their own feelings inside, they may come across to others as having a clearer landscape. And in fact, it seems so to them. Their landscape, however, is filled with so many more subtleties than other spaces.

When Twos take on the depression and sense of betrayal of Fours, that does not mean that they should move away from this experience. Rather, this is the opportunity to become acquainted with this Four space so as to be able to understand what the feelings of sadness and grief are all about. By asking questions of these feelings from the Fours' point of view, they can open up their own feelings and needs. Visiting the space of Four periodically is good for Twos — it helps them to distinguish what is their own, especially in the area of feeling. Here the director can assist them to broaden even further their images of God. Perhaps now they can at least entertain the possibility of the sadness of God.

As Palmer notes, for Twos, being at risk means something about relationship. However, those relationships affected by risk are not the ones that are problematic for Twos, no matter how they feel. Rather, it is their good, secure relationships that are a challenge to them. If they are connecting with someone who really loves and respects them, then Twos are called to greater honesty about themselves, something less evident at the Conformist stage. If they try to run away from this, then they can easily go toward the space of Eight and set up a strong defensive reaction. When Twos are in a highly charged and strongly emotional situation, moving to Eight carries with it the danger of losing themselves. They can too easily switch from their own needs to the needs of others and then find themselves "in charge" of situations and groups.

But there is no reason why the space of Eight cannot provide them with a place to discern something about themselves. There is something about this more belligerent space that makes it possible to strip away the many defenses and masks. The Twos need this high energy of the Eight in order to confront themselves and to be honest with themselves. In the Eight space they are given the opportunity to fight and struggle for clarity, and the director needs to support this. In Eight they will often feel more self-assured, more protective of others, and discover that they can move into an advocacy role without trying to control the people they are helping. Life is more exciting in Eight. The value of moving to Eight is that it helps them to view their personal needs and wants as OK, not something that they need apologize for. Claiming their personal freedom is a main part of their moving toward health.

Direction with the Interindividual Two

Before Twos reach and live at the Interindividual state, which is a more advanced level, there is a period of transition. The director will easily note the changes taking place. As Twos move from the Conscientious to the Interindividual stage, they are kinder to themselves, more accepting of a kind of positive "selfishness," more aware of the conflict caused by not disentangling their own feelings from the feelings of others, more able to articulate and be in contact with their needs, more aware of their desire to move out toward others and their need for self-affirmation, and more attentive to their need to be responsible as they struggle for the freedom they desire. They are better able to intervene to change their attention because they can tell when they are projecting, and they know the direction where integration is found.

Twos in this transitional time have a better understanding of the cause of their anger and are more aware of their chameleon-like behavior regarding their friends. It is their growing ability to discriminate that moves them along in their spiritual journey — for example, they can discriminate between the desire to gain approval and the deeper desire for self-approbation, between trying to be indispensable in someone's life and knowing how to support others in a healthy way, between adapting to the wishes of others and having a sense of the self, between the desire to maneuver and control and real love of the other, between being humiliated by disapproval and a sense of humility that leads to improvement. This is still a transitional stage, and so these discriminations are made within limits. One of my students who believes he is in the Conscientious stage[9] developed a brief meditation that helped him to make this transition and that he still uses to prevent a regression. Here is his meditation in edited form:

I take several deep breaths. I enter into my heart and there do the follow-
ing exercise. I see myself as ill and dependent on others. I am confined
to bed after surgery. I am in my home, but I am not alone. What needs
do I have? I look at my body. What does it need right now? What are
my emotional needs? Somebody walks into my room to ask how I am
and to inquire what I need. How do I feel being asked these questions?
What is my response? Then, I answer the caring inquirer. Can I go back
and review all my needs? Can I identify them? Can I accept them? I try
to stay with the needs.

People at the Interindividual stage are those who are most open to
the kind of spiritual direction that moves beyond problem solving.
These people can go deeply into the spiritual life. Twos in particular
at this stage have an expanded worldview, one that takes them beyond their personal relationships. At the heart of each space's way of
thinking lies a paradox. For the Twos that paradox is the desire to be
free and yet the desire to be attached. They still want to be important
in someone's life, whether this is through love or by being the director
behind a powerful person. But now they can live with it and make
it work for themselves. They can break out of their feeling circle
dominated by relationships, which in the past they supported to get
emotional feedback. They purify their reasons for supporting certain
issues and causes. For example, they take up the cause of marginal
persons with no hope of a reward. My friend who became angry with
me is doing these healthy things. But it has been a great struggle, at
least from my point of view. At this time, I would judge that she still
has a way to go. No longer being important in the life of someone
who has been significant in her life is, in my opinion, probably the
highest form of asceticism for her as well as for Twos in general.

Whatever they became increasingly aware of at the Conscientious
level can now be placed in a social context. Self-fulfillment is not
tied to receiving approval from a loved one or an authority figure.
This greater social awareness means that at the Interindividual stage
the director needs to be particularly discerning. When the Twos were
at the Conscientious level, the task was to assist them to distinguish
themselves from others, from the feelings of others, but now the director must help them bring themselves and others together. Now
the Twos can be drawn to see that they can only avoid the temptation to manipulate and control if they see themselves in relationship
in a social context.

Once the context of a certain pattern or way of living is changed, the elements in the pattern itself change. Since these are healthy Twos, this means that at this time many of their commitments will be reappropriated or modified. As their awareness of their needs grows, the questions of their lifestyle will become more significant. If needs are not being met, then some adjustment will be necessary. They will find ways to maintain their idealistic view of commitment but with greater realism. For one of my students this has meant leaving behind an intimate, sexual relationship that he found pleasant and fulfilling to open himself up to a more permanent and more fully committed life with someone in marriage.

This stage of the Twos is where they are more in love with themselves and need not seek such love from others. And they are trying to bring their inner world of feeling more in harmony with the world of feeling of their relationships. These worlds are distinct but not distant from each other. Twos now see themselves in the different ways that others see them. They have a much more sensitive and sophisticated sense of the dynamics of their relation with others.

In many ways, Liebert's description of the Interindividual stage seems more relevant to the Twos than the other spaces, although, of course, that is only true on a superficial level. Liebert speaks of a greater care of the self where such care is not considered selfish. The care of the self is part of the care of others. The self is in communion with other selves, and so the self must be cared for also. This is exactly what Twos need, and at this level they must be supported in this. To care for others and so care for ourselves is to know that we are distinct. The closer we get to ourselves, the closer we can get to others. And this works in reverse. Again, the statement of Teilhard de Chardin is appropriate here: "Union differentiates." The closer we get to someone, the more we can be our true selves.

The images of God as supporter, helper, and so on, may not work as well now. Other images such as bringer of justice, challenger of a self-enclosed world, and so on, may need to be added. This Twos will do with only a little encouragement from the director. The director here will need to be open to let the Twos "fly" as they move into this deeper area of their spiritual lives with which the director may be less acquainted. The hands and arms are significant body parts for Twos. They should be encouraged to visualize being in God's hands or holding God, caressing God, being touched by God. This statement from a male Two is exemplary for most Twos:

Is there a relationship between my hands and arms and my
virtue which is humility (virtue to be developed by Twos)? Yes!
I love to hold and caress with my hands. I love with arms and
hands, and I love to be held and touched. It is with these that I
accept in total love.

Twos usually are comfortable with hands and arms. The question
that the director can propose to them is: What parts of your body
need further integration into your understanding and sense of yourself? It is best to begin where integration probably has already taken
place, with the arms and hands.[10]

Because the Interindividual stage is an advanced one, some more
subtle differentiation is possible in spiritual direction here. That is,
since spiritual direction, unlike therapy, has the Christian community
as its context, the director can help the directees assume a ministerial
character to their spiritual lives. Indeed, this seems necessary to do.
But now their concern for others will be very different. This more
socially oriented spirituality and its practice in daily life will be freed
from a past attitude of giving in order to get. These Twos will still
bring great energy and enthusiasm to the situation of dealing with
the marginated or deprived, but it is no longer based on an expected
response. Also, they are not attracted to these persons and situations
based on some external pleasing quality. There is no hint that they
are manipulating the persons they are assisting simply in order to
get a positive emotional response. There are fewer mixed messages,
such as saying that they are freely offering their help and yet making the recipients feel like some of their personal freedom has been
taken away.

The director can work with the Twos' anger at this point in a way
that is clearly productive for the Twos since, like on the gut center of
the enneagram, anger is a source of great energy. They will not come
across like Eights or Ones because they bring with their sense of
social justice and correct living an affectionate and loving style. Probably, the most helpful thing the director can do with these Twos is to
assist them to stay with their anger. Being part of the heart center of
the enneagram, Twos more easily let go of anger or let it dissipate
more readily. In order to have a steady supply of the anger needed to
make the wheels of their gospel-oriented activity keep turning, they
need to maintain contact with it. It should be clear that anger cannot
be their only source for committed action for others. It must come

from a recognition of their true needs, in this case a need that is rooted in their relationship with God and not merely in their personality. For ultimately, the most powerful source of energy is their love of themselves because they have first been loved by God.

The struggles the director had with the Twos at previous levels of integration regarding sex, affection, and love now come to resolution. Because there is much less repression at this level, sexual feelings will emerge in their relationships. Here the director can help them to clarify how in the past sex and affection meant love for them and especially assist them to see how they used the language of intimacy but did not develop their capacity for it. Often intimacy was more a matter of approved connections and emotional feedback than of sexuality. Now sexual expression is not a substitute for intimacy or a way of avoiding intimacy but is intimacy itself. Sex, affection, and love go together. Previously, sex and affection may have been equated with love, or they may have been separated from love. It would not be unusual for Twos lacking health to find a hug to be a fuller form of intimacy than sexual intercourse. The freedom to claim their sexual feelings and to open up that part of their lives represents for Twos a difficult task even at this level, and the director's guidance is needed. In the past these feelings were often put on hold so that the Twos could be for the other what they thought the other wanted. Sexuality is now what they want because they need it and not because they think it is a way of fulfilling the needs of someone else. Sexual expression is the way that they care for themselves as well as caring for someone else.

Sexual union can have a ministerial character because it is a way of nurturing oneself and others, and it can be prayerful when it becomes a form of contemplation in which one can love oneself fully. This will often mean that it is all right to feel their own and the others' needs. Focusing on the pleasure of the sexual act itself as a way of staying present to the experience will ensure that this mutual help is not a projection of some kind nor a substitution for the necessary vulnerability of intimacy.

The images of God will be changing although it may be difficult to pinpoint any particular concrete images. I suggest that these images will be more felt than visualized. And the feeling will be about freedom, about relief from fulfilling the needs of others, about a release of anger. God will be that feeling of liberation found in their deep self. The director should let the Twos pick whatever images they like, paying attention more to the feelings around the images and whether or not they are truly freeing.

"Aggression"/"seduction" are the words used to describe the sexual Twos in one-to-one relationships.[11] Seduction is found in the way the Twos alter themselves and make themselves attractive to others. The word "aggression" refers to their determined endeavor to make a connection with someone with whom they want a relationship. Their ability to be many selves for many people can be a virtue as well as a fixation. At this level the director will find it is the virtue that is operative. The thing to keep in mind is that seduction and anger go together. Anger often lies behind seduction.

The couple/sexual Twos bring to their relationships a lot of energy and passion. As committed Christians they initiate relationships to bring about the growth of others and themselves. They productively use their sexual energy to keep their connections alive and active, to accompany people on their paths. Because they connect strongly with individual men and women, they move beyond treating people according to gender roles. For the director it can be a rewarding experience to see how each Two here can claim his/her masculinity and femininity, with whatever mix they have, in order to support the freedom others need to break away from gender stereotyping.

We call the social Twos people of social ambition. When unhealthy, they are active, even aggressive, in the social arena. They not only have ambition to be liked, to be popular, and to be influential, but they also have ambition for others, especially people they think important to promote.

It is no surprise that the Interindividual community/social Twos are the most community-oriented and the least involved in the agenda of their individual friends. These are the real "movers and shakers" of community organizing. These people can move beyond their need for a positive image in the eyes of others and really work hard to potentiate other people. They are usually good judges of what other people can do. They know how to be inclusive, breaking down barriers. Mutual exchange comes easily to them. One woman Two told me that she feels she is good at networking and making connections: "I think if have worked knowing people and remembering people and remembering what they do or where they live, it is to my advantage."

"Privileged self-survival" describes the self-preservation Twos. Palmer says that "privilege is unveiled when you help people to become successful and find that you're angry when there's no reward."[12] These people survive through reaping rewards, gifts, and recognition from the many people they have supported and who have depended on them.

For healthy personal/self-preservation Twos this means that they become more comfortable accepting that what they do for others must also be good for themselves. It is a privilege to work and care for others because this is no longer tied to their needs but springs from their own fuller lives. They are no longer working for rewards and emotional feedback. It is simply something they want to do. One female Two put it this way:

> From my experience of caring for an uncle with Alzheimer's disease I can tell there weren't any rewards. Everything I did he disagreed with, and some of his friends refused to believe the doctors or their assessment of his condition as well. Yet not taking responsibility for his care would have been unthinkable to me.

Twos do not trivialize human contact, but now it is not something they depend on. They want to empower others and be committed to their projects, and they do not feel that if they promote others they lessen themselves in some way. They have grown into adaptable people.

Probably the task of the director here on this more instinctual level is mostly a matter of support. Spiritual direction should not become a time of recounting all the good deeds being done but rather should be a period more akin to the kind of theological reflection that is done in professional schools for the ministry. It is a time of uncovering and making explicit the redemptive character of the Twos' work, the salvational quality of their passions and feelings.

Even at this advanced stage the director needs be mindful that s/he is only visiting the space of Two (unless that is the director's space) but that it is that very visiting that makes it possible to assist the directee. This guards against the possibility of the director operating from his/her own preoccupations. Directors must learn how to empathize with their directees. To empathize means to merge with the other, not by losing oneself in the other but by taking the person inside oneself. Interindividual Twos can assist the director to experience how it is possible to merge but not get lost and so not know who you are.

Chapter 4

The Space of Three

Although they are at the center of the heart center, Threes may enter direction the most out of touch with their feelings. They often have trouble getting to the true self. Their tendency is to move to the surface of things rather than the depths. They are constantly on the go because if they stop, they do not know what will happen to them. Everything may fall apart. It is as if they had no infrastructure. They automatically move to success, progress, and efficiency and not the inner life. The interior world is like a foreign country to them. There is so much outward-directed energy at the conscious level that it is difficult for them to make contact with what is inside. They are often at the center of attention, but if they lack contact with their self this attention causes them anxiety. They have become overly identified with job and position. They have difficulty separating themselves from both. Although they are out there in the public and want people to respond to them positively, they may be afraid that they will expose themselves. Suzanne Zuercher says this about their shadow side:

> The first person they deceive is themselves, because they need to see themselves in so positive a light. They are always capable, functional, in charge, or so they need to consider themselves in the early years of their lives. This is the time when they are building their egos and the self-image they project for other people. It is by this self-image that they want to be known. Reality adjusts to fit that image, which means that their limitations have to be hidden away.[1]

I had a fellow novice who as a Three never seemed to experience anything negative in what he did or what happened to him. His fellow novices would find him in a situation that seemed unredeemable, but he would respond to it by saying: "Oh well. The good part of all this is...."

Threes' contact with their feelings is very superficial. They tend to be very self-referential. They look more self-centered than the other spaces, but that is probably due to the fact that they reveal all that is going on in their minds. They have the need to turn all those near them into an audience. They are addicted to telling you about all the important people they know, mentioning their distinguished friends, and recounting their accomplishments. Self-affirmation publicly displayed and successful relationships referred to in conversation falsely assure them that they are at an important spot in the world. I used to have a colleague who is a Three. He would come into the room where the faculty mailboxes were, open his mail, and then read it aloud to us, especially if it was about getting another honorary degree, about another significant invitation to give a talk, or a buddy-buddy letter from someone famous. Threes are ever performing. This keeps them from looking within, something that they fear greatly. They are afraid that if they do so, they will find nothing. The challenge for them in spiritual direction is to discover real authenticity.[2]

Spiritual Direction with the Conformist Three

Conformist Threes are called performers, achievers, status-seekers, and names such as these.[3] In a less-developed stage their variety shows through. They are very image-oriented and regard efficiency and productivity as primary desiderata. They expend considerable energy trying to succeed or at least give the impression they are successful.

Threes have the gift of picking up the feelings and energies of groups. At the Conformist stage the self is constituted by the groups to which these persons belong. This presents a considerable block in spiritual direction for these persons. They so easily identify with groups that it is difficult for them to find a self apart from those groups. I know a former Jesuit who is a Three and who found a great deal of his meaning in "being a Jesuit." I think finding his true self contributed to his leaving the Jesuits. Threes' attentional style is to move toward the appropriate feeling. It is not that they consciously decide to feel a certain way. They feel appropriate automatically. They feel the feelings of a role. But these feelings are not their own. For instance, they might connect with how a good nurse feels and so begin to feel that way. These feelings are appropriate and appropriated, but they are not their own. They are a block to the true self. The difficulty for the director is that Threes can feel like a good directee feels. Being involved with the true self is what keeps spiritual direction going, but who is the true self here? The director can begin the process of intervention by suggesting they practice distinguishing the true feelings of a loving mother from the feelings they *think* a loving mother should have (the appropriate feelings of a loving mother).

Threes will think like the group or at least the way they think the group thinks. Rather than reaching judgments on their own, they look to the group for their opinions, their evaluations, their conclusions. The director will wonder if the person is speaking or if the group is speaking through him/her. This is problematic because often the groups have been formed around issues that are based on prejudice. Conformist Threes, especially, cannot hold their own in such situations.

It is equally true that the Conformist Threes will take on the norms and procedures of the healthy groups to which they belong, be it family, church, groups promoting justice, or even groups in counseling. The difficulty is the same. Who are these people, and what are they really feeling? The director will need to begin with the difficult task of having them distinguish thought from feeling and both from their job or role. Until that process begins it would be difficult to make use of the forms of discernment. One could use Ignatian discernment only in its most basic form. And here the director may need to begin more conceptually, introducing some nuance in the Threes' thinking. This is not so much the task of opening up the inner spiritual life as it is to build it up since it hardly exists. Threes see their spiritual lives in terms of the particular view of spirituality of the group with which they have identified. Progress in the spiritual life is what others say it is. In many ways any person at the Conformist level has some of these undeveloped Three qualities of relying on external behavior to make judgments and on the group to know how to feel.

The director, in helping them to discover their style of attention, will want to point out to them how they are selective in what they pay attention to. In their case, it is whatever promotes their image, their job, or what they are doing. It would be premature to explore with them the meaning of love in their lives or how it feels to love. If the director is searching for their feelings, it is better to have them speak about their work, what they are doing, and then to listen for the feelings that accompany the parade of words that marches before the director.

The most difficult task in direction with Threes is to help them gain access to the feelings behind the image. The image is so out in front, is something with which they identify strongly, that one gets the feelings of the image rather than the true feelings of the person. For them to love is to do. When I asked one of my students what reality was for her, she replied: "Reality for me is what I do. What I should do. What I'm supposed to do. And even what I can do. I am a doer, . . . a go-go." At the Conformist stage doing makes up the fabric of their lives. Thus, in direction, this kind of Three will first of all try to surmise what the director thinks a successful directee is like and move in that direction. They will feel like a *good and coopera-tive* directee. The director who tries to move these people to depth at this stage will surely be frustrated. Conformist Threes look to the director for guidance, which, is, of course, appropriate. The problem is that for them following guidance means giving the director what he/she wants. These Threes want to look good in the director's eyes. It may not be helpful for the director to reveal too much about what he/she thinks spiritual direction is or what are the sure signs of growth. These Threes can easily shift into what is expected. It may be that by keeping the Threes guessing, they will be forced into some form of self-observation. I suggest this meditation to get at the basic energy pattern of the type:

> Choose some task you have been doing today. Rehearse it in your imag-ination. Now speed it up. Slow it down. Do this three times. Notice the feelings when you do this and note any change of feelings. Is the mind going faster than the feelings? Does the mind tend not to pay attention to the physical sensations that go along with the task? Do you find that too much is going on? In completing this task do you want instantaneous success? Do you find yourself too impatient to appreciate the differences between doing the task quickly and doing it slowly?

Spaces on the heart center have the ability to pick up the quality of other people. Twos do it partially because what they get is based on immediate feelings. Threes pick up the quality of other persons as they are in the world: they are important or not important; they have key relationships or they do not. The Threes' grasp of the quality of another person is more continuous and does not change as readily as the Twos'. The difficulty in direction is that the Three directee can easily absorb the quality of the director's personality and communicate to the director that s/he understands the director. This could be a trap for directors who are not fully in contact with themselves. These Threes are not presenting their true selves but rather their ability to shift into the proper feelings.

The purpose of spiritual direction with Threes at all levels is to help them separate their true selves from their images. At the Conformist level, this project can only begin. Perhaps not much more can be expected than to have the Threes intellectually understand how they might be promoting themselves, identifying with what they do or with their role, or being concerned about the impression they are making.

The director will need to be patient, constantly inviting the Threes to move back to feelings. It might be helpful to have them become more fully acquainted with the system of the enneagram so that they can learn how other people identify themselves as a type based upon meditation and an inner search. Prayer practices and meditation are important at this stage, but they probably should be done alone, for then the Threes will not be able to rely upon what a group is doing. When they are in a group, they automatically sense the direction and values of the group, and so they get sidetracked into the group's energies. Alone, they will have to stumble and flounder around trying to locate some area of depth in their lives.

Since everyone at the Conformist stage appears to have some of this Threeness, it would seem that spiritual direction with these Threes would be especially difficult. It is as if the special blocks of all humanity are summarized in these people. The particular call for the director is to be willing to work with such people. The temptation will be to move them along too quickly or to work with them with a sense of detachment or even to terminate one's work with them.

Many of the directees will be church-oriented and may be professionally religious persons. For them the church as institution will loom large in spiritual direction. For instance, the directees will be well socialized in their religious tradition, will have taken on the ethos of the church, will be intent at being a "successful Catholic." At times the directors will feel like they are taking on the whole church. The temptation will be to try to relativize some of these Threes' desire to always be doing "what Holy Mother Church wants." At the Conformist level it is probably a fruitless endeavor. It is better to begin with the area of life least governed by the church, if the director can locate it.

This locating of authority in the institution makes the pursuit of feelings problematic. Not only do these Threes "think with the church" — they "feel with the church." They understand the church to be guided by the official set of teachings in the public arena without the benefit of theological nuances. Many Threes become spokespersons for the church. To pursue vigorously issues of intimacy and sexuality at this stage would be misguided since those areas have been pushed in a certain direction by the religious tradition, and usually the areas are not open to question at this time. It is better to begin with the least explosive areas so that they can more easily shift their attention, more readily feel their own feelings.

Yet most probably feelings of anger and sexuality will come up. They will be experienced as negative. This most probably is due to views received from parents, the religious tradition, and their own inadequate view of God. To avoid complications at this stage, it is best to stress the forgiveness and loving-kindness of God. But this is also the appropriate time to help them explore that all feelings are good, that feelings are meant to be felt, that it is destructive and useless to try to "get rid of feelings." The problem is not the feelings but acting on them. Just to get the Conformist Threes to feel their own feelings is a great accomplishment.

One danger for which the director needs to watch is that these Threes see the director as the authority. This constitutes a misplacement of authority. Clearly, the religious tradition has an authoritative place in a person's life, but this should not be transposed to the spiritual director. Directors have their own kind of authority, but it is precisely one that should prevent the directee from identifying with it.

Initially, the director can encourage the Conformist Threes to look at all their relationships. Usually, they belong to several groups, and one group can help balance out another. For the Threes who find freedom in the family but are hidebound by the church, the director can encourage a view of the church that is more familial. The same is true in the opposite direction. This will broaden their experience and create the possibility that one group (e.g., the family) that allows and encourages a wide expression of feelings can open up the possibility for fuller expression of feelings in another group (e.g., the church). This is important because often these Threes relate to their groups cognitively rather than emotionally. It is a mistake to maintain that because the Threes are at the core of the feeling center their lives are guided by their feelings. In fact, this means that their own feelings are particularly inaccessible to them.

In the area of belief, the director may often find that now these Threes relate to the same kinds of images of God that they have accommodated for most of their lives. They are in search of an image of God that is appropriate, one socially acceptable, so to speak. What is appropriate for them as Conformists will often be a God who commands, gives orders, or is the great achiever. Doing the will of God will be judged according to some external standards, in this case, ones that produce results and are measured by certain measurable goals. The problem is that this is not really the Threes' own image of God but one they have taken from the public arena. Because Threes are so used to living with a false persona, the image of God may also be a deception. Part of the task of the director at this point is to begin the process of dismantling their own false images. For the believing Conformist Threes this is threatening since removing their own masks is to unmask their God. Whatever may be the image of God — Father, the historical Jesus, the feminine Wisdom, God as energy or process — the question for the Threes is: How can they be true before their God? What is the true way as opposed to the appropriate way to have communion with God? Can they distinguish the two?

What is especially difficult for the director is to get behind the roles with which the Threes identify. Since they would rather play a role than feel, the directees will often present themselves in the role of an enlightened believer, a directee devoted to spiritual growth. Those who belong to specific religious communities will probably be expert in presenting themselves as models of that specific spirituality. Here the director must attend to the rhetoric because that can get in the way of true communication. It would be fatal for the director to mistake an attitude of religiosity with which they are sympathetic for a sign of real spiritual growth.

It is helpful if the director can move them in the direction of the God of emotion. This is not a busy God. This God is not a hyperactive CEO. But it is not enough to move the directee to a God of love. That is too abstract. Here begins the process of relating to an emotional God. Perhaps, beginning with the person of Christ, these Threes can begin to identify with the Christ who felt sorrow, liked a good drink, and had sexual feelings. If the director can assist the person to make contact with genuine feelings, that will be achieving much for the Conformist Threes. As Twos take on the feelings of specific individuals, Threes take their feeling-identify from groups. Making contact with their own feelings will help them avoid switching identities and so never know who they really are.

Spiritual Direction with the Conscientious Three

Some directees enter spiritual direction for the first time at the Conscientious Three stage. Many do not. As Threes move from the Conformist to this new stage, there is a breakup of their worldview in some sense, and so this may motivate some to begin direction and others to intensify it. The experience that triggers this transition can be the realization that they have failed to live up to their goals or that no matter how competent they may be, they may still be passed over. Such experiences are especially devastating for Threes. Basically, the task of the director is to accompany the person in the process of deconstruction. There will need to be a general unmasking in all areas, but the separation from role will be most prominent. The search for the self has really begun. This transition may be more difficult for Threes than for all the other spaces on the enneagram. It involves moving away from group values to find one's own. It means claiming oneself more in personal relationships. It means more self-appropriation. This is true for all spaces, of course. But Threes more than others adopt certain roles and group identification. The question during this transition is: Once you take roles and group identity away, what is left? And often there is no answer.

As noted, older women often begin direction at this stage. Now this may be less and less true, but in the past certainly Conformist Three women had little motivation to move if they were trying to make it in a man's world and in a specifically Three culture, as we have in North America. The futility of making situations work will often be the reason for their searching for a director.

Not naturally drawn to introspection, Threes will need assistance in the foreign territory of going inside. They need to be encouraged to sound the depth of their inner world, their personal relationships, and their experience of prayer and God. Like any other kind of growth, it cannot be forced and requires time. Threes may well see this as another task to be done, something to be efficient about, some area where they must avoid failure. The director can help them see that self-possession has to do more with gradually finding their inner authority and value system. But the most important thing for the transiting Threes is that they find the feelings they have behind all the images they have of themselves. This may be especially true regarding how they now begin to experience their relationships. Although there may be no obvious transition, there will be a time when the director knows that the directee is an adult, is conscientious, is capable of deep reflection, and has a real spiritual life.

The deconstruction of the Threes' world takes place through the tension generated by their, on the one hand, being distinct individuals with their own feelings and goals and, on the other hand, being acutely aware of living in society. This period, then, is naturally one of instability. Questions such as this will arise: If I am not supposed to feel with a group's feelings, or feel according to a role, then how am I supposed to feel? Since "who I am" is such a central question for Threes because they have been in roles for so long, this can be a painful period. Here the director can encourage them simply to follow their feelings (probably even more than their thoughts) and that this will be fruitful in the long run.

All spaces have this critical transition, but for Threes it is very much about discovering new and more authentic images whereby they can relate with God and understand their relationships and most of all themselves. Here discernment must center on feelings because Threes cannot create a new identity unless it is built on authentic feeling.[4]

A conflict may arise at the Conscientious level because so much is done consciously. After all, it is characteristic that at this stage the person is acting according to conscience. But what is needed is contact with true and real feelings. One cannot talk to feelings. Feelings do not reason. The way for Threes to arrive at real consciousness has to be through feelings.

In fact, the Conscientious Threes are those who are creating a self-identity, who are orienting their goals and ideals, and who do have a sense of self. The task is to remove the false feelings and stay in contact with the true feelings. Whatever the director can do to promote this will surely be in the right direction. Sensitivity is needed in the replacement process because Threes can demask themselves only to assume other more enlightened, more acceptable masks. This is because they have lived on the surface for such a long time and now, finding that their past images are not working, they cannot easily integrate more authentic ones because they do not have ready access to the inner world. But if they can stay grounded in genuine feeling, then this will be the time when they "redo" themselves so that they find their own uniqueness. In other words, they will find themselves. I suggest this meditation as a help to them as they create (and find) their self-identity:

> Identify something in your past about which you were or are uncertain. It could be whether you would go for a drive on the weekend, how long it would take for you to discover your enneagram subtype, whether you would finish the next written assignment on time, whether you would succeed the next time you gave a public talk, or whether you would get that job you were applying for. Return to a place of temporary uncertainty. Try to experience the feelings that are present, especially a sense of hopelessness. Try to contact any empty feelings that go along with this hopelessness. Now notice whether this emptiness motivated you to move to action. Are you thinking that it is a waste of time to go back to this emptiness? Is this emptiness leading you to more knowledge of yourself, or are you confusing yourself with what you would like to be, what you hope to be?[5]

What Conformist Threes so enjoyed, identification with a public image of efficiency, competence, and even self-promotion, may be for the Conscientious Threes a source of embarrassment and disgust. But they need not reject the past so much as reorient themselves. They still move to achieve, but now the motivation comes from who they really are, from a "feeling" self who feels with its own feelings. Here is where the virtue of hope comes into play. Hope is neither optimistic nor idealistic; it is realistic. They do not have to do it all, but they have to do something. In that way they can live hope-filled lives without becoming discouraged. Since they are at the Conscientious stage, they can now check their feelings for some guidance on what it is they are to do.

In working with Threes the question of what is really true will be in the background and will emerge from time to time. The word "deceit" is often associated with Threes, but they do not see themselves as deceitful. It is just that truth has a different feel about it, and they have a different standard according to which they judge a situation or an interaction as true. Truth is more action-oriented. It is not an inner concept or an abstract idea. It is pragmatic; it is whatever works. The classical definition of truth as the correspondence between the concept in the mind and the outside reality would escape them. Without being aware of it most Threes operate out of the sociological presupposition that reality is socially constructed and so whatever works is true. The Conscientious level is the time for the director to have the directee examine the Christian tradition more carefully on the meaning of truth. One good way is to provide the directee with some reading on the way the image of Christ as the Truth has functioned in the lives of some of the saints or other major figures in church history. They need to have a larger context for experiencing truth.

A very rich area to explore with the Conscientious Threes is that of their relationships. Because they are more capable of intimacy, because there is more differentiation of feeling, relationships become wonderful opportunities for spiritual depth. These are challenging experiences for Threes since they now know they cannot relate to the other out of some role. They cannot simply act like a loving person. They must actually love. They will see more because they will see themselves in the other person. It is no longer the case of a role reacting to another role. The feelings will be different with each person. These differing feelings fit no appropriate way of feeling. All this drives the Threes back to their true feelings.

This deepened sense of self, a feeling self, will mean that the Conscientious Threes can more readily enter into new relationships and can intensify old ones. But since the basic drive of Threes, to perform, to achieve, is still present, the Conscientious Threes need to take care that they do not overdo this experience of authentic connecting. The person who wants to contribute more, cares more. This care and concern must include themselves lest they regress to a previous stage. It should be no surprise that there will be some ambivalence here. One of my directees, a Three, has been very stable, faithful, and balanced in his relationship with his lover, but he has a great need to connect to different kinds of groups, especially men's groups of various kinds. He shows both self-sufficiency and neediness at the same time.

With the Conscientious Threes the director is dealing with those who have broken through the world of false images, most importantly, their images of God. Helping Threes to reidentify images of God based upon their own deeper connection to their feelings is a major concern in spiritual direction at this time. Groups such as family or church can no longer supply these images automatically. The Conscientious Threes should be able to have feelings about God that are their own and not the result of an appropriate and acceptable way of feeling toward God. The director can expect emotional depth at this level, but only to a degree. Even at this Conscientious level it may not be easy for Threes to enter into those feelings that most undermine their past self-presentations.

When all is going smoothly, Conscientious Threes will be able to see that their self-promotion, being out in front, being in the lime-light, is not a sign of real advancement.[6] The director can support them in not giving into stressful situations, something they may want to do. The director can suggest exercises and forms of prayer in which the body is at rest. At the same time when Threes meet little outside stress, there is the danger of not remaining "conscious." At this time the director may find it possible to have them address issues of intimacy or some other area of strong feeling. Unlike the Con-formists, the Conscientious Threes believe that their own feelings are to be valued. Direction should explore this belief with some depth.

Once Threes have identified their feelings, there will naturally be a tendency to doubt them. "Are these my true feelings?" Their powers of reflexivity and their differentiated inner life will help them through this doubt, but their temptation to work too hard at it may undermine their endeavors. Helen Palmer's point here is a helpful summary:

> The upside of the security position lies in the discovery of real feelings, which make empathy and emotional loyalty possible. …It helps to frame the "unmasking" of image as a useful ac-tivity, to emphasize the positive benefits to health and family life. It also helps to see that doubt can modify a Three's unre-lenting self-confidence. In learning to reconsider, to ponder, and to wait, a Three in stress not only learns to love but can also forgo a quick-fix mentality in favor of authentic creative ideas.[7]

At this level of development the director would de well to pursue with the Conscientious Threes various aspects of their relationships. What are they still avoiding? is the key question. After all, avoid-ance of failure will be a temptation for them no matter their stage of development. They need to repeatedly ask the question of their re-lationships: What is true here? Are they afraid of being seen? What happens when efficiency is not the goal, as in something like relating with others? Is the result an experience of emptiness? What about the spiritual direction relationship itself? Is this only to be another success story, or is it to be real spiritual progress? And what would that progress feel like?

The trust they experience in relationships will help them to trust their self-exploration even more. Exploring the instances in their lives when they received unconditional love more than anything can be the source for the deepest spiritual progress because they have the experience of being loved for themselves and not for what they do or what they have won. If at the beginning of this stage of growth the question of truth is prominent, at the end, the question of what is love may be more so. True loves flies in the face of many of the pre-suppositions of the previous adult stage. Love does not spring from a mode of efficiency. In fact, love requires a seeming waste of time and lack of efficiency.

Some kind of body work, which should be part of the next stage of development, can be very helpful here. In fact, at any level body work with the Three is to be recommended. The question is: At what level will any individual Three be willing to engage in it? But to get at what is real love and what are true as well appropriate feelings for the Three, there must be an opening of the heart. But more is required than intervention on the mental and emotional levels, indispensable as that is. The energy of the body exists at a level beneath the feelings. It is important that such energy continually move through the body. If it is blocked, there is the possibility of physical pain as well as the inhibiting of the deeper exploring of the inner life. Almost any kind of body work will do: Feldenkrais, Rosen, Breema, Tai Chi. Chakra work can be particularly effective in moving the energy through the whole body.[8] What is important is that it be the kind of body work that the Threes cannot turn into some kind of success trip — in other words, the kind of body work that is not dependent on the projection of an image as would be the case with athletics, calisthenics, bodybuilding, and the like.

All this is part of the indirect approach to the real self of the Threes. Since they are at the center of the heart spaces and so are the most identified with the mask they are wearing, it is difficult to address the issue of image directly. Twos might be helped to intervene as they are passing from the feelings outside to the feelings inside. Since they are picking up feelings in a limited way, that is, in terms of one individual at a time, they have something with which to make a comparison. Likewise in the case of the Fours, intervention is possible during those moments when the attention moves from the present to the absent and back again. The difficulty with the Threes is that there is very little room for comparison. But since the body does not lie, if the director can have them listen to the body, some kind of opening will be possible.

Spiritual Direction with the Interindividual Three

There are some signs for the director that the directees are moving into the Interindividual stage. They are more accepting of their reconstructed self, the self without the masks. They know that there is a struggle inside between the desire to succeed and self-promotion and the desire to be more vulnerable and accepting of failure. They are more articulate about feelings, especially those connected with anger and sexuality. They can live with the various areas of conflict — for example, being persons of leadership and initiative as well as taking care of themselves. In prayer and meditation there is a greater experience of distinguishing their inner and outer worlds. There is hardly any need to feel inside in the same way that one might think it necessary to feel outside. Real success is personal development and growth in union with God.

The director will find here persons who are moving toward integration, who are self-aware and more sophisticated about the inner life. This will come as a surprise (pleasant, I hope) for the director who is used to the stereotypical Threes all caught in themselves, constantly polishing up their image before others.

It is a joy to work with Threes moving into this Interindividual level because they can discriminate between moving with a relationship and trying to produce or create one. They can deal with the anxiety that is often present when feelings arise, and so these feelings can move through them more readily. They know that no matter how strong or independent they are, in matters of the heart, they can only be vulnerable. They do not expect their partners or friends to love them for their successes, their public images. They know they cannot make love happen, that a relationship is not like a job. They are more open to the shadow side of their emotional lives. Intimacy is now less of a neuralgic area. It is more than an idea. They can take time with it. They know there are very few big leaps in the spiritual life. They have genuine interest in their spiritual pursuits, and so the director can now move them to the possibly more traumatizing or emotionally charged areas of their lives.

There still will be an incomplete integration of the social dimensions of life in their transitional period. Especially for the Threes, the struggle of how to hold together the desire for intimacy and the desire for achievement takes a great deal of energy. It should be no surprise that the personal and group needs are still somewhat at variance.

Most probably the Interindividual Threes will be older, more mature. They may be involved in some kind of midlife crisis when they come to the direction sessions. The usual disillusionments at this time of life are heightened in the case of the Threes whose whole lives at one time were defined by success, the achievement of certain ideals. Just accepting the limitations of their personal reality (e.g., "I will never be the great orchestral conductor") is sobering for most. For Threes it calls for a life redefinition.

The up side of this experience at this level is that the Interindividual Threes are happy to invite others onto the stage. They need not have the attention only on them. Not only are they now willing to share the stage with others, but the others need not conform to their values. These Threes are so in contact with the inner world that they are capable of collaborating on all levels. Now they experience the need for mutuality not only in personal relationships but also in social issues, especially issues of justice.

These Threes live with ambiguity but also complexity. There certainly is no confusion of the real self and the work role, no matter how intertwined they may have been. Whereas in the past that which was not logical or orderly was seen as inefficient, holding back the achievement of goals and tasks, now efficiency means being more inclusive, more true to oneself and others, more fully aware.

Because discernment at this level is more complex, the directors who are not trained in the school of discernment of spirits and/or are not very familiar with the system of the enneagram may find themselves unable to be of any really meaningful assistance. In justice to the directee, a referral may be appropriate. The directors will probably find that the issues of social sin and social injustice are considered with full force. There is much about the Threes that can be channeled in this direction.

There is a sense of optimism and hope about the Threes that prevents them from being discouraged in the face of so much institutional negativity, war, starvation, and gender and race bias. Threes are likely to become leaders here, and the director will not have to coax and cajole them as would be the case with some others spaces. No longer seeing their value as lying in what they produce or do, they are content to make their contribution to the world order, although it may seem imperceptible. But their desire to have results helps to keep them on track and not give up or escape into theorizing.

Now being more comfortable with sexual feelings, now dwelling in their inner world of feelings, Interindividual Threes have a broader range of relationships. They love in many different ways. At this level they are capable of supporting many different kinds of relationships. No longer does love mean doing things together. Love does not need to result in anything. Love is many-colored, and some of those "colors" are pain and frustration. This is a delicate part of direction with Interindividual Threes. Having become aware of their love and why they love at the Conscientious level, they are now in a position to reexamine the loves in their lives. Having stepped back from any excessive merging with others or with groups, they now need to recommit themselves to that from which they separated. Although these Threes are not likely to be irresponsible here, they need the director to help point the way. All the skills of the director will be called into play, for even at this level Threes can confuse role-play emotions with the real thing. They are now capable of knowing what is more genuine, what is true, but since this is the time of reconstruction, these Threes will need accompaniment on this particular journey. This journey for them can be fruitful in the best sense of the word. There will be much that needs reappropriation since in the previous stages so much had been taken on under "false pretenses," as it were. Threes have to let go of all that. Even at this advanced level, the director is indispensable.

The Interindividual Threes are very much in possession of their true feelings, are definitely on their own spiritual path rather than on one that they take to be the more acceptable one. They do not act simply to be doing something but because they want an outer life that reflects the inner life. It is a long and difficult journey to go from only a public life with an unknown and unavailable inner life to one where the two are integrated. But when the Threes reach this point, all the fixations associated with Threes become instruments of compassion to others and kindness to themselves. There is no need for self-presentation because they themselves are more diverse in the ways they understand themselves. Such ambiguity now implies a way of doing that is just as efficient as their previous more calculated kind. The sense of being in a hurry that had plagued them earlier now is converted into toleration and kindness toward themselves. Their attention span widens, and no one thing or project receives such focus that it imperializes them. The tranquillity of the Inter-individual Threes comes from the fact that they are freed from the need to check constantly the success of the project or to readjust it so that only success will result. Helen Palmer says of Threes: "The key word is *stop*. It's very difficult to stop and listen to yourself once the habit takes over."[9] Interindividual Threes have learned how to stop. In all this the role of the director is one of support and confirmation.

An area where the director may need to be more directive is that of negative feelings. At this stage Threes allow these feelings to arise. The anger that has been there may now be channeled in a number of ways. One way would be to utilize it in helping the Threes move into more social justice areas. At first, however, it will be necessary to help them feel the anger without it seeming to them to be a regression to a prior stage. The anger energy can even be used to help them explore their unconscious more since this is such foreign territory for them.

Sexual feelings now are out in the open. No longer is sex connected with performance, with a form of being in competition with oneself. It is seen not as a way of proving something but as an end in itself. To all these the director must move the directee. A particular challenge for the director comes when the issue of intimacy must be reconstructed. Intimacy is also a threat for Threes who are well developed. Masks, public images, self-promotion — none of these work in a situation of intimacy. Nor does being intimate according to role work here. Threes can easily be intimate if they think they should be intimate. As Palmer puts it: "Doing your feelings is a lot less threatening than turning attention inward and finding an empty place where authentic feelings are supposed to bubble up."[10] But that is precisely what can and must be done at this stage, and the director is the fellow traveler on this more difficult journey for the Three.

It may be true for all spaces at this stage, but it is true certainly for the Threes that they will have to assess the relationship between their needs, which are now far clearer to them, and the lifestyle they have chosen. The director is important here because most Threes reach this stage only after being in a certain lifestyle — marriage, the priesthood, the religious life, the single life — for quite a long time. One cannot automatically presume that they must change their lifestyle, although that may be called for. But even for Threes who married or became priests out of less than worthy motives of public image or identification with some role, it is possible to reintegrate their lives realistically. I suspect that every Interindividual Three will need to look at lifestyle no matter how altruistic were their original motives in choosing it.

At an earlier stage of development the Threes very much identified with the needs and expectations of the group. Because they could so readily pick up the feelings of the group, they found themselves in leadership positions, caring for the group, sometimes in the best sense of the word. Now the Interindividual Threes are able to insert themselves in the group so that they can extend care not only to others but also to themselves. "Interdependence" is the key word here, and what might have been a threat in the past (i.e., the vulnerability involved in caring for themselves) no longer is.

It is difficult to give advice to the director working with Interindividual Threes who are now redoing their images of God. Even before Threes reach this level, it should be clear that the past images will not do. This is an awesome task for all the spaces, but for the Threes, whose whole being, including the relationship with God, has been an assumed image, it is particularly difficult. The director will need to work more intuitively here. If such is not possible, it may be necessary to refer the person to someone else. This movement to new images of God is often obscure and disarming. It flies in the face of everything the Threes used to hold dear: clear image, focused attention, efficient control. Now all is vague, distracting, and out of control. But this is a very fruitful time for the interchange between director and directee. Because the directees are now almost fully in charge of their spiritual lives, the director will need to let them be self-directed. Here the director and directee may enter something like a partnership. Since the Interindividual Threes still maintain their original sources of energy, they should be able to carry this out successfully. Of the many possible images of God available for the healthy Three, I recommend this meditation on one of them, namely, God as lover. Apart from the fact that this image widens our understanding of God, who is easily seen as love but not lover, it moves Threes away from the usual traps they can succumb to in relationships:

> Imagine God as your lover. Your lover may be male or female, the opposite of your sex or the same as your sex. This may take some time to do. If there is any resistance, proceed slowly. Observe what feelings arise when you so picture God. Imagine yourself in moments of passion and ecstasy with God as lover. Make the images as concrete as possible. How comfortable are you with these feelings? Are you judging them? Where in your body are these feelings found? How are you interpreting these feelings: as lust, sex, or desire? Or does your passion mean value, that you find God valuable, and that God finds you valuable? Ask yourself why you love your God. Are there any reasons to do so? Are there any reasons that can explain that love? Can you hear God saying to you: "I love you just because you are you. I delight in your presence. You are precious beyond all else to me"? Can you now see yourself as valuable? Do you value God who values you?[11]

More body-based practices can be useful at this time, especially as the Threes move into more holistic spirituality. For the sexual subtype,[12] where a masculine/feminine image is so important, whether it is through becoming the ideal lover or the expert master of a trade, forms of meditation and body work that support a diffusion of masculine/feminine images between both the sexes are to be encouraged. That way there is no particular stereotypical way of being a masculine or feminine lover. The director should move the Threes to those practices in which they cannot take charge or it would make no sense to do so and where self-confidence or identifying with a role feels inappropriate. Meditation and massage where one simply feels, where there is no appropriate way to feel, are good. Health in sexual Threes is manifested in their becoming leaders or participants who unselfishly promote the good of a group or advance some project. They can now readily support others, and they can take pleasure in the success of others.

The director can help social Threes — who are usually taken up with public presentation, social prestige, being well known, and being highly credentialed and influential — find situations where anonymity is essential. Nakedness is certainly a state in which one is literally stripped of much that makes up one's image, although some Threes could turn this into a body display. In that case it is better to explore areas of their private, more hidden lives in terms of how they can find meaning in circumstances about which most people would know nothing. The director can help Threes find themselves in situations or put themselves in situations where they are not the center of attention, where nobody pays heed to them, and then have them feel what that is like and work with it. To resist "running for office" will produce feelings that can be brought to direction and utilized during meditation and body-based practices. This is a good practice for the Threes because it lets them know what their feelings truly are. Once in contact with their own feelings, the Threes will find no need to adjust to the situation; in fact it would be uncomfortable to do so.

Thus, social Threes can bring new energy to situations that need it, bringing about harmony where there is division. They can move others to a positive common goal. They are unselfishly committed to their work and can rally others around them, moving them out of seclusion and negativity. It is a good psychological and spiritual principle that those who help others in this way are helping themselves in the same areas at the same time.

For self-preservation Threes (survival/security), whose preoccupation is with the security that money can bring, it is important to understand that this security is a misplaced achievement. Emotional survival is not a matter of material possession. Success has nothing to do with an affluent image. Here the director can work with Threes so that they, having reached this stage of maturity, can find it silly to place such value on material things. Encouraging the Threes to find situations of pleasure that have no connection with money or a job and to relish them is one way to unhook the self-preservation Threes from fear that unless they are constantly occupied and advancing, their life is under threat.

Because they are more centered, the healthy self-preservation Threes are willing to risk, to support others, to move to action because they are not inhibited by their own fears and cautions. They will remain with a project and not pull out. They become more team-oriented, moving their group in a forward direction. They are more willing to find security in intimacy and do not find it threatening. They need a friend at this time, and the director can serve that purpose.

Chapter 5

The Space of Four

As we would expect from the heart center, Fours, when they come to spiritual direction, will be concerned about relationships.[1] Usually the concern is about the failure or impossibility of relationships due to their superficiality, their lack of genuine connection, their inauthenticity. There is always something lacking for Fours, and this is especially true in relationships. Because Fours intensify their ordinary experience, it is ordinary experience itself that is lacking. What is exaggerated to others is ordinary reality to them. For that reason they are the cause of the despair they have over attaining a truly human relationship. How can you relate with someone who implicitly denigrates what you experience in your own life? So Fours are left bereft of relationships, which they so long for. What they want most in life is to connect, but then they sabotage the connections by placing impossible demands on them. They expect to be disappointed, and they are.

For Fours a cigar is never just a cigar. Everything is filled with not just meaning but meaning*s*. Their great gift of being sensitive to the symbolic dimension of reality also complicates life for them. Only the highly dramatic presentation of reality seems adequate. This need to intensify means that most things are matters of life and death. Their emotional life is one of extremes, of death and life. Happiness has to be the ultimate to qualify, and despair can only be total. As a result, to achieve inner balance, Fours will take on a kind of philosophical objectivity and aloofness. It is their way of moving away from a messy and disorganized reality that threatens the harmony they so desire. Creating this distance between themselves and the real world causes them to use melancholy as a defense against the possible disruptions of the world.

Fours are often called the artists on the enneagram, a designation that has confused many Fours who seem to have no talent along artistic lines. Suzanne Zuercher gives the clearest explanation of what "artist" means when applied to Fours:

They are often called artists, not because of any special artistic talent, but because they shape and form all of life. Relationships become a problem when others do not respond as planned and scripted.... Fours need to be prepared for encounters. To that end, and to reinforce a sense of security, 4's tend to invite people into their world rather than to go out into the environment of other people. In that way they feel more in charge of shaping what happens.[2]

But life does not go that way. Fours cannot create a beautiful and perfect world; they cannot create that kind of world inside of themselves. And so they despair. Spiritual direction can help Fours to face facts, and this can lead to greater self-acceptance on their part. What is in their favor in direction is their natural desire to grow and achieve an authentic life. Perhaps, then, they can find satisfaction in what beauty and harmony do in fact exist in the world. This includes satisfaction with the beauty of themselves.

Fours can be helped by becoming acquainted with some well-known Four figures. Zuercher has given us a portrait of Thomas Merton as a Four. I have picked at complete random two examples to quote:

The peace movement never did — nor can it, despite the 4 romanticism that would restore Eden — make of our world a rhythmic, flowing whole. As a 4 Merton grappled with limited reality and so became a source of courage and perseverance for many dedicated, as he was, to the cause of nonviolence and peace.[3]

There were many times when he was obviously offended by some of the monastery's modernized ceremonies. In his mind they may well have seemed a bit overdone if not orgiastic. Romantic 4 nostalgia for the Latin liturgy never left Merton, who as an artist, retained an understated style that echoed in the strains of Gregorian Chant.[4]

Spiritual Direction with the Conformist Four

I suspect many directors find it near to impossible to work with a Conformist Four.[5] In fact, they might find it difficult to work with most kinds of Fours, but certainly at this less developed level some directors could be harmful. Hopefully, a director will know when to move a Four to another director. These are romantic people. Sometimes they are called "tragic romantics." Their emotionality is both their gift and their weakness. They live in a world of emotion. Relationships of all kinds figure constantly in their lives, and they seem always to be leaving one or entering into a new one. They lead driven lives, driven by the desire to connect, to feel complete, to be fulfilled in someone. Directors at times will feel like they are being caught up in an emotional web.

The Four space is a complicated one in itself. What complicates matters even more is how the Conformist Fours operate. Because there is so little differentiation of feeling at this level, because every situation is seen as one that is either/or, because there is little nuancing in their judgments, and because there is so little connection with their own authentic feelings, they appear to be living very superficially. This is difficult enough in itself, but when it is also done dramatically, with lots of flair, with mood changes of the roller-coaster style, it may simply be too much for some directors. However, those directors who keep on the journey with Conformist Fours and assist them in their growth process will be rewarded with people who have a beautiful inner world and who can connect deeply on the feeling level.

Because Conformists are unable to engage in any serious introspection, the Fours at this level seek their fulfillment in terms of external things and activity. As the director listens to them speak of what they long for, what they think is missing in their lives, what they envy in others, s/he can only wonder how people who consider themselves special and who are unhappy with ordinary life can be so caught up in trivia. The astute director will sense that behind this external display of feeling and mood, behind this longing for happiness in terms of absent friends and lovers, material wealth and reputation, there is a somewhat hidden desire for God. All this impatience with daily life, this desire for peak emotional experiences, this endless search for meaning in trying to create an aesthetic environment are their ways of trying to touch God. But because they are still disconnected from their inner lives, they are left unfulfilled and unhappy.

It is as if these Fours live under a double jeopardy. Even when they are healthy there is a sense of longing, attraction to what is missing and unavailable. Indeed, at this level, they are *really* missing something. There really *is* something that is unavailable. There really is *something* that is absent. And that is the connection to their own feelings, to their own inner life. This lack of connection then only amplifies the questions they have about why others seem so happy and they are not, why life is so unsatisfying, why no one loves them.

The discerning director will sense that this yearning is not simply for something or someone. It is yearning for a connection, for meaning, for something higher, more visible, and more concrete. It will help if the director has them examine the experience of yearning in itself without attention to what they think are the objects of their yearning. This constant yearning brings about a lack of interest in the ordinary. It triggers this constant search for more quality, something richer in experience. The theme song of these Fours could well be "The Impossible Dream" from the musical *The Man from La Mancha*. This yearning seems to be the origin of their sense of melancholia. Most Fours will probably be able to distinguish being melancholy from being sad or depressed. Sadness is specific, and depression can be tied to some other feeling such as anger. But melancholy is more like the background music in the Fours' lives.[6] It is these subtleties that require sensitivity and nuance on the part of the director.

It is important that in the sessions the director allows the Fours to ventilate their feelings. There are real feelings here. It is not all playacting, although the feelings may be dramatized. The question is: To what are these feelings connected? In that sense, we can ask the same question we must ask about Twos and Threes: What are they really feeling? Who is the true feeling self? Probably a good entrance point for the director is to pursue the area of envy. This will help the director to understand the worldview of the Fours because they see the world through this filter of envy. It is important to note that this is not the envy that one might discover in Twos or Threes, where the envy would be about what the others, either individuals or groups, might have. The Fours are more centered on themselves, and they do not want to have what others have in terms of concrete things. It is rather that the happiness of others reminds of them of their own unhappiness. The Twos and Threes may not even know that they are lacking something until they notice what others have and they do not. But they would see it as a simple matter of getting the things the others have. In the case of the Fours it is far more subtle. They actually do not want what the others have, except, of course, for their happiness. They are missing the happiness and contentment; they are not missing the things that others have. They may say that they do want those things, but that is because those things are symbols of happiness.

Things are not so simple, however. Indeed, at the beginning, at the Conformist level, Fours have so little connection with their inner world that they can think and give the impression that they are interested in getting the concrete things that other people have. And so the Fours will do what Twos and Threes would do, namely, try for the external things that seem to produce happiness, whether it be money, profession, or a partner. But there is another twist here for Fours. Since it is not actually things that they find missing in their lives, but contentment and fulfillment, when they finally are able to gain recognition or a mate, they end up disappointed — they discover that what they wanted wasn't really that new dress, that riding costume, or that new lover. They are missing something much more profound, something more spiritual, and in fact, they enjoy this absence despite what they may be communicating. That is why there is the push/pull effect in their relationships. Once they have something or someone, they no longer want it, and so reject it. But then when it is no longer there, they believe that they really do want it and need it.

What can the director do to assist the Conformist Fours at this time? Here is where the styles of attention are important. I am not sure that working directly with the actual or assumed feelings of the Fours at this level is profitable. Their emotional setup is so complicated and so unreflected upon that the director could only be frustrated. Rather a more "heady" approach here might work. If the Fours can begin to notice how their attention constantly moves toward that which is absent, that which is unavailable, that from which they are separated, they will have made a beginning. It may seem to the director that the Fours are aware of how they attend in their hankering after the unavailable, but in fact the Conformist Fours need help in noticing that they long for the absent precisely as absent. That is why they engage in their cycle of longing, getting, and then rejecting.

The director should not expect that an intellectual recognition of Fours' style of attention will produce the answer to their issues or immediately launch them on the path of growth. Conformists find it difficult to notice what is going on in the inside. But if they can at least discover some kind of movement between absent and present, then the director can assist them in making some comparisons among their feelings. They can notice how they feel when a desired object or person is present and when it is absent and contrast the feelings. This will probably take a long time since Fours will resist the implications of noticing something simply because it is absent, being attracted to something because of its absence. They will find it difficult to believe that the things that other people have are not the answer to their happiness. The big black hole of what is missing in their lives is in themselves, and nothing others have will fill it. Once Fours can begin to imagine that big black hole of loss inside themselves, they are on the way to discovering their lives. I suggest the following meditation as a help for Fours to explore their inner world of feelings:

> Bring your attention inside and notice whatever feelings you may be having at this time. Try to feel these feelings inside. You may have to roam around inside for a while to connect with the feelings or to stay with them. Pretend you are in an airplane and that you are flying back and forth over your inner world of feelings. In this plane you are drawing a map of the land below. Map your feelings with each kind of feeling imaged as a mountain, dry land, a river, or a fertile field. What is the picture and structure of the map of your feelings? Now which feelings show up on the map more clearly and are more finely delineated. Do the negative feelings stand out? Does your map remain stable, or do you find that there is always something missing? Is there a part that you cannot map? Is there a black hole somewhere? What do you think that means?[7]

Much of what is usually described as characteristic fixations of Fours will show up at this level. When the director points out to some of these directees that they are automatically selecting the positive aspects of the absent, it may come as a surprise to them. But this is also the time to help them explore their emotional center, what it is that is missing, what is it that they long for. They probably will not come up with a correct analysis in the beginning, but it is an opportunity for them to become more familiar with their inner emotional life. The following reflection can be helpful here:

> When you are in a group of people and find them to be superficial and ordinary, a waste of time, ask yourself: What, concretely, are these people missing? What, concretely, are you, as a Four, missing?

Happiness is the not the proper answer because it is too abstract. There must be something specific to bring them home to their own emotionality.

There will be the temptation at this level to do what other spaces, such as Threes, do here, namely, go in for status symbols such as collecting art or specializing in some exotic field. Fours do this not so much to get the applause of others à la the Threes but to discover for themselves the source of happiness. Ironically, in doing this the Fours act very superficially — precisely what they accuse others of doing. Christian — especially Catholic — Fours can pride themselves on special devotions, church tasks, or even somewhat idiosyncratic beliefs. This is partly due to the fact that at this stage their meaning is still tied to external behavior and the need to react to the group in some way.

Church regulations are often quite important to Conformist Fours because they define themselves in terms of them. It may seem that self-definition through regulations constitutes an unusual way of belonging to a group, but for them it is a way of connecting. They are actually looking for approval because authority is important to them. This can easily happen in the church, where we tend to be tolerant of people who have special displays of piety. Because some saints have displayed such eccentric behavior, we often give these Fours the benefit of the doubt as people who might well be holy.

The Fours' envy, melancholy, sense of abandonment, mood swings, and impatience with mediocrity all conspire to make them very critical of themselves and others. This criticality only makes it more difficult for them to enter their own world of feeling. They may say that they are not angry, but this is only because their sense of their feelings is so vague. They may say that they have transcended sexuality, but this is only because something so emotionally dense puts them in conflict with an image of God they might have or with an idealized view of themselves for which they are longing. The director can help them have an appreciation for all their feelings without discrimination as a way of opening up the possibility that later they will deal with the feelings individually.

Often the director will sense the pain in the Conformist Fours. They desire to belong, but they do too many things that put them at odds with various groups. They can only relate in terms of external behavior, and since this behavior can be alienating, they are in a catch-22 position. Because friendships are defined more in terms of actions and because acting with a friend makes that friend present, the Fours have trouble relating since they focus on the negative traits of the friend who is present. Because their relationships are not deep, Fours have nothing to maintain the relationship, since what they see they do not like.

Most directors will find it a real challenge to know what to do with Conformist Fours when they are speaking of God. For Conformists in general, God is concrete and personal as well as strict and demanding. But God is also far away. Because God in some sense is absent, that is, not perceived as the person next to them, Fours may speak of God with considerable feeling, giving the impression of a deep connection. The question is: To what degree is this due to their attraction to the absent? They might be less happy with a more concrete God, such as the one found in all those ordinary people with whom the Fours are surrounded.

Because Conformist Fours do not have their lives in hand, have not yet discovered who they are, and are hidden behind their own special antics or by identifying with marginal groups, the director may be frustrated in moving these people to more self-appropriation. But if the director is patient and continues with the Conformist Fours, s/he may be rewarded when working with those persons at a later stage.

A word of caution is in order when working with Fours at this level. It may be that the director will have to address other issues before s/he does the direction in terms of the enneagram as such. For instance, the directee who comes to direction may be in great pain. This must be addressed first. Before the Four directees can explore their lives, they must face issues of behavior first. This is especially true of concerns that involve self-blame and shame as well as pain.

Spiritual Direction with the Conscientious Four

Some directors will have pursued the melancholy of the Fours at the previous level. I would tend to do that at this stage. Why? Because melancholy is not simply a negative emotion that needs to be challenged. As Palmer defines it: "Melancholy is the sweet sadness of separation. Although based on a perception of loss, melancholy is a sweet and evocative stage."[8] At the Conformist stage it may be that the Fours' melancholy will be a solace to them, a kind of stable source of identity as they deal with the issues of external behavior. Also, the melancholy of the Fours is subtle. It is not simply sadness — once the source of sadness is discovered, it dissipates. Melancholy is part of their very constitution, and so dealing with it requires greater self-awareness. It is at the Conscientious stage that such awareness is present. The growing introspectiveness, the greater individuation, and more depth in relationships and ideals prepare the ground for some fruitful work with the Fours' melancholy at this time. A concern about their melancholy may be the key to discovery for the Fours as they move into the Conscientious stage. As they move toward greater self-appropriation and sense of themselves in their relationships and their work, as they become more fully conscious of their particular journey, it is very helpful to have them ask themselves what it means that they are melancholy people.

At this point the director can assist the Fours to experience areas where they can feel satisfied. Connected with the melancholy is the sense of loss, the feeling of being different from others, searching for the unattainable. By discovering areas of satisfaction the Fours can relativize those aspects of melancholy so that this characteristic can be expressed more through sensitivity to others, the ability to accompany others in painful situations, and helping others to deepen their own spiritual lives. At the Conscientious level the Fours have relationships and are not defined by them. Relationships are a fruitful place to explore for the experience of satisfaction. Unlike Fours at the previous stage, these Fours are highly reflective, and they can find satisfaction in relationships, rather than in external connections such as reputation or wealth.

If on the Conformist level the directors were able to remain stable during the mood changes and push-pull pattern of the Fours, at this level they will find the Fours open to exploring these changes and this push-pull pattern. They are more capable of mapping their feelings and seeing the consequences of them as well as placing them in the larger context of their relationships. They will begin to notice themselves acting to support their various fixations such as dramatic self-presentations, the depreciation of ordinary experiences, and looking for a lifestyle to help their self-esteem. This will cause some emotional and even intellectual instability for them. Having related in these ways in the past, now how do the Fours relate? If they have been tragic romantics at an earlier stage, now how do they act at dinner parties, decorate their offices, and address God? The director is necessary to assist them over these rather rough times.

This can also be a time for religious trauma for some devotional Fours who now question the validity of some of their religious practices that they had taken on as part of their "special" relationship with God. These practices could be anything from devotion to some unusual saint or some antiquated (in the opinion of others) form of asceticism to the ritualization of their private meditation period. Clearly, this is the time of what might be called a paradigm shift in religious sensibility. I suspect that this will register more strongly among Fours than among most other spaces on the enneagram. And for the discerning director this can be both a challenging and a rewarding occasion — challenging because it is not possible to predict the outcome of such critical passage and rewarding because the Fours may emerge from the experience with more mature values, a greater sense of their inner lives, and a fuller claiming of their spiritual identity.

Much will fall away during the Conscientious stage. Now that Fours see themselves more according to their interior lives than external behavior patterns and are ready to articulate their long-term goals, the director can help them to discover what is really important in their lives. If previously they tried to live in a beautiful world inhabited by few others, tried to surround themselves with what is of high quality and, at times, even an outrageously aesthetic environment to mask the emptiness, the sense of loss, and the feeling of insignificance inside, now their gracefulness and originality can be grounded in an authentic sense of themselves as human beings. The goal of the director is to move them to find their uniqueness before God as creatures and not in external paraphernalia. But in order to achieve this end, the Fours need assistance in deciding what of the possibly flamboyant past should be maintained and what discarded.

At the Conformist level the Fours were caught in this endless search for something deeper, a more authentic human experience, a more completely satisfying relationship. If Ones are critical of their present experiences and Threes are trying to reorganize present experience toward a successful outcome, Fours are always asking the question about the quality of the present experience. At this stage the Fours are ready to explore why significant experiences never seem to take place in the present. They are always past or future. These Fours are ready to ask this question because at this stage they are also capable of more intense relationships, more communication, more objectivity about themselves and others, and so are readier to experiment with finding a satisfaction in the present based on seemingly trivial things.

This ability to relate to something ordinary and find happiness there is crucial if the Fours are to develop an adult relationship with God. It is true that Fours need to feel themselves unique before God. But how can that be done when their uniqueness is based on their creaturehood and there are all those millions and millions of other people who were also created unique by God? What is so special (in the Four's mind) about being a creature when everyone else is? Will the fact that creation is unique to each of us be enough for Fours? The temptation will be that the Fours will look around at all those other uniquely created people and remain unhappy as they perceive those other creatures enjoying life.

At the Conscientious stage directors can effectively use Fours' sense that their pursuit of God is unique to them. Fours feel alive and passionately involved when they are in pursuit of some goal or person. To search for meaning and connection gives them meaning and connection. And since one cannot complete the search for God in the same way as one can with a person or some object, there is a sense in which they are always in pursuit of God. The director is advised not to stress this with the Conformist Fours because it would only intensify their fixations, but since the Conscientious Fours know what they are doing, they can see that they can act authentically this way. This is still something in the nature of a crutch and may not be necessary at the next stage. Hopefully, the director will have sufficient theological acumen to assist these Fours at this time. Giving a "pat" solution and suggesting a quick-fix supported by platitudinous religious statements will be very destructive of the director/directee relationship.

As the Fours move more deeply into themselves, as they become more self-possessed at this level, as they develop a more differentiated emotional life, the director can help them find satisfaction in their very melancholy. There is, indeed, something special about them. All the others spaces on the enneagram have their specialness too, but it is not the same as that of the Fours. Palmer describes their melancholy as "the mood of preference. A sweet recollection of missing things. A felt connection to absent people and distant places. An understanding of death Preserved within the preoccupations of their own neurosis, Fours never gave up the realization that we are all connected at the level of essence."[9] Their melancholy is their way to God. The purpose of their taking on the projects of life more consciously is not simply to remove their depressions, although it does do that. This melancholy is now more about the way they possess integrity and truth. It becomes a tool of compassion and discernment for them. It becomes more a virtue giving them greater sight and insight and is not a (possibly distorted) personality characteristic.

The director can be sure that Fours have shifted from the Conformist to the Conscientious level when they fit Palmer's description of the Fours moving into the space of security (the space of One):

> The first security signals look like a relaxation of the focal issues. Sadness lifts and feelings of oppression lessen. Projects seem both interesting and possible. Relationships settle into a realistic perspective in which both positive and negative elements are apparent at the same time. Any situation that renders satisfaction breaks the Four's habit of focusing on things that are missing in life. It's the shift to seeing a half-full, rather than half-empty, glass.[10]

For Conscientious Fours this is more the usual state of affairs rather than an occasional trip to the One space.

Finding satisfaction in almost anything will be helpful for Fours because the sense of satisfaction in one area will allow them to experience that feeling of satisfaction in other areas. This is the foundation for the movement to the next level. As long as Fours are preoccupied with themselves and their longings and are concerned about what other people possess, they will not be able to move out to others and the world in which they operate. Good Christian spiritual direction can never be satisfied with individual growth alone. It implies a commitment to the Christian community and the participation in Christian (usually church) life. Their desire to be different and the lure of originality of the Fours may militate against this kind of involvement. The director will want to move them into commitments and areas of participation where such originality can be most utilized. Some of these Fours would make good directors themselves, and the director would be remiss not to suggest that or analogous work to them.

The director should encourage Conscientious Fours to pursue more imaginative forms of prayer and permit them to play around with more idiosyncratic images of God. At this point they need the freedom we give to artists to experiment. The Fours moving to health are less likely to lose their way or become confused. Just as in the creation of an art object there is a moment of clarity for the artist when it all comes together, so Fours will bring clarity of vision to their search for the "unusual" God and religious experience.

The director will find that Conscientious Fours possess a beautiful inner world. I describe this inner world as a cave. The analogy for the experience of entering a Four's inner world is that of the passageway through a deep cave with all its various rock formations, its dark, deep pools of water, its mineral-colored walls, its stalagmites and stalactites. It is the winding pathway of mystery and beauty. The director should encourage them to move out of it, and although they might not yet be ready to share it with the larger world, they can at least let that world peep inside.

I have used this example in my courses on the enneagram and spiritual direction. One of my students, Helen Barnes, constructed a Four meditation on the image of the cave. Directors and directees might find it helpful, and so I quote from it here:

> I enter the opening of a cave along a long black tunnel following a faint light ahead. This light draws me onwards and inwards until I arrive at a spacious cavern. Here there are many people gathered around a glowing fire. From the fire comes light and warmth and comfort. The flames throw light and shadow upon the faces and forms of the community. I find a spot to sit, for as soon as I am noticed room is made for me to sit. The flickering flames highlight the characters and personalities of each person. I become absorbed in the features of the people, which reveal much of their life journey and struggle. In this place emotions are strong, and I am caught up in the wonder and fascination of the storytelling that is going on. As the fire burns down, the people drift away, first the mothers and babies and last the old and wise ones. I am eventually left alone with my thoughts and memories. I reflect upon all that has happened since I entered this sacred place. I hold the stories in my heart and ponder their meaning in the light of the greater story of humankind's search for wholeness. My fear is that the fire will die out and I will be left in the dark. To prevent this I place more wood on the dying embers. When dawn comes outside and people begin to wake, the fire is burning brightly and ready to be stoked to begin the day's work. I feel good about this and return to the outer world refreshed and empowered by my own inner source of energy.[11]

Such a meditation can be the agenda for an entire session. The director can treat it like a dream, and so a dream analysis on the response of the directee would be appropriate.

At the Conscientious stage the director should pay particular attention to the panoply of feelings that is going on in Fours. They are now ready to look honestly at their sense of helplessness, blame, anger, guilt, and boredom as well as their buoyancy and sense of being alive. At the same time the director must be aware of his/her own feelings to make sure the Fours do not confuse their feelings with those of the director. The particular gift of the Fours is their ability to mirror back the feelings of others to them. They can pick up your feelings, run them through their own feeling system, and then mirror them back to you. That is why many good actors are Fours. The problem for the Four directees is that there is the possibility that they will confuse the feelings of others with their own feelings. The feelings of others get caught inside them, and then they can no longer mirror the feelings back, nor can they match the feelings of others. These feelings of others have become entangled with their feelings. The director should look for *caught* feelings. Caught feelings break connections and so intensify the sense of alienation many Fours feel. It is like an actor who steps outside a role. The actor assumes a role to have the audience respond emotionally. The audience may cry, but if the actor breaks down in tears, s/he steps out of the role and ruins it for the audience. If the actor needs to cry as an individual, then s/he should cry before or after the show, not during. Otherwise, the actor cannot mirror the feelings to the audience and can cause confusion between his/her own personal feelings and the feelings of the character being created in an aesthetic mode for the audience.

Despite the fact that these Fours now are not consistently governed by the fixations associated with them, there is still a need for the director to be with them in certain areas. One of these is intimacy, which can still be tension-filled for them since loss and abandonment have been so much the pattern at the previous level. What they need is a trusted guide who will not let them run away but will encourage them to continue to explore those points of satisfaction that they have already experienced.

Spiritual Direction with the Interindividual Four

There are signs that Fours are moving into the Interindividual stage. They grow into complex people with rich inner lives. There is very little of the envying of others because they seem to be happier; there is less of self-presentation that says that they are God's gift to the universe. The director will know that s/he is dealing with someone who feels deeply, but that depth can now be seen through the calm clear water rather than being obfuscated by a stormy surface. Although Fours at any level can portray their feelings vividly, at this level this is done with greater understanding of the self in terms of the origins of the feelings as well as with the kind of self-reflection that allows them to integrate these feelings.

This transition for Fours is characterized by their ability to discriminate between how they can alter themselves for others when they are threatened and their healthy moving into other people's lives in a ministerial way. They are very much aware of the inner conflict that is produced by an attentional style that searches for the absent and longs for the beloved who has gone away. These Fours live with the ambiguity and paradox that are caused by their constant seeking for something deeper. "Being deep" is not a way of avoiding the pedestrian, not a substitute for ordinary feelings, not a way to escape from present reality. It means contact with God in the present moment, no matter how ordinary that may be. No longer are these Fours trying to find that unfulfilled dream, that pot of gold at the end of their life search for meaning. Now they take satisfaction in the very search, the spiritual journey itself. Being on the journey is for them in some sense the attainment of what they have longed for. Now they have what they have envied other people for.

It is not always the case that the director works with someone beginning in the Conformist stage who then moves through the Conscientious to the Interindividual. Some will come to direction transiting into this latter stage because they have had to confront reality. They realize that they cannot live at a constant level of profundity, that not everything in life has to be or can be of high quality, that being defined by toss-and-turn feelings is no way to live. Fours at this level want and seek more mutuality and equality. They are ready to deal with intimacy issues. And they feel called to move into the larger world where social justice issues are in the forefront.

At this level the director's task with the Fours will be mostly one of discernment of certain complex issues. The emphasis is on complexity. All spaces at this level engage in these areas of ambiguity and paradox, but Fours bring to situations their own kind of complexity springing from their automatic movement to depth, their search for the really real, their viewing reality through their aesthetic filter. They will find a way to hold together the contradictions they experience, and the director can support them as they look for ways to discover the beauty of God in ugly situations and how they might confront conditions of injustice in new ways. In many ways, "beauty" is the key guiding word at this level. The director needs to know that this search for beauty does not mean that all Fours like to go to art galleries or that they are going to promote justice by writing songs or poems about it. The beauty they discover is the aesthetic quality of human commitment to "renew the face of the earth" whether this is through ecological concerns or harmony in the family. For Fours at this level their God is beautiful, and this in the sense of God as artist. Fours see themselves as art objects at the Conscientious level. Now they happily see others as art forms too.

Fours will want to bring together the inner and outer lives, which will often mean for them a change in external behavior. At an earlier level the external drama was a way of dealing with the inner sense of loss. Now being in touch with their inner beauty will manifest itself in more subtle ways on the outside. The director has the opportunity to help them find ways to act accordingly. The areas where the director can encourage Interindividual Fours to go for full embodiment include the arts as well as the beautifying side of ecological concerns.

As in the case of all the spaces, Fours at this level will want to and need to deal with intimacy and sexual issues. At the Interindividual level the unconscious has fuller play than at the previous two levels. Dealing with intimacy will entail some new understanding of their ideals, their lifestyles, and their commitments. Of course, these issues are centered around feelings for all the heart-centered people. Twos become entangled in the feelings of individuals with whom they are relating and Threes with the feelings of the group and feelings expected in certain roles. But for Fours the reaction to feeling is more complicated. Helen Palmer puts it this way:

When the heart is touched, Fours have an impulse to follow those feelings, to abandon caution, to be emotionally met. This profound requirement makes ordinary relating difficult. Because connection is the focus of their existence, fours want absolute emotional presence from a partner. They want unwavering devotion, and they get extremely tense about abandonment.[12]

Clearly, this description belongs more to the Fours at the Conformist level and to some degree at the Conscientious level. Interindividual Fours know that their search for love is nothing more than a device that in actuality keeps them away from intimacy. The unhealthy Fours simply set themselves up for disappointment by being dissatisfied with the actual person or situation. The connection is not of the quality that they had hoped for, and so there is now the possibility of loss and abandonment. This results in withdrawal from intimacy. But the absence makes the heart grow fonder, and the process of trying to connect begins again.

Interindividual Fours are willing to risk hurt in order to stay present to an intimate connection. The director can help them stay concrete in this area by reminding them not to distance themselves from present sources of intimacy in their lives and not to exaggerate their attractions when the person is absent. Having learned at the Conscientious stage to commit themselves in less provocative areas, Fours now can enter into commitments fully. The anchor that prevents the push-pull pattern of the past is their own emotional lives. Having learned to stay in the present by learning to appreciate some present reality that is not emotionally charged (e.g., their flower garden), they can stay present to the person asking for commitment now. Eventually, the person seeking the commitment will be the stabilizing force in their lives, but only because the Interindividual Fours have already made a commitment to themselves as works of art worthy of such commitment. They can hold a steady line and need not immerse the other in an ocean of feelings because they have no need to drown themselves in feelings. Under the steady guide of the director these Fours will easily shift to what they do have rather than to what they do not have. They can enjoy the present and what the present has given them. Their lives are a blessing, and they enjoy that. There is a meditation that I suggest Fours use to keep themselves on track in the area of intimacy. This meditation can also be used at the Conscientious level:

Call to mind someone you really desire — man or woman. Are they really inside of you? Can you feel them inside? Where in your body are they located? If they are not located in some specific part of the body, they are not there. Now check for some feelings. Any depression? Do you feel ashamed? If there is any shame or sadness, is it because you know that far inside you two have not really met? If that person is inside you, is she or he there as a guest? Who will take a message from you to your guest dwelling in you? How do you know when you have built a bridge so that you can carry a message to your beloved? Suppose there is no bridge and you cannot build one. Can you take life without the beloved? Can you believe that humor holds the answer to that question?[13]

Often the spiritual director will be the bearer of the message to the beloved who is inside the Four lover.

There is a peculiarity about the Fours that is significant at all levels of development, and the director will need to be aware of this phenomenon. To what degree the director becomes explicit about it on the Conformist level is an individual judgment call. The reflection on it should be present at the Conscientious level, and it must find some resolution on the Interindividual level. This peculiarity is called introjection. This psychologically explains a great deal about Fours' behavior and attention. The Six *projects,* and the Four *introjects.* Unlike projection, where Sixes take something from within themselves and place it on something or someone outside themselves, when Fours introject, they take something outside themselves and bring it inside. It may be a feeling; it may be an abandoning parent; it may be anything that represents a loss in their lives. It exists as a foreign body in Fours because it is not integrated. It is like having a heart transplant that is not working. They cannot connect with it. So there is this ever-present sense of being disconnected, this yearning for what they do not have, this grieving over what is absent. I find it difficult to believe that Fours can move to the Interindividual level without first learning how to intervene in this process. A good director will assist them in introjecting God/Christ, with whom they already have a strong connection. Much of spiritual growth now will be their finding ways to continue that connection once they have brought the God/Christ into their very selves.

The sexual Fours in their one-to-one relationships are characterized by the word "competition." This quality is quite obvious at the Conformist level, where it has a negative character.[14] Their relating can, however, be enhanced to the degree that they can assist the other person to improve his/her lifestyle and surroundings. Because Fours can recognize quality where others cannot, they can find ways to bring beauty to a relationship. At this level the Fours can bring intensity to relationships, whether this be sexual or not. Healthy Fours are able to have a deeply emotional relationship with someone without it being sexual, but at the same time they can also bring both beauty and intensity to the sexual act.

The director can encourage and support these Fours to develop their spiritual lives in terms of their relationships. There is much in an intimate relationship that the Fours can use to image their God in prayer: that God is beautiful, that God is full of possibilities, that God will see them through critical moments of their lives, that God will help them to change over time, that God patiently waits for them to develop through the various stages of their lives, and that God is their primary example of how to let go of negativity.

The central experience for the social Fours is shame. Because Interindividual Fours are in contact with their true selves, they no longer feel misunderstood or out of place. Rather, they use their gift of sensitivity in feeling to assist others. For the director this can be a temptation to switch roles and to become the directee momentarily in the sessions. Fours at this level would be good spiritual directors themselves. I should think that male Interindividual Fours would be very good working with other men because these Fours can express tender feelings. Men might expect women to do that as the director but might not have that presupposition about other men. All Fours at this level would be good in helping people in painful situations, ones that are filled with a lot of feeling.

Interindividual Fours possess authenticity at its highest level. All Fours long for the authentic, but these Fours really can recognize it. They can detect the phony in others (directors beware!) as well as discover those who have outstanding qualities for certain jobs and forms of leadership. The director will have little difficulty convincing these Fours that sexual activity can be a form of prayer and that being fully sexual is one of the most significant ways to move along the spiritual path. Because of their own histories these Fours move well with the differences of others and know how to integrate idiosyncratic behavior into a relationship.

"Dauntless" and "reckless" are words to describe the self-preservation Fours. Having survived a philosophy that life must be lived on the edge and no longer needing to create the possibility of loss, these Fours now can devote their full energies to being creative. They know how to make the ugly beautiful. The creation of something beautiful usually involves some kind of risk, and these Fours are natural risk-takers. They will take as a purpose in life to fill in that which is missing, to make life more complete. The director may not need to do much to assist them in their personal journeys of filling up their own lives but can be of real assistance in helping these Fours do that for others. Probably no other group on the enneagram can build a spiritual life on the Pauline principle of "building up what is missing in the body of Christ" as much as these Fours.

Self-care for them is to fill up their own lives with God's beauty so as to do that for others. Their vision for a renewed world is very much the vision they have for themselves. Their sense of being a co-creator with God will have reached a highly sophisticated level. But that does not mean that they disdain the mundane. Like any good artist these Fours will revel in the textures, colors, and sounds of life.

I would suggest that the body work for all Fours of whatever subtype be of the kind that establishes contact with the environment. Where they walk or run is just as important as the exercise itself. The director can encourage them to sense when they are being manipulated by external stimuli to move to the absent (roses if one is running by a rose garden) and when they are able to ground themselves in the present.

Chapter 6

The Space of Five

Suzanne Zuercher makes a good point about Fives in direction, namely, that the director should not presume that they will be "necessarily intellectual or bookish."[1] Rather they are observers who are looking for meaning in life often by collecting information, organizing data systematically, discovering a mental structure that gives meaning to the outside world. For this reason they treasure what inner order they have established and are threatened by anything that disturbs this order. New information can do that. I know a Five who, when told by a friend that he was going to get married, responded not by congratulating him but by saying that he would have to think about it. One of the reasons that Fives withdraw both physically and psychologically is that they need time to process anything that comes to them before they can respond to it. They take it into their minds, organize it, and integrate it into their interior system so that they can go out and feel safe when they confront reality.

The director needs to be sensitive to the special needs of Fives. They need time to integrate information into what they already know, time to synthesize any feelings and facts that they are taking in, time to prepare for going back out into the world to deal with that information. When Fives feel disoriented, they find that they are vulnerable. This vulnerability has led to painful experiences in the past, and so they are on the alert for anything that might put pressure on them or interrupt their established order. The director should resist being too directive with Fives. It is best to wait for them. They will not usually be very verbal. The director should resist the temptation to fill in the blanks. They tend to mull over matters and come to their own conclusions. The problem is that they do not bother to tell anyone about these conclusions. Because they have overdeveloped their observing qualities, they tend to depreciate other forms of communication, such as speaking. If the director can encourage them to expand on their remarks, amplify their observations, and listen to themselves, s/he can help usher them out of their private worlds and into a larger life. Speaking is a way for them to contact external reality.

We call Fives the stingy people on the enneagram. And they are stingy with their thoughts, their feelings, their emotionality, and their sensuality. It is the way they feel safe. They believe that if they move out and share experiences, feelings, and sexuality, they not only will be hurt but will lose something. Growth for the Fives takes place when they allow themselves to love someone and then experience not loss but gain. Like every enneagram space, their weakness is their gift. They may withdraw to be more reflective, to discover themselves, to be in communion with God. They may also withdraw so that they end up isolated, lonely, lacking in affectivity, and sterile in their humanity. This withdrawal is the most difficult part for the director. It seems like resistance. It calls into question the value of working with Fives. It seems a waste of energy and time. But if the director can remember that deep within every Five is, in fact, the desire to join the real world, to be part of life, to be a person who connects, to have a lot feelings, to be able to express love externally and physically, s/he can find ways that will allow the Fives to do their own kind of spiritual direction mentally even while in the direction sessions. If they sense that they have space to do it themselves, they will not withdraw and will connect on a deep level with the director.

Ultimately, the director wants to get the Fives to enlarge their perceptions, their sense of themselves, and their range of emotional response. A large part of direction will be helping Fives to put words to their experiences. This will make the experiences more real for them. Fives need to verbalize what is going on inside. That way they recognize that the real world is not their mental world but the world outside themselves. When they find themselves in a safe environment, they can become very communicative. It is this naming of their experience that helps them to get on the train of life, to connect with others, and most importantly to move toward greater intimacy.

The American poet Emily Dickinson is often considered a Five. So is much of her poetry, as the first few lines of one poem illustrate:

> The Soul selects her own
> Society —
> Then — shuts the Door —

To her divine Majority —
Present no more — [2]

Spiritual Direction with the Conformist Five

Conformist Fives, and all Fives to a lesser extent, bring to direction an outlook that creates difficulties for the director from the beginning.[3] Their real world is the mental, private one. Direction, of necessity, demands a situation of openness and transparency. Fives tend to operate out of the motto, "I'll tell you as little as I can." Direction works when the directees are willing to be articulate about their inner world, including their conflicts. Fives have the ability to compartmentalize their feelings. This means that they can be aware of their feelings without being in touch with them. Usually, when people become articulate about their feelings we assume that they are in contact with them. Not so with the Fives. They can observe their feelings, speak about them clearly, and still be distanced from them, still detached from the feeling dimension of their lives. Much of the time in direction the director will be trying to discern what is not being said and what else is being said in the few words being offered. This observing attitude means that at times Fives will give mixed signals. Their withdrawal may look like they are "playing hard to get."

Since Conformists are not nuanced in their thinking and judging and are simplistic in the distinctions they make about life and human behavior, it should not surprise the director to find Five directees who shut themselves off from the rest of the world because they see so much of the outside world as fearful. Rather than get involved with a world that they see through a sentimental filter or in terms of unattainable ideals without qualification, and so a world that makes demands of them, these Fives retreat into their inner world to do their own thing, to be safe from the interference of meddling people. This is a rather superficial view of external reality, but Conformist Fives will operate from this perspective. For all their intellectuality they are not yet equipped to see beyond and behind the areas of external behavior such as reputation, wealth, or the lack of them.

At the Conformist level the self is constituted by the group to which the person belongs. For Fives at this level, whom many people would consider antisocial, this takes on a quite different form. They belong to mental groups. They belong to groups who possess a certain kind of knowledge, something in physics or art, or knowledge about something specialized like certain kinds of snakes around the Amazon River. The members of these groups are bound together by the power of specialized information. This does not necessarily mean that these groups meet monthly or annually, although they might. Often it is a purely mental bond with people doing the same specialized thing. The Fives may know these people or not. They may have actual contact or not. Today, they might well keep in contact through the Internet, which is the Fives' great delight: a way of communicating in which you can hide as much as you want.

This attitude of noninvolvement and emotional control might baffle some directors, annoy and frustrate others, and confuse some others. What directors need to realize is that although Fives are very mental people, belonging to the head center of the enneagram, Conformist Fives are not good at introspection. Going into one's head is not to be equated with profound self-reflection. These Fives are most probably quite alienated from their actual feelings. In fact, they might not be able to observe them accurately. Whether they are looking out at the external world like a fox from its hole or observing their interior landscape, they do not have the depth to see things with insight. What feelings they do see they probably cannot accurately differentiate from their thoughts. Directors and therapists may find that they must do even more preliminary work with them before they can distinguish thought from feeling.

What the director can do is to help them understand how they pay attention and that not everyone does it like they do. For good reason they are called observers. But that is all they do. During the session they observe the director; they observe themselves; and they observe themselves observing the director and the director observing them. This is where the director can help: s/he can help the Fives become aware of the style of their attention, which then helps them become aware of their inner lives. And even though these Fives might not be very discriminating, at least they can detect inner movements. There will be some feelings attached to these movements. Contact with these feelings is a good beginning. The difficulty for Fives is that they can pay attention to something like pain but can also let the feeling go away. They watch the feeling rather than feel it. I would recommend this meditation by Helen Palmer:

After quieting yourself, identify some feeling. It can be any feeling such as being tired, physical pain, warmth, anxiety, frustration, anger. Focus on the feeling. Stabilize it in your attention. Now let go of it. Find a way to be non-attached. It may be helpful to concentrate on your breathing at this time. Try to feel yourself letting go of the feeling. Notice if you are watching the feeling go away. If you are, you are still attached to the feeling, although it is going away. In non-attachment you stop watching even your feelings go away.

I think it is best to elicit from these Fives some reflection about their prayer. It will probably be primarily mental and self-constructed, at least to the degree that they have distanced themselves from the forms of prayer that they find out in the real world, at least those kinds that require them to be more publicly transparent. They will not be very good at describing what is actually going on in this inner world, but even a somewhat confused contact with feeling at this point is an opening. Many Fives will pray externally. But the director should not be deceived that this is really all that external. For instance, Fives could well be engaged in the prayer of the liturgical hours. The prayer structure is set; it has an ancient tradition; it has a certain "specialized" quality about it; it is not open-ended. It is done in community, but the individual participant can remain hidden behind the liturgical form. Involvement with the ritual is not the same thing as involvement with the other participants in the ritual.

Conformist Fives also participate in groups through adopting certain identities, values, and status symbols. Especially important to them are symbols of knowledge such as academic degrees, a plentiful personal library, computer literacy, and personal connections with experts. Here the director needs to take time to discern the meaning of these elements in the Fives' spiritual life. These symbols of knowledge can also represent superficiality. It is easy to detect the superficiality of the Threes' having the best computer or the Fours' idiosyncratic dress fashions. It is more difficult with Fives, but whenever knowledge is equated with what is most real, the truly essential, the deepest dimension of these Fives, the warning sign should come on for the director. The key question for these Fives here is: What is beneath this desire for more knowledge? In fact, it is a deep desire to understand and love themselves. They have a hunger for love in their lives, and this love could nourish them, but they are afraid of it because they think it will overwhelm them.

Often Conformist Fives will come across as devoted sons and daughters of the church. And externally they may be just that. But it might be a loyalty that is overintellectualized. External practice that is in no way deviant is a way of protecting their privacy, keeping away those human invaders, and avoiding the entrance of any feelings and desires into their mental system. But mentally they might be quietly deviant, very disobedient to the church, as it were, but no one will ever know. It would not be surprising if the director found that these directees who are seen as good Christians, practicing Catholics, are in fact seriously deficient in the faith. Although there might be conflict there for these Fives themselves, still they continue as they are because to reject church participation might require that they step our of their little hidden worlds, interact with others, get reactions from others, and change a well-known external terrain. All this might bring up their own needs.

When desire enters the Fives' inner world, the alarm system goes off. Why? Because their method of remaining hidden is done through scarcity and nonattachment. Fewer needs and fewer desires maintain them in their castle, fortified from the outside world. The recognition of needs brings up their desires, and they find themselves being pulled out of the shadows and obscurity. It will be very helpful for directors as they negotiate this private world of the Fives to realize that the external emotional withdrawal, the obvious stinginess, and the low level of involvement are only skin deep. Just below the surface are many strong feelings and real desires not to just have knowledge but also to be involved sensually and sexually. They long to be connected, to be part of the real world, to jump onto the train of life, to be passionately involved. But that is so frightening and so totally threatening (because their armor is so thin) that they retreat into as much unavailability as possible. It would be disastrous if the director attempted to tear away this thin protection at the Conformist level. The first step is to help these Fives with some understanding of how they operate in avoiding as much feeling as possible. Because they are emotionally stingy, which is their way of avoiding involvement, and because they operate so interiorly, they have less motivation to change behavior. The director can recommend that they practice exercises that will connect them to the outside world and that will require them to externalize their inner world. The following meditation can be helpful here:

Quiet yourself. Imagine that you are at a national convention where you know no one. You are going to the opening banquet the first evening. There are no assigned seats. How do you feel as the time for the evening meal approaches? You are now walking toward the dining room. How do you feel as you approach the dining room? What are your feelings as you enter? What is the first thing you do as you enter? You notice that there are a variety of round tables seating from four to eight people. Some have people already at them but with spaces. Others are entirely empty. Some tables have animated discussion going on. Others are quiet. What are you feeling as you see all this? Which table do you chose to sit at? What attracted you to that particular table? What do you feel as you approach the table?[4]

Conformists who are recognizable by their rigidity in following rules, whether they be the more public ones such as the laws of the church or the more interior ones such as methods of prayer, are concerned with controlling their impulses. For Conformist Fives this is especially sensitive since they have some notion that these impulses are not too far below the surface and could easily erupt. Authority and institutional identification become supports to avoid the display of emotion in the public arena. These Fives can then present themselves as those who have achieved that kind of spiritual detachment that the Christian writers have spoken about. It probably does little good for the director to try to relativize church regulations or spiritual restraints from the kind of absolutism these Fives give to them. Rather the director can help them to see that detachment from emotion is not the same as detachment as it is usually understood in the Christian tradition. The directors who are trained in the Ignatian method will have resources at their disposal to deal with these Fives on this point.[5]

Trying to get these Fives to deal with the strong emotions of sexuality and aggression at this level will not be easy. It may be quite counterproductive. It is not just a matter of embarrassment; it is more a matter of the fear that prevents them from making contact with these feelings. As Palmer notes, those on the head center (Fives, Sixes, and Sevens) have fallen into fear. Fives fear that their inner passions may break out with the slightest provocation. However, at the Conformist level Fives may not even be aware of any real strong feelings inside. They have so defended themselves by separating themselves from those feelings and they have so retreated into their own conceptual world that the fear they experience is more of a free floating kind rather than one tied directly to sex or anger. These Fives are much more likely to say that they feel very little inside, that they do not feel passionate or angry at all, that they can locate very little emotion about a person or an issue. That does not mean that these feelings are not there. But these Fives have almost no contact with that part of their lives. It is better for the director to move them to examine their method of prayer, their views of God, what they mean by the spiritual life, their connection with the church, and so on. All of these considerations are for the most part conceptual. In the area of the intellect these Fives feel secure because they can rely on their mental world to maintain balance and there is less danger that they will be exposed. It may be helpful to have them explore praying to a God who has feelings and relating to a Christ who did not hold back his feelings, who felt very deeply, and who showed and communicated his feelings without fear or in spite of it.

Conformists want to belong. They want to be connected with groups. They feel secure belonging to organizations. But Conformist Fives fulfill these desires in a way others spaces do not. Palmer's point about the way Fives relate in public is instructive here:

> Fives can go public and still be distant. When thought is un-hooked from feeling, you can watch emotional events. You don't need closed doors or elaborate ways to avoid entanglement when you can detach from your feelings. You can talk and respond to people without really being there. You can be far away even when you're in front of a crowd with everyone looking.[6]

The director can easily be led astray here. These Fives look like they are involved. For instance, in the direction sessions they can appear to be quite engaged. The deceptive thing is that while discussing feelings they may seen quite immersed in them. In fact, these Fives are not. They are watching themselves talking about feelings, which means that they are in fact detached from them.

Or they may appear to be quite involved with their friends. In fact, they are usually absorbed in the ways that they are doing things with these friends. If there are deep feelings present, they probably are unable to detect them. Fives want these human connections with groups, friends, and a director, but at the same time they fear them and so detach from them. The director needs patience working with

Fives at this level so as to be able to assist them in exploring their feelings about God. They may quite readily and easily talk about a deep and even emotional connection with God and think they are actually feeling this relationship. In fact, what they are doing is observing it and mistaking that for feeling it. But gradually the real feelings that are there will keep struggling to come to the surface, and this is what often moves these Fives into the next stage of growth.

Spiritual Direction with the Conscientious Five

Fives who reject the possibility of growing, who live life at a distance from God, who out of fear choose to remain hidden in their mental world, may never move into the Conscientious stage. They can spend their entire lives in a highly repressed state. But for Fives who want to become better human beings, who seriously desire a relationship with God, who want to participate in church community life, and who want to pursue a life of prayer, spiritual reading, and the like, it will be impossible to stay at the Conformist stage. They will find it increasingly difficult to maintain the privacy, the detachment, the stinginess that they have so highly prized. More and more there will be eruptions of feelings. Drives that they have considered undesirable and best hidden will keep demanding recognition. Maturity lies in developing relationships with the world. This is a critical time in working with Fives. All spaces on the enneagram will be tempted at this time to batten down the hatches and regress to the previous stage, to redouble efforts to gain control of unruly emotions and conflicts. But Fives will be tempted most of all to do this. The director needs to support them at this time with a great deal of encouragement, but not in an intrusive way. The director can help them become not too dependent and not too independent. S/he can assure the Fives that if they continue on with this transition, a very rich and deep life awaits them.

It is probable that the director who deals with a number of Fives will find most of them at the Conscientious level. For these Fives there is less hiding in a private space, less concern about what society sees as qualified people, less exclusivity in relationships. Most importantly, the director will note a greater willingness to make a commitment. Fives share with Fours a sense of loss. For Fours the loss is always there. Fives feel they are losing something when they commit to something. Once they can internalize that commitment is a gain and not a loss, they are on their way to greater health. Commitment involves intimacy, spontaneity, and stress. Fives will need to stay engaged in the presence of these three and resist the temptation to go into the head and process what is coming to them. It is difficult to see how they can maintain commitment unless they stay present to strong feelings.

The Conscientious Fives are both more ready to enter into strong feelings and at the same time more likely to resist them. It takes a lot of energy for Fives to commit themselves. And what looks like minimal commitment in the view of those who are not Fives looks like considerable handing of themselves over (thus loss) to another on the part of the Fives. Here the director has an invaluable role to play. S/he can help these Fives to feel supported as they enter into relationships where commitment is demanded. Commitment to someone or something outside themselves goes against the grain and is a struggle. Their fear of commitment is obvious in the way many Fives do not like to say where there are in a relationship with someone. Yet this commitment is their salvation. When Fives enter into commitment, they can take as their motto the Spanish saying: *Vale la pena* (It is worth the pain).

What other spaces have developed in the Conscientious stage Fives already have at their disposal — that is, the ability to introspect. But there is a special trap for Conscientious Fives here. Because people at this stage are honest and concerned about relationships and because they have an ordered sense of values, there is the temptation to settle at this level. Fives can do it with a sense of satisfaction that they are growing or have reached a personal vision, a depth in the inner life, a certain freedom from outside restrictions, and a certain vigor in their spiritual lives. There is a self-appropriation and claiming of their inner authority. Is that not enough? is the question the Fives put to themselves. Having chosen scarcity in the past, this seems like a luxurious spiritual life.

But this is not enough for Fives. All of the above is done in a conscious and mental way. They have not tapped into their intuitive processes, much less their bodies and strong feelings, especially their sexuality. In the long run it will not work to remain at this level because the directees are also interested in future development and are self-consciously creating a set of ideals. Because they are aware of themselves in a more nuanced way and because they are more at home with a wider range of feelings, Conscientious Fives will find that this stage does not offer them what they would be most comfortable with, namely, the opportunity to be safe and hidden but now at a more religiously acceptable level. They now know that if they wish to continue to grow they must become increasingly transparent. Here the director can help them to discover what lies behind their defensiveness, although some of this discovery should have taken place at the Conformist level.

Because the Conscientious stage is a transitional one to the Interindividual, it is a time of shifting ground, and the directee knows it. Directors will often find that working with anyone at this stage feels like crisis management. For these Fives things are less and less mental. Feelings are now beginning to be more felt than thought. It is not quite so easy to run away from passion and situations of strong feeling because the Fives are now aware of their automatically doing that. They are becoming aware of inner desires, some of them very unsettling, such as sexual ones. They are increasingly aware that to resolve something in the mind does not mean that it is resolved in the outside world. They are less and less satisfied with remaining uninvolved and so detached. At the Conformist level it is difficult for the director to take advantage of the Fives' emotional needs because then they often are unaware of them and frequently do not feel any because they are so distant from that part of their lives. But now at this level many of these needs emerge, and the director should help the Fives give birth to these needs. If the director can establish a relationship of trust with the Fives so that they will be willing to try to make contact with the feeling and physical sides of themselves, then the director can suggest exercises that will have a strong feeling, even sensual, content. One suggestion would be prayer that is tied to movement and/or music. Some Fives are open to an experience of massage done in silence and then are willing to reflect on it later. Often those reflections will surface in the spiritual direction sessions themselves. The reason is found in the Fives' method of self-defense. Palmer notes:

> Moving away from people is a strategy for survival, and privacy feels good and safe as long as there's someone on the other side of the door. Noninvolvement is an active choice when there is some reason to guard yourself; *but when nobody knocks on the door, privacy can feel like a prison.*[7]

The atmosphere of spiritual direction provides the kind of privacy in which there is no enemy or source of fear on the other side of the door, and so the Fives become uncomfortable with their own privacy. They know there is more to life, more to spiritual growth than their noninvolved way of proceeding. They are now more willing to explore that emotional turmoil that lies just beneath their surface. They will do it consciously at this level, and the exploration begins when they start to feel more involved in life. As the fear of invasion diminishes, the director can encourage these Fives to be more transparent with the feelings that they can connect with, to be more generous in what they share about themselves, to learn to feel free in public, and to let others have more of them instead of the bits they parcel out because of their stinginess. I recommend the following meditation to learn about the Fives' desire to enter into life.

> Image in your mind your half extended hand. If helpful, extend your hand on your knee till it feels half way. Open the hand half way. What does it feel like to be unable to reach and unable to pull back? Does feeling bring desire? Does the desire bring disappointment? Do you feel needy but also need to remain independent? Do you want to make a connection with others but cannot feel in the presence of others? Do you want to indulge in pleasure but feel more secure with scarcity? Do you feel any pangs of loneliness but still want to maintain your limits and boundaries? Would you like to participate in life, live a less restricted life? But how can you do that if it is important to predict the behavior of others and so you cannot be committed to them?[8]

Apart from the safety of spiritual direction, Conscientious Fives might find that there is a person in their lives who deeply loves them. Like the safety of the direction sessions this person helps the Fives to experience the loneliness of their lives when they withdraw and live in seclusion. Some Fives at this level will embrace this relationship as an opportunity for spiritual growth by letting the feelings emerge that the lover triggers in them. They will try to remain attached to the person when the two are interacting. They will try not to withdraw emotionally in order to reevaluate in private what is happening. They will take the risk of exposure with this person. They will let feelings come out and be expressed on the spot as spontaneously as possible. They will be able to tell the person what s/he means to the Five. They will be willing to discuss the relationship.

This is a considerable challenge for Conscientious Fives. Directors can assist them and encourage them in this direction. Directors can point out to them the wholesomeness of the relationship, the long-term value of the relationship, and how holding out against this person who loves them is holding out against God. But the director cannot push here. Many, if not most, Conscientious Fives will find it very difficult to respond fully to this relationship. That does not mean they will reject the person. Rather they will respond fully in some areas, partly in others, and not at all in others. Fives still find these relationships threatening, even though the person who loves them is not threatening them. Fives are usually threatened by the sexual dimension of the interaction. Often Conscientious Fives will understand that sexual commitment and involvement could be a great source of spiritual energy for them and that withdrawal from this more bodily and sensual experience is a hindrance in their movement to deepen their relationship with God. But because they are not sufficiently emotionally grounded in their bodies, these Fives will choose to withdraw to the safety of a nonsexual relationship if that is possible. This is understandable since this stage of growth, while marked by deeper awareness, is one of uncertainty, of changing images of God and value systems. These Fives are still trying to create their own spiritual identity, and often they hope that this can be done in a somewhat disembodied way.

Although in search of their identity, these Fives are also able to create it. They have internalized their goals in life, and their inner world is not confined to the mental dimension but has a fuller emotional component. As these Fives become more and more secure in who they are, they have a tendency to be controlling people. But at this stage the director can help them to recognize that and avoid moving in that direction. What can take place is that the directee becomes more relaxed and less defensive, making it easier for the director to pursue other issues, issues that Palmer has summed up very nicely:

Secure Fives participate physically and emotionally. They can be outgoing, get angry, and hold their ground in a fight. This is often described as tapping into a healthy rush of power, a feeling of waking up, and being fully alive. Secure Fives are every bit as immediate and forthcoming as Eights. They move into action rather than retreat.[9]

Because the Conscientious stage is a time of discarding much that worked in the past but no longer does, all the way from petty defense mechanisms to the images of God, these Fives are at the point of greater opening up, and the director needs to note this. These Fives are tired of withdrawing. Isolation is no longer so sweet. Although the outside may appear calm or even exuberant, the inside is filled with tension and turmoil. Now like Sevens they allow themselves more options and lots of external activity.[10] And like the Eights they need to become more external, increasing their connections with others in order to feel that they are bigger, that they are taking up more space psychologically. The time of shrinking into invisibility is over.[11] The issue for the director at this time will be how to prevent the Fives from feeling isolated in all this external mix. It will be important to help them relax through this process and not to judge the outer world from an inner-world perspective. Because at this stage directees are often hypercritical toward self and others and because there is confusion about the direction of their lives, these Fives may be tempted to run away from all the activity, consider the outside world superficial, and become fearful that they are losing themselves in all this.

This need not be the case. This is also the time when there is the possibility of greater reliance on God, and they can let all this internal and external activity become their way of handing themselves over to God. Enjoying options, the flurry of activity, and surprising situations can become for them their special character before God precisely as Fives (and not as Sevens, who do these things naturally). It is a forged identity, and the director can help them in this process.

The move to the next stage begins at the Conscientious level, where the issues of intimacy have already arisen. More intense and more authentic relationships will be developing at this time. By helping the Fives to distinguish among their feelings and by helping them to identify their strengths and weaknesses in relationships, the director can move them in several important directions. Fives need to learn to bring their intimacy out in the public more. By that I mean that they need to be able to express their feelings explicitly with another person, rather than hoping that the other person will guess how they are feeling. Fives also need assistance in learning how to move toward the person they love rather than waiting for the other person to make contact with them. They need to learn how to initiate and how to be vocal about their feelings in a direct manner. When these Fives can say to the other that they both want them and need them for their spiritual growth, they have made their entrance into the Interindividual stage. The challenge for the director is how to encourage the Fives along this path while at the same time making sure that they do not hand themselves over to the other in such a way that they are not caring for themselves. It will be the director's task to ensure that as the Fives integrate each intimate relationship into their lives more fully, there will at the same time be a deepening of their friendship with God. The two friendships must go together. They are the same reality for these Fives: love of God and love of the beloved. And although it may still be difficult to express sexual and aggressive feelings in prayer, the director can move the directee to feel "as much a possible" in formal prayer.

Spiritual Direction with the Interindividual Five

As Fives move into the Interindividual stage there are still key areas of their lives where they have not yet achieved integration. They still struggle over how much to give of themselves to others and groups and how much to keep for themselves. They still wrestle with, on the one hand, their desire to move into intimate situations and, on the other, their wanting to live a more "efficient" life that is not complicated by a relationship. But these lacks must be balanced with what is achieved now, such as a greater comfortability with themselves and their bodies, an expression of feelings that also means that they are in contact with those feelings, and a willingness to live in an outside world that is often out of control and frequently confused. Most importantly, these Fives know how to intervene when their style of attention takes over. As they become more aware of how they operate in terms of their attentional style, which is to be an observer, to watch themselves watching, they become more understanding of themselves in relationships, more nuanced about their inner worlds and the feelings that are there, and more aware of what they need to do for further growth.

The Interindividual stage is one of high spiritual and human maturity. Probably the greatest obstacle for Fives in reaching this stage fully is the belief, which they often hold on to tenaciously, that their surest and most secure way to God is through meditation, reflection, and prayer. Enneagram writers often use the word "castle" when speaking of the Fives' tendency to withdraw emotionally and find refuge in their mental worlds. One could just as well use the word "monastery." They may actually go to monasteries,[12] although most carry their monasteries around with them or try to create the monastic experience in their secular lives. The crisis that may bring these Fives to spiritual direction at this time or that at least moves them to intensify their direction is disillusionment in making their "monastery" work. Their approach to God increasingly collides with their greater awareness that they cannot go through life alone and that, for instance, social justice issues are becoming increasingly significant for them. But most importantly, there is a growing awareness that God is asking them to come to God in a way that is not the most congenial to them, that is, in a way that is different from reflection, prayer alone, meditation, and certain ritual practices.

I hope it is clear that the director is *not* to discourage the Fives from doing these more private and reflective spiritual exercises. These are ways to God that are common to humanity, and all the spaces profit from meditation, prayer, spiritual reading, and ritual. And for some of the spaces, such as the Threes, these methods are the primary forms to move to God. But because Fives do these things naturally, something else is being asked of them.

Now living life more deeply and expressing themselves more concretely, these Fives will find further areas in which they are challenged to grow: the importance of sexuality, especially in a one-on-one relationship, the larger social context in which they can live an expanded life, and a reexamination of their commitments. The director will want to assist the Fives as they move into a very deep spiritual life. But the way that some Fives will want to go because they feel it true to their calling may cause the director some apprehension. For instance, a Five may decide to get a divorce or leave the priesthood. Especially in the area of sexuality the directors will be most helpful if they keep themselves open to expressions of sexuality that they would not choose for themselves. For instance, a Five could begin to relate genitally with someone who is already a close friend. Rather than denouncing this, it may be best for the director at this stage to trust that the Fives will be realistic about themselves and will act morally because they are operating out of a desire to overcome the dichotomy between their inner and outer worlds. Like all spaces at this stage, Fives will be able to live with the ambiguous far more easily than before.

When Fives are unhealthy, psychologically and spiritually, they avoid strong feeling as a defense. They simply do not feel. They remove themselves. They become absent. In speaking of Fives who are less healthy Palmer says:

> Detachment has protective value. It softens unexpected jolts of emotion and cushions unpleasant events. Life is quiet and pleasant when you're unemotional. Why entertain strong feelings when they are the source of pain? Separating from emotion does neutralize negativity. But, over time, cutting off your own reactions can seem like an amputation. By denying yourself the wellsprings of emotion, you deprive yourself of experience.[13]

Perhaps the Fives became detached because they were rejected in the past, possibly in a past relationship. They learned to disengage from their feelings. Now it has become habitual; they enjoy detaching from feelings. They have become attached to detaching from their feelings. At the Interindividual level they can become aware of this kind of psychic isolation and remedy it. They must detach themselves from their detachment.

I believe Palmer is speaking about those Fives who are moving toward health and a deepening of their spiritual lives when she says:

> Sex can be an important area of security for Fives. It's high level nonverbal communication that lasts for an hour or so and then is done. Although they are primarily mental beings, secure Fives can be quite at home in their bodies. They like physical sensation, athletics, and sexuality, and may even enjoy an occasional fight.[14]

At the Interindividual level the Fives are ready to pursue their spiritual lives through sexuality and intimacy with another person. They are already expert at spiritual practices such as mediation, contemplation, *lectio divina,* various devotions, and liturgy. But these are usually not enough to break through their defenses to make themselves totally vulnerable to God. Although Fives would prefer to do so, it is not possible to think themselves into that vulnerability. Since the healing of Fives in terms of styles of attention involves staying in the presence of strong feelings, a relationship in which there are experiences of strong sexual passion with some regularity will be the key that opens for them the deepest experiences of God. In the arms of a loved one they can let go of all that holds them back from the spiritual life: the fear that their privacy will be exposed, the feeling of being possessed, the fear that they are being run by their emotions, the sensitivity to being dominated, the mistaken belief that if something is not said, it does not exist. Blessed are those Fives who have someone who loves them enough to provide the security of an intimate relationship for them. One can only hope that the director will be supportive and nuanced in what is done and said when these Fives bring this matter to the sessions. Paradoxically, these Fives can also teach us how to be alone without being lonely. They have achieved a degree of freedom by having gone through the loneliness in their lives. The following meditation is meant to help Fives open themselves to more intimacy:

> Quiet yourself. Be attentive to and stay with your own breathing. Call to mind some desire that you are experiencing or have experienced recently. Imagine someone coming to you and offering you what you desire. How much will you take? Then, they offer you even more. Can you accept more? What would that feel like? They offer you even more. Can you accept even more? What would that feel like? When does it become too much? How do you know that? Can you enjoy such an abundance? What feelings do you have when you have too little? What feelings do you have with abundance? Imagine yourself embracing the abundance.
>
> Now repeat this meditation, but in place of something you desire, insert love and affection. Imagine someone coming to you offering love and affection. How much will your take? Suppose this person offers something more, such as time together; sharing of deep secrets, personal goals, and visions; common projects; and leisure time. What would that feel like? Would you accept it? Suppose this person offers even more, such as physical intimacy, sexual union, becoming lovers, marriage. How does that feel? When does it become too much? Why? What feelings do you have if you say no to any of these offers? Imagine yourself embracing the abundance, that is, full physical intimacy. What takes place in your mind, your feelings, your body?

On the Interindividual level Fives will no longer appear antisocial. Rather, they will be very concerned about social issues, especially as they touch upon the need for education and justice. They can bring to these often highly conflictual situations a sense of calm and balance since they have securely worked out in their minds the goals and the means to attain them. They have already processed the information needed and have run it through their own discernment process. Here is where their weakness, detachment, becomes their gift. They are able to remain emotionally distant in order to do a proper evaluation. At this level they are less likely to do what they would have done earlier — that is, wishing to avoid conflict, they would have decided in private what was the best way to go and then would have announced that decision without consultation or warning.

Although this is a high stage of human growth and spiritual advancement, that does not mean that there is no pain. Like all the spaces, when Fives reexamine their life commitments, goals, and ideals and discover that these in the past have only supported their fixations, they have now to integrate them in a new way. There are no easy answers here. However, the director can rest assured that at this level the Fives will bring to the conversation a greater inclusiveness so that groups and individuals will be included in their lives. Fives will be as caring for themselves now as they are for others. As the name of this stage suggests, Fives will deal with their feelings, their concern for justice issues, their life commitments, and their reconfiguring of their images of God in terms of this sense of interdependency. This kind of work will be beyond the competence of some directors, but where the directee and director can profitably work together, concrete suggestions for the ways the Fives might move will probably emerge from the intimate experiences in their lives. This highlights the importance of considering the religious experiences of the various subtypes as they are emerging at this stage.

The key word to describe self-preservation Fives is "home." The word is self-explanatory for the reclusive Fives. But when they have reached a high degree of health, these Fives can be warm and friendly. "Home" means not the defensive castle but refers to being "homey." Because they are Fives, there is still the desire not to be in the public realm. But they are very good in giving support to others in a more hidden way and also can carry on work by themselves without requiring support from others. The director will now feel as if these directees no longer need or want a spiritual companion. This is partially true. But they still need the steady support of the director to help them to continue to invite people into their homes. They may need to be reminded to invite in a person with whom they are intimate. They may "forget" to issue the invitation. If God is to come to dwell in their home, that home needs to be peopled by those with whom the Fives are intimate.

The key word for the sexual Five is "confidence." As the word suggests, these Fives make good confidants. They are also willing to take into confidence their spiritual director. They feel confident about themselves, but because they are now people who have claimed themselves, they can also inspire confidence in others. In a situation of intimacy they will not feel overwhelmed. They can remain independent in connecting with a good friend and in an expression of affection. They can confidently enter into a relationship. They can embrace the passionate and will not substitute fantasies for their real desires. Palmer notes that "Confidence Fives say that they're drawn to sexual expression as the antithesis of intellectualism."[15] In other words, it is their way of being healthy and holy.

The key word for social Fives is "totem." The word can be confusing. But when one considers that totems are the means by which native people connect the forces of the universe with their own minds, one can see how this applies to these Fives. They see the mind as the source of power, and so they connect with "those in the know." They are attracted to systems of thought that tend to give universal explanations. When these Fives are healthy, they bring to social groups a sense of authenticity and quality. They more willingly share themselves in groups and set up a strong sense of group intimacy. They introduce clarity into relationships, and their commitment is strong and perduring. They bring these same qualities to the relationship with an intimate. And because of that their relationship with God can be described in the same way. They have an authentic and intimate connection with the greatest force, the God they worship.

Chapter 7

The Space of Six

Of all of the directees, the Sixes are the most ambivalent.[1] They are ambivalent about themselves, about direction, about the director, about the pursuit of the spiritual life. The fear that makes them so ambivalent will soon be obvious to the director. Fives and Sevens operate out of fear also, but they express it more indirectly. The Sixes' hesitation causes them to procrastinate, to delay their decision making, to check things out constantly. They are the "projectors" on the enneagram. We all project on to reality to some extent, but Sixes do it as part of their daily lives.

One of the difficult things for directors is to determine the kind of Six they are dealing with. This ambivalence shows up in the double personality of the Sixes. They can be sticklers for the law, and they can also be the ones who most deliberately set laws aside. They are often as preoccupied with trying to do the right thing as Ones are. But the difference is significant. Ones know what is the right way; Sixes are never sure. The lack of certainty springs from their fear, not from ignorance. That is why getting the Sixes into their feelings, especially fear, early in direction is important. Addressing some issue rationally with a Six may result in the appearance of a solution, but in fact there may be no solution at all. The fear will kick in the next time the Six must make a decision in the same area.

Some say Sixes are playful. As a Six I can attest to that. There is a certain kind of openness about Sixes. They have the innocence of the child but also the fear of the child. Creating a warm, friendly environment is a way of getting the protection they think they need. Because Sixes are looking for the sources of fear in their lives, they develop a certain ability to discover the unseen and the unspoken. In my own life the combination of friendly joking and intuitive insight has gotten me into trouble because I will engage in humor with someone while I also reveal to him/her something about their own lives, and they then become defensive. I have always found it difficult to "just joke" without something else being implied.

The fear behind the Sixes' friendly manner comes through when they are not consciously trying to be playful and teasing. When I am lost in thought my face becomes grim and serious and people say to me: "Smile, you look like you're unhappy." And then when I smile they say: "You have such as wonderful smile. It's so open." There is no evidence of fear in the smiling.

It is axiomatic that Sixes fear authority more than anything else. This sensitivity to rules and regulations can mean that Sixes are constantly looking over their shoulder to check if they are doing the right and dutiful thing. This can become oppressive. This comes through in my life clearly every day at one moment, when I am opening my mail. If there is a letter from some authority, a bishop, the provincial, some government agency, I automatically experience a rush of fear. My presumption is that the letter will contain something harmful to me, something that threatens my present position, someone calling me to task. Usually the letter contains mere information, something quite trivial, but that does not prevent the fear from rising at the next letter opening. After all, sometimes the letters do contain bad news!

The director who is dealing with Sixes who have not dealt with their fear will sometimes wonder if s/he is dealing with a Five. The discouragement that comes from their feelings of inadequacy can move Sixes to withdraw like a Five. The greatest gift that a director can give to a Six, and the most effective tool in direction, is trust. An atmosphere of trust will help a Six to open up on several levels to look at fear. When they trust someone who trusts them, they will check their projections. I was fortunate enough to begin my therapeutic work with a therapist who was able to establish that kind of ambience in his office. Often, when I was pondering with considerable anxiety whether I should say something, he would ask: "What will happen if you do that? Will the sky fall in?" The question was effective for me because of the relationship of trust. This created the atmosphere to move more intentionally to my feelings. From this feeling level I developed a confidence in my self. From this confidence I was able to move to claiming my own authority.

Spiritual Direction
with the Conformist Six

Sixes[2] are usually divided into two categories: phobic and counterphobic, those who are authoritarian and those who are antiauthoritarian. Perhaps that is one of the reasons there has been a changing nomenclature for Sixes. Riso uses the term "The Loyalist," while Rohr describes them in terms of a need: the need for security/ certainty. Palmer's first major work uses the title "The Devil's Advocate" while in her volume on love and work she uses "The Trooper." This may serve as a warning to the directors that when dealing with a Six they cannot automatically presume that they are dealing with someone who follows all the rules, a kind of "Oliver North" mentality whereby the person passes all responsibility on to the law and persons of authority.

What the director will find is that these people are fearful, and fear is part of the very fabric of their lives. Trying to get them to eliminate fear from their lives is counterproductive because to eliminate fear would destroy their very personhood. The concerns of the Sixes that Palmer[3] lists mostly come from this fear. Palmer's list is also a description of the Conformist Sixes. Some of these traits are: letting thinking replace doing; imagining the worst; having anxiety peak with success; being ambivalent about authority; being afraid of anger; having a doubting mind; and finding the world to be a threatening place. The style of attention is to scan the environment for possible danger.

It will be easy for the director to recognize in all these traits at the Conformist level the common characteristics of Conformist persons. They judge according to an external norm. For Sixes this is some authority or an antiauthoritarian stance. The world is black and white without much differentiation. For Sixes this means there are friends and there are enemies. Conformists have a poorly developed inner life and find introspection difficult. They must rely on external behavior for evaluations. This means that Sixes at this level will move toward or away from people based on little knowledge of who these people really are. They might flee from people who want to connect with them but whom the Sixes perceive as threatening, or they might become sentimentally involved with some persons who themselves lack an inner life. It may be a case of the psychological principle that "water seeks its own level."

The director must begin by establishing a situation of trust with the Sixes, or no further work is possible. While trust is indispensable in all spiritual direction, trust is the single most important element for Sixes, even more than love. Both types of Sixes are fearful and doubtful, and that is the way they will begin their relationship with the director. The directors represent authority whether they want to or not. Only a person who has no interest in spiritual growth picks an incompetent spiritual director or goes to a director who, under the misguided notion that s/he must be completely equal to the directee, refuses to offer anything other than "presence." Sixes will want to know what the directors really want and what they really mean by their questions and suggestions. They may try to provoke the directors as a way of checking them out. If directors avert their gaze during the session, this could be interpreted as fear by the directees. They will be looking for any weakness on the part of the director because Sixes have difficulty accepting weakness. Thus, there is value in beginning with the directee's style of attention: the scanning mind. Otherwise, in the sessions the directees will be so concerned with what might threaten them, with whether the director can be trusted, or with asking the constant "What if..." questions, that it will be impossible for the Sixes to hear, much less act upon, what the director is saying. It is pointless to be offering advice to someone who is drowning in doubt. Sixes must learn to trust themselves so that they can trust other people. You can only trust others to the degree that you trust yourself.[4]

If the Conformist Sixes can begin to recognize how they operate out of fear, how they are constantly checking for the fearful, how they become fearful if there is no danger detected, and how their minds are like a flashlight surveying the environs of the pathway in the dark of night, they have made an important step toward health. It is their entrance into their interior worlds. The director might suggest that Sixes begin to observe how their fears affect their prayer life. This would appear to them to be a safer place to begin than with something like strong feelings. Because Conformists are not that good at introspection, moving Sixes to investigate the inner world in general or certain fearful issues would only paralyze them with the fear of discovering something they do not want to uncover. Forms of prayer with which they have become comfortable might be the place for them to start the experience of distinguishing the inside from the outside. After that, it might be possible to ask more general questions such as: How do you feel when you are not fearful? Why did you feel fearful of something after you had checked it out and found that there was no real cause for the fear? These Sixes' dominant feeling is fear. The question is whether the director can lead them to distinguish among their fears so as to introduce some differentiation on the feeling level. The director might find the following meditation helpful with Sixes trying to locate the fear in their lives:

> *Quiet down and recall some fear this day or in the last few days. It need not be a large or dramatic fear. Pick something relatively inconsequential. Try to recall when the danger came up. It is important to understand the context in which the fear arises. Where in you did the danger first become known to you? In your thoughts, feelings, bodily sensations? If you felt it in your body, where did you feel it? Any particular organs of the body? Did it make you indecisive, cause you to hesitate, or remain in a state of waiting? Did you find that you were trying to understand and explain the internal fear?[5]*

If anything defines the Conformist persons it is that their self is constituted by the groups to which they belong. When the Sixes can trust a group, they easily take on the philosophy of life of that group and imitate the behavior that the group values. If the director challenges this kind of unquestioning identification with a group, the Conformist Sixes may lose their trust in the director, and so it is better to have the Sixes begin their inner explorations by looking at more neutral areas. There will be plenty of trivial matters about which they are fearful. The point is to get them to look at their projections. Sixes more than most of the other spaces have a tendency to project. If they begin to look at how they project and when they project, they can create an opening that will allow them to look at other areas of their lives and how they defend themselves. They may then begin to look at their relation to certain groups.

Some Sixes may come across to the director as very conservative persons, as people who always toe the line, who are waiting for the next command from above, who spend their time following the rules and are upset when others do not. Obviously, Conformist Sixes do act that way. It is their way of belonging, and belonging to something is important in a threatening world. Authority is very important to them because it represents security and stability. It is their defense against chaos. It is their protection. Helen Palmer says that Sixes overestimate the authority of other people.[6] It is not surprising that one finds many Sixes in religious life and the clergy of the church. And for ordinary Christians there are plenty of rules and authorities to which they can hand themselves over. Catholics may seem to stand out here, but that is only because the rules and regulations in the Catholic Church are so specific. But Protestants can be just as concerned about a kind of Puritanism, and Anglicans can overvalue the authority of the Book of Common Prayer.

One way for the director to begin with these Sixes is to have them look at the reasons they have committed themselves to some external authority. Why do they need authority? What have they given away to authority? Do they not have their own authority? What are they avoiding when they submit to authority? How can they deal with the fear of standing on their own? What are the conflicts they are imagining when they think about standing on their own? What are the different kinds of fears that arise when they look inward? Conformists are hard on themselves and others, and Sixes are no exception. Life cannot be pleasant when it is filled with so many shoulds. The director will have to disagree with some of their judgments at times. This might help the Sixes to broaden their view a little. As all Conformists do, Sixes will exclude from consideration negative feelings such as sexual or aggressive ones. Not only are these feelings fearful to explore, but they also raise doubts about the Sixes' commitment to something like the faith, the church, and personal integrity. At this stage Sixes have too much fear to be able to distinguish among these various feelings themselves as well as the causes of these feelings. The director will meet with embarrassment and resistance if s/he delves too much in the areas of anger and sexuality. But the director would be amiss if s/he did not pursue seriously with the Sixes what their image of God is and how much of that image is shaped by their fears and their issues with authority.

Like other Conformists, these Sixes like to belong to different groups. The director will often be dealing with people who are deeply involved in parish organizations. Obviously, the religious who come for direction are already part of a group, and the Six characteristic of loyalty will be there from the beginning. This loyalty may reflect their solid commitment to religious life, but it could also be what some have mistakenly called "Jesuit blind obedience." Whatever may be the case, groupiness is a way for the Sixes to feel safe. The Sixes' doubting mind is soothed when there are ten or fifteen other people who are doing the same thing. It is the "there is safety in numbers" approach to life. Directors should realize that when Conformist Sixes respond positively to their suggestions that does not necessarily mean they have interiorized these suggestions. This positive response is their way of eliminating doubt. It is important that the director maintain a consistency of support when working with Sixes at this level. Because the directees' relationship with the director will be very much on the conscious level, they will be both looking for approval and trying to observe any change of behavior on the part of the director.

What Liebert notes about people at the Conformist level regarding their images of God as well as the way they deal with religious authorities applies par excellence to these Sixes. They may feel close to their God, but it is a God who is playing a parental role or is at least the one who gives them the certainty they are seeking. A God who is both loving and compassionate as well as all-powerful can help these Sixes to have at least one example of something that does not fit into the worse-case scenarios that they are used to. But this may also be too abstract for them, and so they will try to make the spiritual director fulfill the same function of bestowing the longed-for certainty. This will place enormous expectations on the director in the beginning. S/he will then, as part of moving the Sixes to the next level, gradually wean them away from such an attachment.

As Conformists these Sixes easily move outside themselves to connect with authority figures and institutions. This has a certain Five quality about it since for them it is a way of remaining hidden. They have not yet found out who they are and are looking for connections that will create their identity. This is problematic for these Sixes because it is accompanied with so much doubt. And there is a catch here. Precisely as Sixes, and so people with considerable doubt, they tend not to take the external, the outside, as the really real. Or if the outside world is acknowledged as real, it is suspiciously so. They follow authority at the same time that they doubt it. They are plagued with the question: What is really going on here? They love to delve beneath the surface, looking for hidden motivations, unearthed sources of danger. A harmless remark from the director can lead them to question the whole relationship. Why did she say that? What was intended? Does he not really like me? Is she bored with working with me? And on and on. To doubt means distrusting the obvious. The famous Freudian remark that "sometimes a cigar is only a cigar" is not one that the Conformist Sixes would ascribe to. This is a difficult area in working with Sixes because so often in our world people do hide their true motives, do try to sweep things under the rug, do try to hide behind the external. But the electricity going out does not necessarily mean that there is a conspiracy afoot.[7] The director will often be asking these Sixes to check the real situation. Check reality. Check whether they are projecting. Sixes love to check things out, and so they may as well check out their own checking out.

There is a gift hidden in the midst of all this doubt. That is the Sixes' ability (when freed up and developed) to be intuitively aware. If the scanning of the environment can be made conscious and can be controlled, it can be the Sixes' source for their religious discernment. The problem is that they are constantly trying to find out other peoples' intentions. Palmer puts it this way:

> The Six mind doubts, repositions the refined propositions, and doubts again until there is no doubt. It's the appropriate state of mind for sleuthing. Sixes are impressive troubleshooters; doubts are confirmed when the obvious turns out to be devious or mistaken. They see the holes in an argument and inconsistencies in reasoning. They see the context that influences the discussion. Most of all they see intention. What are the motives here? Are they oppressive or kind?[8]

The two areas where the director can encourage these Sixes to grow in order to move into the next stage of adulthood are deepening their experience about their style of attention and directing their growing intuitive powers toward themselves and their inner lives.

Spiritual Direction with the Conscientious Six

Although it is difficult to detect clearly the movement from one stage to the next, there are some signs that indicate Sixes' movement to the Conscientious stage. One is a stronger sense of the self, even though it is still a doubting self. Some times this will take place because the Sixes are developing a more conscious commitment to individuals and this is relativizing their excessive loyalties to groups. Often they will be more willing to look at the laws and regulations they have been following with a more critical eye. But self-reflection is definitely going on. And it is a reflection not motivated solely by the fear of danger. The director must support this growing flexibility in their lives. Conscientious people are open and honest and really interested in spiritual direction as a way to grow. The director will find these Sixes more confident, more willing to take the initiative. And with some help from the director they can be mobilized into action. They are melting from their previous frozen stage at the Conformist level. Or at least, the ice is cracking. Now is the time for the director to suggest to the directees that they try some spiritual direction on their own in certain areas of their lives, some areas that are less neuralgic and where they can feel what it is like to live with some uncertainty. This is preliminary to their accepting that the pleasure and success in their lives are not possible land mines that they must avoid at all cost less they be harmed.

The more spiritual part of spiritual direction begins in this stage. Because these Sixes have a more reflective sense of the self and more connection with their inner world, they can pursue the spiritual life more intentionally. In fact, this pursuit will be quite conscious now. If real trust has developed with the Sixes in the earlier stage of spiritual direction, they will be able to recognize and negotiate many of the difficulties they have in relationships. They will be less suspicious of the support the director gives. They will be less likely to doubt the director's interest in them. They will probably not stop wondering what the director really thinks or feels about them, but they now have the ability to intervene sufficiently to pay attention to what the director is actually saying. The director can promote trust in the relationship by encouraging Sixes to move away from a black-and-white view of the world where relationships are defined by a kind of all-or-nothing approach.

At this stage Sixes are less likely to be immobilized by their fear of rejection. In the past this fear has caused them to avoid coming to conclusions about their life issues. It was a way of keeping themselves distant from the possibility of rejection. Sixes can talk about something, such as feelings, without really taking about it. This is also a form of distancing. Here the director can intervene to help them understand what they are doing. The director should not dismiss their fears because these fears have some basis. But the director can assist the directees to reduce their fears by looking at what they are imposing on their environment. To reduce the fears they must reduce the projections.

The temptation will be to handle fears by thinking them through. It is what was done at the previous level. At this level Sixes need to deal with fears consciously, and they need to do it with a stronger bodily component. They need to go into their fears, befriend them, feel them. They must do more than think about them. If they can feel themselves in the fear, if they can go through the fear, they will come out the other end with courage. Much of the imaginative work in meditation can be devoted to this moving into fear. There is a great deal about fear in the scriptures. Using the appropriate Psalms in meditation can prove to be beneficial.

Pleasure is a problem for Sixes. It raises a lot of doubts and conflicts for them. Where Ones, who also have difficulty accepting pleasure in their lives, would be likely to ask when a specific pleasure is permissible, Sixes will see pleasure as a source of danger. Palmer puts it this way: "Sixes find it frightening to have their own desires aroused, to realize that they are vulnerable to what others do. They prefer to show strength by assisting others to attain their goals, are capable of significant self-sacrifice.... They expect hurt when their guard is down."[9] Although the full integration of pleasure into their spiritual lives is more a task for the Interindividual stage, some important growth movements are possible now. However, it probably is best not to begin with the actual relationships these Sixes might have, romantic or otherwise. There is a whole world of pleasure that can be explored where the possible explosiveness of a relational aspect need not intrude. For instance, do these Sixes have doubts about spending money? How do they feel about the time given to sports, exercise, going to the theater, sleeping later than usual? Is there more uncertainty and anxiety about some rather than the others? The point of these questions is not to solve one or other area of unrest but to help the Sixes to enter into the areas of their discomfort, which will in turn help them look at their constant need for reassurance, which in turn leads to their ever-present searching for the hidden factor, which in turn leads finally to their fear. Although it would be extremely harmful for the director to move the Sixes to try to eradicate fear from their lives, they do need support in finding ways to make that fear work for them. Fear will remain part of the fabric of their lives, but it need not be an obstacle to communion with God and a profound life of prayer. It should in fact be the necessary energy that makes abandonment to God possible.

Although it is a cliché to say about Sixes that thinking replaces doing, it is nonetheless true. For Conscientious Sixes this habit will be one of the main foci of attention in spiritual growth. The positive side of this is that at this level the thinking is much less stereotypical, much more socially oriented. These Sixes can see the consequences of their fixations. They recognize the paths they have chosen. They are dealing explicitly with more feelings. This is especially true of the feelings surrounding fear and, of course, fear itself. But this is also the stage of greater doubt. It is relatively easy to knock holes in the doubts of the Conformist Sixes. But doubt at the Conscientious level is more subtle. They are now aware of the real confusions and uncertainties in their lives and how many of these originate from fear. They know that some of their fears have a basis in reality. Some of these fears are characteristic of this level of adulthood where the ground has been shifting and where much has been relativized. God will not be spared. These Sixes will be tempted to revert to a kind of God who takes over the responsibilities of their lives, or they will try harder to resolve their doubts without God.

The reason that "real" spiritual direction begins here is that at this stage issues of faith can be fully engaged. This is where Sixes must make choices about their lives based upon religious values. This is where these Sixes will have to jettison past images of God and of themselves, as well as former ways of operating, including prayer forms. This is obviously a sensitive time for these Sixes. The notion of a crisis of faith takes on a special meaning when dealing with Sixes. Faith is what enneagram experts say is one of the qualities of the essence of Sixes. Their doubt is a loss of faith. They need to develop their faith moving from their cowardice and doubt. Having faith is a sign of their growth and maturity. Faith transforms their lives. The director will have no cause to dispute what enneagram writers say about faith and the Sixes. But in spiritual direction the word "faith" will become much more specific than one usually finds in books on the enneagram. There often faith means a kind of psychological commitment to certain beliefs. But for the Christian, faith implies much more. There are beliefs to be firmly held, but the beliefs are very specific, and they usually have an internal consistency in that they are part of a larger worldview that is much more comprehensive than a personal worldview. Christians participate in a church or worldwide community vision. Their beliefs are not simply their own. They participate in the beliefs of many others, both of those who are living now and those who have lived and embraced these beliefs since the beginning of Christianity.[10] It is at the Conscientious stage that the internalization of these beliefs must take place. Here the director needs to assist the Sixes to lay aside their fears and integrate these beliefs into their very self-identity. Part of the work will to be to deconstruct their religious past beliefs, but this must go hand in hand with a reconstruction of these beliefs in terms of their deepest values and commitments. This does not mean a rejection of a belief in the Trinity or real eucharistic presence, but it does mean that these beliefs must be consciously held, must be articulated in a form in which those who hold them do not feel like they are setting aside their intellects for such beliefs. These beliefs must make some kind of concrete difference, at least in terms of personal growth. All this requires considerable discernment. This is something that these Sixes can do best if they have accompaniment in the form of the director. I suggest the following meditation as a way for Sixes to look at the quality of their faith, how they have increased in faith, and what is still lacking:

> Imagine that you are getting married. (Whether you are marrying a man or a woman will depend on your sexual orientation. What is important for the meditation is the marriage commitment.) Let your imagination supply the place and the details of the setting (church, rose garden, a courthouse, or something more unusual like a ski lift). Wherever you are, picture yourself with your spouse-to-be. Hear yourself say the words of a marriage formula. Perhaps it is the more traditional one of promising to be true to each other in good times and bad, in sickness and in health, and so on. Perhaps, the vow formula is of your own making. Feel the love in your heart for the other person. Are you also thinking of such things as: What are my real motivations for marrying? Will this love last when so many marriages do not? How will I react if our love cools after a while? What if the other person is disloyal in the future, will I continue to love him/her? Will I remain faithful if the other does not? What does believing in this other person really mean to me? Is there something in my past experience that shows me that I can be loyal and trusting in the face of betrayal? Do I feel (emphasis on feel) that I can trust God, have faith in God more than my spouse? Try to identify some of the qualities of your faith in your spouse and compare them with the qualities of your faith in God. Locate any areas of resistance here. In what ways do you treat God like you see yourself treating your spouse?[11]

This is the time for a deepening of personal relationships. Although, as already noted, it may not be advisable to concentrate on the specifically pleasurable aspects of close relationships, there is much in this area that can be material for discussion, reflection, and prayer. The most significant area would be the projection that goes on in any relationship. Sixes will have little hope of achieving intimacy in their lives if they do not check their tendency to project. Yet it is true that their fear of intimacy often is due to past rejection. Real intimacy is based on trust and on the truth of the relationship. Objectivity is required if real communication is to take place. There is no possibility for intimacy if communication is lacking. Since a person can only be as intimate with another (including God) as they are intimate with themselves, the director will want to deal with the issue of self-intimacy as s/he leads these Sixes through their fears to greater communication in their relationships, and hopefully to greater mutual intimacy. This is not an easy task since so few people seem to know what self-intimacy is.

In the place of security (an issue on which the Sixes take on some of the characteristics of the Nines), there is at this stage a definite sense of letting go of many fears and paranoid feelings and preoccupations. It is important that this relaxation be strengthened. Relaxation can be hard work for Sixes, and the director should devise various practices to enhance this sense of tranquillity where the body is not waiting for an attack. The fears will not go away. But there comes a point when the Sixes are comfortable with them. They expect them to be part of life, and the fears become more diffused. For instance, in the case of the Six receiving a letter from someone in authority and assuming the worst before opening it with all the attendant fears, the Six can entertain other possibilities why the letter has been sent.

Palmer makes a significant point about the attention of Sixes that I believe will come into play in an important way at the Interindividual level. She says that many Sixes seem to (do?) lose their focus of attention, their sense of vigilance, when they are relaxed. Attention moves from the mental state to the body, and so the Sixes feel spaced out and unfocused.[12] The director would do well to encourage these Sixes to practice remaining in this state of greater body awareness and enter into the feelings of it. Developing this will enhance their own intuitive powers, which can be very helpful for them in the deep spirituality toward which they are striving. It can allow them to move into more body-based forms of prayer. Like Fives, their spiritual advancement and their richest contact with God will be through bodily experiences, especially those that are pleasurable.

There is still the possibility at this level that these Sixes could retreat in fear from this unguarded situation to a place of lower energy, to the self-narcotization of the Nines. But spiritual direction is a very good place for them to explore the other possibility, namely, being open to intimacy, the enjoyment of the physical whether it is fishing or ballet, and pleasure, especially sexual pleasure. At first it will feel strange and disconcerting to be consciously distinguishing being in the body and being in the mind, but this experience is basic for all the mental types.

When these Sixes are dealing with stress in their lives, the director will need to pay more attention to which kind of Six s/he is working with. Phobic Sixes will find it more difficult to move out on their own and will hope that the director will resolve the issues for them. At the Conscientious level it is possible for the director, through a kind of talk therapy, to help these Sixes to relativize their fears and to move through the stress with greater equanimity. But that will not be enough. They will also need to start in the body. This means releasing the tensions in the body that may be preventing stress-originated feelings from freely flowing through the body. The director could profitably recommend the directee seek out a massage therapist.

There are some very positive qualities in Three that can assist Sixes in dealing with stress. Moving to Three, they do not freeze in their tracks. They can feel energized, and so the tension has some place to go. In many ways, being active and in motion à la the Three is a way for Sixes to move into the body. But it is no substitute for actual body-based practices or direct experiences of pleasure. It is simply the first step to getting out of the mind. Getting into their instinctual part will help Sixes stop the scanning. Although it will be more difficult for phobic Sixes to relax into the activity, both types can find some valuable energy in the Three space, which they can borrow at times of stress, the latter being a factor that can too easily make them regress into a Conformist mode.

Spiritual Direction with the Interindividual Six

Working with Sixes moving into the Interindividual stage is both a challenge and a learning experience for the director. The challenge is knowing how to support them as they find themselves increasingly comfortable around others, more self-confident in situations that in the past would have triggered their paranoia. They will easily recog-

nize the difference between reality and their projections. They will
be able to sense true danger. They have a fuller understanding of
how their particular psychological mechanism of scanning the environment works. They can discriminate between what comes from
themselves and what comes from the outside. They can distinguish
among their feelings. They can tell what fears have a grounding in
reality and which do not. What will need further encouragement
at this point is their entering more fully into pleasurable situations
without hesitation, doubt, and fear of being aroused. Or if fear is
present, they need to be encouraged to find a way to integrate it into
the pleasurable situation.

The director can learn from these Sixes something about the more
intuitive aspects of the spiritual journey. Good directors will be able
to deal, sometimes very creatively, with the directees' conscious aspects of spiritual growth, union with God, and experiences of prayer.
Fewer will be comfortable with the hidden factors that are involved.
For instance, the Sixes' tendency to scan the environment to look for
sources of danger; their automatic inclination to seek out the hidden
aspects of people, events, and issues; the ease which with they move
to the invisible, oftentimes missing the obvious surface realities —
all these help them become very good intuitive readers of others and
themselves. The director at times might feel as if these Six directees
are operating with some hidden source of information. It is as if
they have access to sources of knowledge that the director does not.
Highly sensitive Interindividual Sixes may make the director feel, if
not "spooked," at least a bit quizzical. But the director need not follow these Sixes into their intuitive spaces. What the director needs to
do is to help them verify that their intuitions are correct. And even
highly intuitive Sixes may still have difficulties with accepting pleasure, which would be something to have them work on during this
period of direction.

As in the case of all the spaces at this stage, these Sixes now
have a broader understanding of their place in the world. They are
more socially aware. They see themselves as part of a larger context. They are ready to be challenged to articulate and choose what
will be their path in life. These Sixes are more capable of mutuality
and intimacy because they are less fearful of others and of interacting with others. They are developing to a high degree the virtue of
courage that Sixes need to have. It is this courage that allows them
to be both independent and interdependent. Like other spaces at this

stage, their sensitivity to social justice is growing. They are more willing to take risks in this area. These Sixes also have an awareness of the various ways in which biases are hidden in the very texture of our society, and they can unearth injustices in situations where it would not be obvious to others. While all spaces at the Interindividual level have good powers of discernment, each space practices discernment in a different way. Healthy Ones, for instance, have excellent gifts of discernment based upon some objective standard. What Sixes do is to bring to bear their ability to locate the hidden part of reality. Now that they are more comfortable with ambiguity, they need not project, and so their discernment is more accurate. Their natural intuitive powers come into play and assist them greatly in their perspicacity.

At this stage of growth the director should not hesitate to challenge these Sixes to deal directly with the matter of pleasure in their lives. Hopefully, a good foundation was laid at the Conscientious level, and now it is a matter of building on that. If at that level the Sixes could affirm that pleasure, especially sexual pleasure, is OK, at this level they should be able to embrace it as a positive good, something intrinsic to their prayer life. Often Sixes have powerful imaginations and vivid ideas that help them to express their feelings more graphically. Because of the expanded sense of self now, these Sixes are less likely to respond to situations of intimacy with a lot of fear, with fantasizing about it but not doing anything about it. I suggest the following meditation as a way for Sixes to evaluate how they are integrating pleasure in their lives:

> In your imagination choose something pleasurable. If you can do it without causing too much distress or interference, choose genital pleasure. If that is not your choice, then choose some kind of identifiable sensual pleasure such as eating, dancing, or swimming. Focus on the pleasurable sensation directly. Drop down from your mind into the body itself and sense the pleasure in the body. Notice any other feelings and thoughts that occur. Can you name them? Are they true impressions coming from yourself, or are they projections of your mind? Which are which? Move back and forth among several pleasurable experiences and notice which ones you are most comfortable with and which you are least comfortable with.[13]

What at the Conformist level was indecision now is changed into necessary ambiguity, an ambiguity with which these Sixes can live.

Although they know what they want, have a clarity about their desires and the directions in which they would like to pursue them, there is still the ever-present doubt. They are able to see through any mere surface reality and they are not taken in by the outward appearance. This creates doubt.[14] We can also say that it is this doubt that is their heuristic device to discover their passage into the spiritual life. The point is that at the Interindividual stage the Sixes have the resources to live with the doubt and to turn it into a good force for honesty and clarity in a relationship. It is this that allows them to accept and embrace fully the pleasure involved in a relationship.

While the support of the director is important as these Sixes allow space for the pleasurable in their lives, the director can also be invaluable by helping them to look at their ongoing relationships in order to reassess them. This may mean getting closer where there has been distance in the past to make the relationship safe. It may also mean moving away from a relationship that has become codependent because it brought a sense of security. It will definitely mean no longer projecting on someone a quality of relationship that does not actually exist, and it will mean no longer trying to potentiate someone into a closer relationship.

With these Sixes the director is able to address the issue of their ministerial commitments. What can they do to advance the spread of the gospel? Their special contribution will most probably be linked with their ability to find the hidden sources of both good and evil that lie within ordinary human living. Because they can locate that reality in themselves and others, they can become truly compassionate. No longer the victims of their wavering between belief and doubt, they can assume the position of a spiritual guide for others. They can recognize the cause of doubts that others have. They know the value of trust and how that must be present for others to be able to love and to live with their doubts and questions. Sixes are less likely to try to resolve the doubts of other people as if they are something to be gotten rid of as one gets rid of a cold or throws out old clothing. The director can point out to these Sixes that they must now do to others what the director encouraged them to do at an earlier stage, namely, to befriend their doubts and bring them into their journey as companions. Because they are such loyalists, healthy Sixes are capable of considerable self-sacrifice for others. Sixes are not seduced by image as are those on the heart center, so they can both challenge and support others at the same time and still communicate a sense of commitment.

Now spiritual direction is at a place where the director can help these Sixes to distinguish themselves along more intuitive lines while moving them to more body-based spiritual practices. The words associated with self-preservation Sixes are "warm" and "affection-ate" because it is situations described by those adjectives that give meaning to their lives. Palmer describes the more fixated Sixes when she says:

> Given encouragement, warm Sixes are devoted to friendship. When your safety is tied to other people, you want to under-stand them. You get close to people by disarming their anger and allying in friendship, by sticking up for them, by taking their side.... Because safety is tied to friendship, a change in af-fection is very threatening. It is like being thrown back into a hostile world again.[15]

Interindividual Sixes can be very supportive in an affectionate rela-tionship because they are no longer threatened by the presence of these kinds of feelings, and they will open their heart in a relation-ship. The director can encourage them to enjoy their tender moments with the other. These Sixes are not manipulative but in fact are very loyal to the person toward whom they have warm feelings. Good questions to ask regarding these Sixes are: What happens to these warm feelings as the Six scans the environment? Can the Six main-tain this tenderness while knowing what the other person is really like? When the Sixes can maintain that warmth in those situations, they are ready to use focusing on the warmth of sensual/sexual plea-sure as an object of meditation and prayer. Can they locate God in the warmth of this experience? They most probably have already integrated a friendly and trustworthy God in their spiritual lives. Can they now extend their experience so that God is the one of warm sensuality?

The words "strength" and "beauty" are associated with the sex-ual Six. This may mean that they may develop power as a way of dealing with fear, especially in a relationship. It may mean a concern for aesthetics as a distraction from their feelings of anxiety. Palmer describes them thus:

Strength and beauty are a show of power, a mask that covers inner doubt. The motive is to attract and command allegiance. The power of beauty. The mastery of strength... The reason for this preoccupation is that a beautiful and wise environment offers reassuring feedback. When the environment is lovely and people are humane, you can relax.... A preoccupation with strength or beauty may well be common with other personality types, but for Six the motive for being strong or beautiful is anxiety management.[16]

But at the Interindividual stage these Sixes are more comfortable with themselves, with their bodies, with their being a man or being a woman. They know how to engage in an appreciation of beauty to enhance their lives. They are willing to work on the "aesthetics" of a relationship. They are also models of strength. They can bring a sense of well-being to others. They use their intuitive powers to find ways to assist others. They know the hidden sources in others that will advance their growth and happiness. Sixes are known for having a "preferential option" for the underdog. They can be strong and loyal supporters of those less favored or those who are marginalized. The director would be remiss not to take advantage of the strength and beauty that these Sixes bring to their one-to-one relationships and have them apply these to their images of God. The power of God would be purified with a God who is "powerful" in her caring. God's beauty will no longer be abstract — rather the very commitment to God becomes an aesthetic experience. The beauty of God is found in the analogy that these Sixes can make with the beauty of their own intimate experiences with others. This presupposes that they are now in contact with the beauty of their own self-intimacy.

"Duty" is the word that characterizes the social Six. At the Conformist level, these Sixes obeyed the rules, followed without challenge, and dealt with authority by doing their duty. Duty creates a safe world for them. As Palmer says: "This is a way to contain fear through mutual obligation and commitment. The needs of the group govern behavior so we know what to expect. Self-doubt lessens when opinions are confirmed and backed by the power of collective authority."[17] At the Interindividual stage, however, Sixes' loyalty to work and friends moves into commitment to social concerns; they move beyond their own groupings and the familiar. Their highly developed sense of the intuitive and their insight into how others live and function serve them well in bringing together the inner and outer worlds of both themselves and others. Their ability to sacrifice for others and for a cause is now a way in which they become co-creators with God in improving this world and advancing humankind. Their suspicions of authority now become their instrument for confronting the sinful structures of our world. Projection is transformed into an objectivity about their relationships that makes it possible for them to be more mutual and intimate. And duty becomes obedience to their true selves. At this point the director can have them see that the pursuit of pleasure is a form of that obedience.

Finally, the director should note what may be a very subtle form of avoidance that may still be present. Are these Sixes using personal integration as a form of defense? Do they engage in the process of growth to keep themselves safe? Do they grow in some areas to avoid growing in others? They may need to be challenged to even fuller integration.

Chapter 8

The Space of Seven

Over the years that I have given workshops or taught courses in the enneagram I have found to my amusement how many people wanted to be either Fours or Sevens.[1] This is based upon a superficial understanding of these spaces. These people wanted to be seen as special and most definitely as the people in the world who have the most fun. Sevens want to have the most fun and try to make that happen, but in fact, it may be some Fives who are enjoying themselves more. That we would never know, of course. Most of the Sevens I know are very outgoing and willing to engage you in some way.

What seems so strange is that Sevens are as afraid as Sixes. But like Fives, Sevens cover over the fear in ways that Sixes could never do. They drown their fears by stimulating themselves with experiences. Sixes exaggerate what is going on outside of them. Sevens enlarge their experience by flitting from one thing to another. They have an insatiable thirst for experience, but they do not drink deeply. They taste a bit here and bit there. Like Fives and Sixes, Sevens need a director with whom they can feel safe because of their fear. It may take the director some time to cut through all the "tossed up sand" to get at the fear, but if s/he is patient that time will come. Fives, Sixes, Sevens, and Eights seem to think that unless they themselves do something, the world is going to descend into chaos. But this fear that there may not be any meaning to life at all is only an indicator of the tenuous connection they have to their inner life. The director can help them to see that things may not be as bad as they suspect they are.

Once I was planning a trip with a Seven. He went into lengthy descriptions about the details of the trip. The good part of all this was that he liked to plan and so did all the planning for the trip, relieving me of something I would find bothersome. At first I was puzzled by all the options he presented to me, the detail in which he gave them, and the presumption that I would need considerable time to think about them all. Actually, I was usually ready to make a decision immediately. Then I realized that behind all this talk was a fear that I might not like the plans he made, and behind that was his usual Sevenish fear to prevent any possible breakdown of structure.

The director needs to intervene in such situations to point out what the real motivation might be. If we, as directors, let ourselves be mesmerized by Sevens' plans and experiences as well projections for the future, we are no help to the directees. We need not grind their noses in the pain they are avoiding, but we must get them to glimpse it with increasing attention. We need to watch whether spiritual direction becomes just another "experience" for Sevens, another thing to plan for, even enjoy. The sessions can become a "chat time" with a "captive listener." They can be an excuse to relive past delights. This is especially a problem for those directors who are reluctant to intervene in the process.

It is helpful for the director to note the different ways those in the head center deal with such things as pain, limitation, and frustration. These ways may be revealed when others set limits on Sevens, accuse them of something, or get angry with them. Fives will tend to retreat into themselves even more deeply. Sixes will react by checking out ways to safely break away. Sevens are the most likely to respond with a burst of anger. All three will find ways to accommodate themselves to the situation. Fives will externally conform through personal scarcity. Sixes will conform in order to feel safe but check other areas where they may find some freedom. Sevens will try to find out what the others think and want so as to be able to reestablish a harmonious social relationship. For Sevens harmony means order, safety, and control.

The task for any director of Sevens is to find ways to help them to stay in the present. They can be present, but not for very long. This is a very difficult thing for them to do, and usually it requires some kind of meditative practice. The director might suggest that they look at the various gifts of their lives, express gratitude to God for them, and try to savor these gifts in their present form. They need to resist the temptation to imagine their gifts in some future form. It is not only that the Sevens fear present negativity. They also flee from present enjoyment by not treating it with depth. It is as if they are afraid that if they enjoy something in the present, they will so enjoy it that they will get stuck in the present. At this time the director can encourage them to explore the feelings that accompany this experience.

In direction Fives may withdraw feelings and may even withdraw from the direction experience itself without the director ever knowing. Since they can talk about their feelings without feeling them, the director can easily be deceived. Sevens can be equally as withdrawn, although it looks much different from the outside. They seem to be engaged, but they are really distant. They are afraid to withdraw like Fives, fearing what may be inside. So they move out, whether in the direction sessions or not, in such a way that they remain emotionally detached. This is done by treating the feelings superficially. But this can last for only so long if they want to grow. Very soon in the direction process they will learn, at first intellectually, that love involves delayed gratification, pain, suffering, and sacrifice.

Spiritual Direction with the Conformist Seven

Spiritual direction with Sevens can be a fun experience, at least for the first five or ten minutes.[2] But the director will meet with strong resistance as soon as s/he wishes to move beyond the chatter, the jokes, the endless topics of discussion. There will be a lot of energy coming from the directees in different ways. All of it is designed to keep life stimulating and keep their fears at bay. If Sixes replace doing with thinking, Sevens replace feeling with thinking — thinking about their plans, their future(s). Thinking here is a matter more of fantasy than of analysis. These are the "wow" people on the enneagram. The one thing the director needs to clearly remember — as the Sevens are speaking about their pleasant experiences, all the enjoyable things they have done, are doing, and will do, all the extroverted activities they are involved in — is that these experiences are very "heady." Like the Fives and Sixes these are mentally based people. If for Fives the real world is the inner and hidden mental one, and if for Sixes the real world is the one they mentally project outside themselves, then for Sevens the real world is their idea of it. To have an idea of something is equivalent to accomplishing it.

The director should expect to be annoyed after the initial "fun and games" of each session. What Conformist Sevens find engaging will seem so trite. They will come across as simplistic in what they think is important or worth spending time on. Everything of value seems to be outside themselves. There seems to be little nuancing in their judgments. "The more the better" seems to be the guiding principle. So different possibilities and ways of doing things, imaginative ideas and creative approaches to what life sets before them, are their source of happiness. What is disheartening for the director is that these people are so obviously superficial, so clearly scattered, so manifestly out of contact with their inner world. The director might ask them some of the usual questions that come up in direction, such as: How would you describe your prayer? Do you sense the Spirit of God working in you in your present life? It is impossible to predict what the answers will be. The response of the director should be compassion rather than irritation. These Conformist Sevens are desperately trying to avoid anything like deep feelings, because such feelings usually bring pain. If they come across as excessively self-referential it is because they want to avoid paying attention to the needs and pains of those around them. The pain of others reminds them of their own. All Conformist people evaluate on the basis of external behavior, reputation, and material possessions. These Sevens are no exception. And they are more likely than the other spaces to become sentimental or overly idealistic in their view of the world, themselves, and the things they are doing.

From the beginning the director needs to remind the directees that they have an interior life, that they need to discover and experience it, and that it is not identical to the outside world or to what they ideally would like it to be. Acquainting themselves with their style of attention is the single most important task in the beginning. Mentally they are jumping all over. They live in a world of options, alternatives, planning, possibilities, and creative ideas. The problem is that they do not stay with any one thing very long. It is like the butterfly alighting on this flower for awhile, then moving on to the next, and to the next, and to the next. It is not that they are not present to the reality they are attending — it is rather that they do not stay long enough to achieve any depth. A helpful exercise would be to have these Sevens observe what happens when they are praying in traditional and well-known prayer forms such as the rosary or the Psalms of the Divine Office. Do they find that they are looking for ways to make this interesting? Where does this tendency pull them? Are they preoccupied more with trying to make the prayer interesting than with where it is leading them?

At the Conformist level the director could conceivably confuse these Sevens for Threes. They stress appearances, and group identification is very important. Sevens try to gain group identity by bringing a lot energy to the group, keeping it entertained. Being the happy member is as much a status symbol as having a well-appointed office. As Palmer points out, often these Sevens are narcissistic because they overestimate their influence and their ability to stimulate the group. The director must content him/herself with the fact that at this level spiritual direction will be dealing with the Sevens' outside world. If the director wants to get them to focus in prayer, it would be best to begin with the more concrete forms of prayer, which are often devotional practices. If the director can help these Sevens to stay with a form of prayer and grasp the quality of it, the depth of it, a great deal will have been accomplished and progress will become evident. The danger for all Conformists is that they confuse nonessentials for essentials. These Sevens do this in spades.

Ordinarily it is important to encourage Conformists to think for themselves, to separate themselves from their overidentification with their groups. The idea is for them to find their inner authority. But with Sevens this presents a special danger. They naturally equalize authority. They are experts in getting around authority. They already feel superior inside. They are used to charming themselves out of difficult situations. They deal with their fears by making a lot of friends. The director can challenge them to look at whether this is really independence or avoidance of hurt, a way of doing their own thing without much challenge from anyone else. And although it may seem as if they are flouting the rules and operating out of their own inner convictions, in fact, they are definitely subject to authority outside themselves. They are only faking their independence because they are seeking the approval of others in the way they negotiate through life. And although it may come across as all very spontaneous, in fact, they are afraid that their approach may not work, that somebody will call their game. Feeling superior inside is not the same as having inner authority. The problem with Sevens is not so much to get them to think for themselves but to get them to stay long enough with any of their own thoughts to gain some insight and depth. Having them do something like the simple Jesus[3] prayer may help them to get the experience of distinguishing between trying to elaborate on something simple and achieving greater spiritual depth.

The director can take advantage of Conformists' desire to belong. If their weakness is the escape into alternate thinking, the gift is the ability to make connections, often quite unusual ones, and to present creative alternatives. This can bring life to a group to which they belong. There is nothing wrong with bringing a sense of lightness to groups. Others will appreciate their optimism. People like to associate with those who have a sense of a bright future, who provide a world filled with engaging experiences, and who find the pleasurable alternative. But a director should ask his/her Seven directees a few discerning questions: What is in it for them? Are they providing others with a world that they themselves cannot fully participate in? Why are they doing this? Out of the joy of the good news of Jesus Christ? Because they feel that they are in contact with the Spirit of God? Or is it to stuff one's life so full of experiences that there is no room for pain and disappointment? Are they really involved with their group, or are they using the group to get appreciation? Are they really present to the group? Or is the group an excuse to launch off into more ideas and planning? What about the pain in the group? What are they doing with that? How do they deal with it? Is it just another fascination for them? Are they there but not there much of the time? Is the group experience another way to glut themselves on experience?

Although early in direction the task may be just trying to get the Sevens to focus in a more concentrated way, it will be helpful for the director to note the areas of denial. We know that Sevens want to avoid pain because pain raises areas of fear for them. The avoidance of pain is their way of dealing with fear. They are as caught up in fear as are the Sixes. When the denial centers around sexual and aggressive feelings, as it does for Conformists, the question is why are these feeling necessarily connected with pain? Sexual feelings are pleasurable feelings. Ordinarily, the movement into pleasure is a movement away from pain. Pleasure is often a mental experience for Sevens. Real pleasure is something else. Conformists tend to feel embarrassed at the presence of these feelings, and this could be a form of pain for the Sevens. The director can best explore this issue with directees by entering into a discussion with them about the images of God that may be dominating their lives. The reason is that frequently these images of God are connected with strong feelings such as anger, sexual pleasure, and various forms of sensuality. That is, the images of God are constructed as reactions to these feelings, sometimes accepting of them, but unfortunately, very often as condemning them.

Sevens at this level may find the structure of spiritual direction annoying, depending on the form of spiritual direction being used. It may represent for them some kind of limitation, whether it is beginning and ending on time, staying with certain feelings and thoughts throughout one whole session, or responding to the questioning of the director. Being clear would represent to them a restriction, a limitation of their thought. But spiritual growth must start somewhere, and for Sevens it best starts with staying with present experience, in this case, the experience of direction itself. The healthy Sevens at later stages will develop depth in these areas, but presence is still required. The director needs to note that when Sevens come in with their plate full of activities, it does not mean that they are actually doing those things. The point is to think about doing them so that they feel free and unlimited. It is having options rather than doing them that gives them their sense of enjoyment. If the director can help them slow down and stay with some one thing in order to find the possibility of pleasure in this one thing, then a considerable step has been taken. Conformists have a lot of "should" in their lives, just the thing that Sevens abhor. "Should" means limits. This translates differently for Sevens in that they believe they *should* have options. They *should* belong to like-minded groups. They *should* see their friends in terms of people with whom they do things. They *should* avoid pain.

Pain will be the most concrete of the issues at the Conformist level. What Palmer says about pain and the Sevens can be very instructive for spiritual directors who must confront the Sevens directly on this matter at some time before these directees can move to the Conscientious level. Sevens reframe their pain into something else, such as a "good" experience from which they learned something. If they cannot distract themselves from it, then it becomes a learning experience.[4] The director could easily misunderstand this since to have a directee talk about painful experiences as growthful seems to be exactly what is desired. The problem is that for the Sevens this is all in the head. The directee will need to search for the feelings that are present. This is not easy because Conformist Sevens may have little access to any real feelings, that is, ones that are clearly distinguished from their thoughts. The difference between feeling something painful as growthful and thinking something painful as growthful is that in the former there is the greater possibility that the

Sevens will need to let negativity enter into their lives, and at this level this will be fearful and threatening.

Since this is spiritual direction, these Sevens will be more inclined to talk about God. Because they are Conformists, this relationship will be concrete and personal, but it is also one that carries a heavy concern to do God's will and to follow religious authority. Sevens at this level so distort and manipulate this view of God that the director will surely wonder what is going on. Their God is a demanding one who makes no demands. God is a strict parent who sets no limits. They invest scripture, spiritual directors, and the church with authority, but what this authority means in the concrete is so unpredictable that the director will get lost if s/he tries to follow it more closely. At this level the director must look at the larger picture in terms of the style of attention and the nature of the avoidance because trying to grasp the connections the Sevens are making according to their own sense of logical structure will be baffling. Sometimes the director can use characters in movies and fiction as a way of helping the Seven to focus. Many Sevens are attracted to these two art forms.

The director who knows how to proceed with the other two spaces in the head center will be able to assist the Sevens through the maze of possibilities they have constructed. With Fives it is important to get them out of their thinking world by having them stay with strong emotion. With Sixes it is important to get them back into extramental reality by going only with what is actually out there and not their projection on to that outer reality. With Sevens it is important that they learn to stay with the quality of the "out there." They need depth. Sometimes these Sevens seem like Fours because they become disappointed with present reality. But the two experiences are quite different. Sevens are unhappy because staying with present experience is inhibiting and boring, while Fours are unhappy with present reality because it is present, even though it may be deep. I recommend the following meditation for use at the Conformist level:[5]

Bring your attention inward. Review the past week regarding the various ways you looked for relaxation. Did you settle on one or two things or did you end up doing several projects? Did you easily get bored or did you maintain your involvement doing nothing? Now repeat this meditation on the recreational events of last week but do it more quickly. (Pause.) Now repeat this meditation but do it very slowly. (Pause.) When did you experience anxiety in all this? In this meditation was it when you slowed down or when you speeded up? As you recall the past week, do the positive memories outnumber the negative ones? What have you learned from this?

Spiritual Direction with the Conscientious Seven

Sevens will not display some of the usual signs of transition that other spaces do when moving from the Conformist to the Conscientious stage. They already have so much pluralism in their lives that introducing it does not cause them to reflect more deeply. Failing to live up to an ideal, which can cause some change, is often a sign of this transition, but Sevens have an automatic response to this failure by substituting many other possible ideals. What will be familiar to the director is the way that the Sevens are going to have to deal with feelings. Although the directees will be tempted to remain in their splendid world of possibilities, they will still have pain in their lives. One suggestion is to have the director begin with the pain of spiritual direction. The point is that this is one place where these Sevens cannot have their own way completely, nor should they be allowed to have it under some misguided notion of what spiritual direction is. Apart from the necessary limits that spiritual direction places on directees, there are some necessary redefinitions that need to take place. What is fun for Sevens may not be fun for others. That may be news to them, but it must be communicated. The paradoxical thing about Sevens is that for all their ability to find options, to make connections, and to see variety as what constitutes our world, they find it difficult to understand that other people may not like what they like, might not think the way they do, might not be entertained by what they find entertaining. Their pluralism is excessively mental.

The usual sign of moving into the Conscientious stage is greater personal commitment and more dependence on oneself. This is usually manifested in an attitude that rules have exceptions and that group values need not be dominant. This commitment to self takes a somewhat different form with Sevens. They have always thought that rules have exceptions. But now they are beginning to call into question some of their presuppositions. In other words, they have had their own exceptionless rules such as pleasure is always good, love conquers all, and guilt has no place in life. As their sense of honesty grows, as they begin to create for themselves what it is they want their lives to be, these Sevens will seek spiritual direction as a way to discover what is beyond what they have valued to this point. For instance, the quality rather than the fun of a relationship will become more important. And while this is done in a somewhat self-conscious way, it is also self-reflective and indicative of a growing inner life.

These Sevens are moving away from optional thinking to more complex thinking. These are not the same. Having a lot of options is often a way of avoiding the more complex issues of life. Having alternatives does not necessarily mean that the person sees the consequences of these alternatives. These Sevens now do. And while Sevens at all levels have a wide range of emotions, it is now that they are beginning to discover the quality and nuance of these emotions. At the Conformist level they dealt with their feelings in an intellectual way and altered their personalities according to their understanding of feelings rather than according to the feelings themselves, as the Twos would do. It is at this time that the director is most useful because s/he can help these Seven to stabilize. They are the least grounded of those at the head center. This is the time when many presuppositions are called into question. They will resist having to cast away their basic rule that life should be fun, an adventure, a constant peak experience, described by such words as "full" and "friendly." Many, many times the director and the directee will need to return to the issue of pain.

I have one caution for the director here, and that is to resist the temptation to have the Sevens reframe their pain in terms of the pain of Jesus on the cross so that the pain seems to be an end in itself. We want to avoid an attitude that "it is great that Jesus and I are suffering together." Rather, it is more significant to have the Sevens do something with the pain. Jesus suffered to redeem the world, to take a drastic step to proclaim his relationship with God. Suffering moved to change and liberation. A spiritually positive way of reframing the Sevens' pain would be if the suffering involved in personal growth, in developing relationships, and in staying with present experiences would motivate them to take more personal responsibility, especially in the area of social justice. Toward what good is their pain directing them? Is this a better world because of their suffering?

Conscientious Sevens have taken their life task in hand and are creating who they are. Spiritual direction is a way of sorting out who they are among the many identities they have already created for themselves. What once were considered ideals turn out to be mere distractions. As they deconstruct much of their past, a lot of the "wow, isn't life great" will go. Successful spiritual direction will help the Sevens to become "high" on their true selves rather than on the ones created out of their fantasizing. They need to search for their true sources of nurture. This is the stage of self-appropriation, of claiming one's uniqueness. Uniqueness implies some one way of being, not twenty-five. Part of the job of the director is to help the Sevens to find in the journey of the spiritual life that stimulation and adventure they so enjoy. They may easily do that. The problem is that this spiritual adventure might remain only one adventure among many. They need to prioritize and choose among adventures when that is called for. The spiritual growth adventure must take precedence.

Since this is the stage when much that worked before no longer does, this is the time for Sevens to allow challenge in their lives without trying to dismiss it or make fun of it. They need to be encouraged to pray to God in a more focused way. They probably already have a whole treasury of images of God, but each image is appropriate at a certain time, and they should stay with an image as long as it is needed. These images should not be moved around to make the Sevens feel comfortable for the present moment. I suggest the following meditation as a way of providing Sevens with an appropriate image of God:

Imagine that you are young again. You are preadolescent, perhaps five or six years old. You are at a party and you are enjoying yourself. You go from table to table to be with different people, to listen to what they are talking about, to taste the different foods they offer you. You are totally carefree and totally absorbed in what you are doing. You are happy here and now, and you are not thinking of the future. Then suddenly you see your parents and they are quarreling. They leave, taking you with them. You sit in the backseat crying while they drive away still arguing. You are left alone in your sorrow, and your happiness has suddenly gone, but memories of those totally absorbing moments comfort you. . . . Now come into the present. Imagine you are at party with your wife (or husband) and two children. You go from table to table enjoying the conversation and the food. But do you do it the same way you did as a child, being totally absorbed in the experience? Or are you only partially present? Then you notice your two children are fighting, and you and your spouse decide to take them home. As you drive away they are still in the back-

*seat fighting. How does it feel to have your pleasant party destroyed by
these two? What has happened to the happiness of the party now? Is
it forgotten? Do you think back on it, exaggerate it, become absorbed
in it as a way of moving away from the unpleasant scene in your car?
Where is God here? Is God the one who wants you to find happiness
in the here and now as you did as a child? Have you let the darkness
of the unpleasant experience of your children fighting make it difficult for
you to find the God of happiness in the present? Does not God want the
unpleasant episode to deepen your experience of God as being happy
about you?*[6]

A good indicator of how much Sevens have allowed their standard
of evaluation to become internal is the degree to which they allow
guilt in their lives. I am not speaking about guilt as a feeling. Guilt is
the result of a judgment one makes about oneself and one's actions.
Guilt is often avoided because of the feelings that accompany it. The
director can help these Sevens to distinguish between their guilt and
the feelings surrounding it. Not only will this help them to proper
discernment in telling right from wrong, but having separated the
feelings from the guilt, they can now rely on God as the forgiver of
their guilt while dealing with the feelings at a different level. When
the feelings are isolated from the actual guilt, both lose a lot of their
power, and so these Sevens can work on both in a spiritual context
with less fear and threat.

As with all the others spaces at the Conscientious stage, the matter of intimacy comes to the fore and must be integrated before
movement to the next stage is possible. Having learned how to differentiate their feelings in other areas, Sevens can now transfer that
ability to the area of relationships and sexual intimacy. There is
greater capacity for intense relationships. There is less fear about
relationships. These Sevens come to them with a sense of having
something to offer, from a sense of fullness rather than emptiness.
On the Conformist level, Sevens' idea of relationships was all fun and
pleasantry and quite self-centered. It was more taking than giving.
Now they can be more open to focusing their feelings. They must
zero in on the present pleasure of intimacy. At an earlier stage they
moved their pleasure in the future, where pleasure is not accompanied with pain. They actually reduced the feelings in the present by
diffusing them. Now they need to have a concentrated experience of
present pleasure.

The beginning work on a relationship will be easier for Sevens. They are more likely to enter one easily and will bring a lot of energy to it. The point is to get them to stay with it. Although the director might be tempted to do otherwise, s/he needs to work with the Sevens on their negative feelings. The one thing we can all be assured of in a relationship, no matter how good, is that we are going to feel hurt, disappointed, bad, frustrated. The point is not just to feel hurt and disappointed. There is no value in that except insofar as all feelings have value. The point is to feel the quality of feeling bad, the quality of feeling hurt. Unless Sevens can enter into the depth of the negative emotions they will have no way of knowing if they have entered into the depth of their religious experiences. That means that the director needs to be with them while they do the hard work of not running away into the future, of not thinking of some pleasant alternative, of not fighting to break out of seeming limitations. This is not easy work for either the director or the directee, and I would encourage the director to keep in mind these words of Palmer regarding Sevens:

> Sevens will typically try to find many different solutions and many different exits before they reach the point of anger. It's hard to pin them into a corner when they're looking for a way out. They're committed to a positive outcome, they're committed to feeling OK about themselves, and they're verbally slippery.[7]

At this point the director may want to recommend some group spiritual direction for the directee. In such situations the Sevens can observe how others make their connections, and they can discover the many ways they disguise their feelings through their mechanics of multiple associations. The Internet is a perfect example of how they operate here.

At the Conscientious level Sevens can profitably visit their stress and risk points of Five and One. Choice is a problem for Sevens since choice means narrowing the options or cutting out alternatives all together. But commitment to the spiritual journey is impossible without restricting possibilities. Both Fives and Sevens experience commitment as some kind of loss. And commitment presupposes choice. It may be necessary for Sevens to experience a sense of loss in order to be able to pray.

For many Sevens, moving to the Five space will be the only realistic way they can engage in the meditative process. It may become the usual place for them to do their personal discernment. They may need to retreat there to become more conscious of who they are, to understand what their direction in life is, to perform certain religious rituals, and to use certain methods of prayer. Spiritual direction sessions may be a Five experience for many Sevens. Palmer points out that "the security point appears when Sevens get to withdraw from sensory overload and from an overstimulated mind. It's a time to center and redirect attention to priorities."[8] It would not be unusual that the annual retreat of a Seven would be a very Five experience. For Sevens to remain quiet and focused when in the Five space it will still be necessary to have some external helps (unlike Fives). In that case many Sevens are helped by the creation of a certain type of atmosphere. I know some Sevens who are very much influenced by a sunset, a Zen-style garden, or some art object. These make it easier to let the imagination settle on one thing.

There is no danger that the Seven will turn into a Five, and so the director need not address that. What s/he needs to watch is whether the Five characteristic of emotional stinginess is reinforcing the Sevens' tendency to move away from any depth in the feeling area. The Conscientious level is the time when the directees consciously try to uncover their needs. Moving to Five in such a process can be hazardous. They could pick up Fives' negativities and so deaden themselves inside. This could lead to a kind of depression in their lives. They need a different kind of energy for opening up the area of personal needs.

The director will be quite familiar with the process of Sevens moving to One. Because of the highly reflective character of spiritual direction, Sevens will be examining themselves, especially at the Conscientious level, and will be making comparisons with others with the attendant judgmental quality. But as Palmer points out, Sevens do not judge in the way that Ones do. They are concerned not about what is right or wrong but rather about being limited, not having enough, the restriction of pleasurable experiences.[9]

Just as often these Sevens will need to draw upon the strengths of the Five space to enter into a world of prayer and worship, so they need to seek energy from their relationship to the One space when it comes to putting into practice the fruits of their prayer. For from One they can operate with greater clarity, more dedication. They are committed to the ministerial aspect of their inner lives. They may have to visit One if they are going to stay with present experience in order to plumb the depths of that experience. The quality of One can be most beneficial for Sevens as they try to maintain the direction of their spiritual journey and not be distracted by so many other possibilities along the way.

Both stress and risk spaces are very helpful to strengthen the qualities of the Conscientious stage: a differentiated inner life, a life of reflection, self-chosen goals, and an adult conscience. They will visit these spaces often as they move away from a self-centered world, as they learn to deal with the pluralism that inevitably is part of their lives, as they advance toward integrity, and especially as they avoid the temptation of both the Conscientious level and the Seven space: "getting side tracked into a search for inner religious experience."[10]

Spiritual Direction with the Interindividual Seven

These Sevens will appear to the director to be very different from the ones s/he dealt with on the Conformist level. These are highly appropriated and focused people. Probably one who is judging people's space on the enneagram in terms of external characteristics would not see these persons as Sevens. But there is a period of transition into this stage, and it will be the support of the director that will help the Sevens to remain focused for this transition. The particular strength of this time is the ability to discriminate. To discriminate is not the same as having options. The Sevens' alternate thinking pattern lacks discrimination. But fortified with the experience of knowing the difference between their inner and outer worlds, with their understanding that other people differ and do not regard as pleasurable all that they do, and with an increasing social awareness, these Sevens can now discriminate between true pleasure with a basis in reality and an imagined pleasure that is purely mental.

These Sevens can freely visit the space of Six, where they will have a powerful resource to assist them in their focusing. This will help them stay with the present moment, especially if there is something negative about it. Both healthy Fours and Sevens must stay with the present moment. Fours need to focus on the present with both its negative and positive qualities, refusing to refer the positive to the absent. Sevens must be willing to stay with the present with the possibility of the negative — that is, they need to be open to the negative being there, although it may not be in any given case.

For other enneagram spaces this transition involves what Sevens do naturally, namely, the toleration of contradictory possibilities. Sevens will concentrate not so much on the coexistence of opposites but more on the quality of the feelings that these opposites cause. The struggles with intimacy and the awareness of the mixed signals Sevens send when in relationships are signs of movement into this Interindividual stage.

As the Sevens become more integrated into this stage of both personal autonomy and mutuality, the possibilities for greater intimacy open up. Paradox, ambiguity, and complexity are now calls to experience their own depths, not forms of distraction as they were before. Their social awareness, which was only incipient at previously levels, now flowers to a greater degree. They are no longer led around by some kind of vague principle that one must be true to oneself and that this means that all options must remain open. Now they can sacrifice options so that justice may be pursued. Injustice and social sin are specific in their consequences. Now the issue becomes reaching out to the marginated, abused women, and illegal immigrants with the attendant lack of pleasure and possibility for pain. These Sevens can see that among the many possibilities to which God is calling them this one must be given priority. And they can also see that while sacrifice is involved, there is also for them a certain kind of pleasure in having assisted others and living with a broader worldview.

The Interindividual stage is one of high spiritual growth for all spaces, but with Sevens it takes on a certain kind of nobility. People at this stage have deep inner lives; they know that the spiritual life is more than following one's conscience. They have a great sense of compassion for themselves and for others. They can see themselves in many ways. Now the fixation of the Sevens and their preference for endless options are put to the service of others. They, more than most, will have ideas of how to make this world a better place. They will stay with the pain of those who are suffering and have ways of dealing with it. Where others might have all the will in the world to do something to correct a wrong situation, these Sevens will also be able to bring to the situation a lot of information that they can put to use to alleviate the pain and distress of others. They can give voice to the longings of others, help them claim their own vision, and rally them to move into action to remove themselves from destructive situations.

This is the stage at which all spaces must look at their ideals and adjust them to what is realistic. Life carries its own limitations. All personal histories have certain parameters. This exploration is painful for anyone. But it is especially so for Sevens, and the director needs to note that. These Sevens must do in their personal lives what the United States as a whole must do as it moves into the twenty-first century: learn to live with limits. The United States is usually described as a Three country, but in terms of the so-called Reagan philosophy (which comes out of the U.S. tradition) that life can get better and better, with unlimited options for the future, it must do what any Seven needs to do to move to health: that is, to realize that in the concrete there are few options, and not all of them are glamorous; that, in fact, much about the past may have been better than what the future holds. U.S. citizens are recognizing this as they understand that they cannot have the same amenities their parents had.

Sevens may have an advantage over the other spaces as we all move into a more limiting world in that they can take fewer options and make more out of them. They will see possibilities in the very limits themselves. They will be more willing to experiment although they must remain within clearly defined parameters. At this stage the Sevens are likely to move from idea to action and also to maintain their momentum during a project. The director's task during this time is to help the Sevens to remain focused and to provide a time and place for them to speak about their difficulties and seek the further clarification that they might need.

The self-care necessary at this stage as well as the expected changing images of God are connected with greater intimacy. Like Fives, these Sevens must embrace commitments to enter into greater intimacy with self and others, and so with God. Once Fives have worked through their fears and have learned to stay with strong feelings, they can commit. Sevens can commit once they focus and accept the pain of intimacy's journey. They will do this best when this commitment, although a present reality, has an alluring future and a certain adventuresome quality. When Sevens appreciate the many demands made on their own lives, they are exercising self-care. When they value the many dimensions of others, they are moving toward intimacy with others. And when they can positively embrace what God is asking of them, they are moving closer to God. The directee might find the following meditation helpful at this point:

> Imagine yourself preparing a savory meal that you will share with a friend. See, touch, taste, hear, and smell the whole experience. Meet your friend and serve the meal, including a bottle of your favorite wine. Note what is on the table – taste and smell the items. What does it feel like to eat such a delightful meal with a treasured friend? Hear the music playing in the background. Look into the eyes of your friend and speak to him/her with your eyes. Can you understand what is being said without words? What does this feel like? Reach out and touch your friend lightly on the hand to let the person know that you are enjoying yourself in his/her company. Is the time passing slowly or quickly? Tell the person how you are enjoying his/her presence with you. Savor the moment. After the meal as the person is leaving, emphasize how you will cherish the evening and this friendship. How do your respond to their gratitude? Breathe deeply and now return to the present moment.[11]

After this meditation, which the director and directee might do together during one of the sessions, the director should take the opportunity to ask the directee some reflective question such as: What has this experience taught you about your relationship with God? Our hunger and thirst for God is often described in terms of food and drink. Where did you find your hunger and thirst for God in this meditation? God's happiness is found in revealing love for us. Where is the happiness of God found in the meditation? God wants us to rejoice in God's presence as at a banquet. Where is that present in the meditation? Has this meditation helped you to discover a richer image of God?

As with all spaces, this more advanced ability with intimacy must be accompanied with a stronger social sense. For Sevens, this means letting go of much of their imaginings and avoidances so that they can accept the autonomy and humanity of others and so that they can build more mutual relationships. At an earlier level many social issues did not arise for the Sevens because they were so set on avoiding personal pain. They did not attend to social forces that create a kind of societal pain. Now they are willing to do this. This will also influence a change in their images of God. They will be far more economical in how they describe God since their relationship will be more realistic.

Many qualities of the Sevens that at the Conformist level were inhibiting to growth now can enhance it. Their highly relational way of paying attention, their parallel thinking, and their general creativity now stand them in good stead. They can do their own spiritual direction and far more creatively than most directors can. This is especially true in the ways they can find to drop into their unconscious world. So much energy is there for them. No longer are they *seeming* to be having an experience. They are actually having it, and it is rooted in the unconscious life.

The words associated with the sexual Sevens are "suggestibility" and "fascination." First connections with others are immediate and filled with a lot of energy. Often interrelations with others, at least in a less reflective stage, are electrifying. It feels like powerful connections are being made. The problem is that they are mostly mental, the result of a hyperimagination. Even when relationships become sexual, the sexuality can be primarily mental.

But at the Interindividual level the director will be dealing with someone who is creative and can work and relate in imaginative ways. These Sevens can connect with a more healthy sexuality. They know how to bring relationships alive, how to keep the energy constantly flowing. These qualities must move over into their spiritual lives so that they can keep the spiritual pursuit interesting, filling it with new experiences and connecting it with other areas of life. They must remain focused because being creative in the spiritual life is also a temptation for them to revert to their basic fixation. Personal intimacy with another becomes a way of helping the attention stay with the quality of present experiences. The pleasure of commitment outweighs the pain of commitment.

"Social sacrifice" is the term to describe the social Sevens. These Sevens like to have an ideal group with which to associate. They enjoy being with like-minded people and will make sacrifices to be with such groups. They are confronted with a typical Seven conflict — namely, there is pleasure in being around others, and yet others introduce limitations into their own lives. They feel held back by others in the group although they find the group also provides them with much of the ambience that they enjoy. They find ways to maintain their personal freedom in any group to which they belong.

The evolved social Sevens can enhance their group relationships by injecting energy in to them and keeping the mood of them lively. And at the Interindividual level they are models of how to subordinate one's own needs to the needs of the group in a healthy way. Of all the Sevens these are the ones who are most likely to maintain their commitments during projects and relationships. In some ways these Sevens are good examples of what many feminists claim authority should be, more egalitarian, more democratic, and more consensus-building.

"Survival through a family of like-minded defenders" is the way that Palmer describes the self-preservation Sevens.[12] Like Sixes of the same subtype, who use warmth with others, especially their friends, to ward off their fears, these Sevens seek consolation from their "family" of friends who come to their defense when they feel threatened by the narrowing of options. These people are dream-partners because their goal is to keep their dreams alive. The inner "home" of the self-preservation Five is made visible and public in the self-preservation Seven.

At the Interindividual level, Sevens bring warmth and joy to their work and relationships. They are congenial people, and that congeniality spreads from them to others. They are enthusiastic and can present creative possibilities. They revive the mordant interests of others. They help others to begin anew. They have staying power, and this power is positive.

Chapter 9

The Space of Eight

THE STORM

The wind has shifted to north by east
  and blows in a wintry gale,
The sea is charged with angry waves
  and there's ice on the riggin' and sail.

The sky is grey and filled with clouds
  that boil in vehement motion,
And all about is a feelin' of dread
  cast like a veil on the ocean.

The vessel shivers as each new wave
  pounds with incessant fury,
Exploding spray leaps o'er the bow
  and is gone in as much a hurry.

The riggin' creeks and the timber moan
  in a ghostly song of discord,
And about the ship, eyes are strained
  for the welcoming signs of shore.

A lone figure stands at the salt-covered helm
  baring his back to the wind,
He looks ahead at the angry seas
  then back at compass again.

It shows in his eyes and it's etched in his face,
  he's fought this sea before,
And though he's made it safely home,
  he can't remain ashore.[1]

The lone figure in the poem encapsulates so many of the characteristics of Eights. There is the controlled energy, the sense of aggressiveness, and the passion and commitment to what they are doing.[2] The lone figure is independent and intent on survival. Like other Eights he is on his own. He is confidently in charge of the situation. We admire his courage, his directness, and his sense of moving forward because he "can't remain ashore."

As with Nines and Ones, anger is the central emotion for Eights, but because they are so focused, it seems as if anger is the only emotion they have. Because all feelings come out as anger, they seem to be angry all the time, whether for worthy causes or to control other peoples' lives. The conversion of the Eight is indicated by the conversion of their anger, whether into effective leadership or into exposing the hypocrisy of others. Because they are so narrowly focused, their strength becomes their vulnerable point and vice versa. They seek integrity, honesty, openness, but when they narrow this search too much, they can be vindictive and close-minded. Because of the need to present such a strong front, they hide their tenderness; thus much of the rough and tough attitude is a cover for a softer inside. They are capable of real commitment to a person in need but can also be personally uninvolved as they pursue some cause mercilessly.

The director must always bear in mind the two-sidedness of Eights. They can be gentle, warm, magnanimous, passionate, loving. And they can be the opposite: cruel, severe, harsh, lethargic. They will move away from these latter qualities if they adopt an attitude of mutuality with others, not fearing to yield to others' desires and needs. Conversion of feelings is the name of the game here. They hate being bored and so will look for stimulation. Under some direction that drive for energy can be put to good use. Their natural tendency is to move into an excessive amount of activity and pursuits. The task of the director is to help them to find ways to convert that energy into something useful and spiritually beneficial.

Direction with Eights can be engaging but directors need to be sure of themselves so they can be almost brutally honest while manifesting real care for the directee. Eights like any other human being will not open up fully about their feelings with the director unless they trust the person. For Eights trusting the director involves being sure that s/he can handle the Eight. Because they are gut people Eights will be open to working along more imaginative lines such as dream work, some kinds of body work, and anything that has to do with symbols. There is so much energy in the Eight space. The director has no other choice but to encourage the directee to explore all this energy letting it go where it will. As Eights move to health one of the goals of Christian spiritual direction, by which it is often distinguished from therapy, can readily be achieved, namely, the pursuit of justice and the empowerment of others.

Spiritual Direction with the Conformist Eight

The director will probably have little trouble recognizing the Eights when they walk into the room.[3] They fill up the space and tend to take it over immediately. If the director is easily intimidated or thinks that people should not act that way or is surprised that there are people with such strong personal positions, the direction is probably not going to work. It is important for directors to remind themselves constantly that Eights really want truth in their lives and long for a kind of "original innocence." If they try to wrest control of the sessions from the director, the director needs to maintain firmly his/her own position as well. Sometimes a director will give in under the false assumption that the directee may leave. That may work in many cases, but with Eights it is a disaster. If Eights leave because the director is also strong in maintaining what spiritual direction is about, those Eights are not ready for spiritual direction of any kind. Whichever way it goes, the director will be dealing with a lot of energy during the sessions. Power is an issue. The director will hear a lot about justice and the eradication of injustice at this point, but the question for discernment is: Whose justice are we talking about? The confusion for Conformist Eights is that they think what they need is what the world needs. It is helpful if the director can always remember to see the child in the adult Eight. It is the child who is trying to maintain contact with that original state of innocence; it is the child who protects itself against the weakness of innocence;[4] and it will be the child who will be in need in the process of growth later on.

The deceptive thing about Conformist Eights is that they are not as powerful and strong as they think they are or as they present themselves. They are defined as much by the groups to which they belong as any Conformists. The difference will be in the groups. They will gravitate toward groups dealing with issues of justice, groups that have as their agenda matters of equality and fairness. Eights are working for members of Congress, are ecological lobbyists, and paradoxically are leaders in circles of both war hawks and pacifists. What is the same is the energy with which the issues are addressed. Certain social movements can be characterized as Eight in feeling. This does not mean that the majority of members are Eights. But the narrowing of focus that one finds in more radical feminism, among liberationists, and among those committed to maintain the memory of the Holocaust communicates an Eight's style of attention. Clearly, there are real issues of justice involved in each example. But it is also difficult to interject other points of view in these situations because the members see that as watering down the full force of the evils they are confronting. During the 1960s and 1970s, when there was considerable conflict over the wars in which the United States was involved, a great deal of Eight energy emerged communally. "My country right or wrong" and "If you don't like it, leave it" were Eight slogans voiced by those who disliked what the protesters were doing. Those who were pouring blood on files and demonstrating outside munitions plants and the like often took the attitude with others that their actions were a necessary extension of what they believed. There did not seem to be any other possibility. The lack of flexibility on both sides indicated that the Eight energy was operative. The director may discover that kind of thinking in an Eight directee but in less dramatic form.

The thinking style of Conformists is very Eight in quality. I think most directors will find Conformist Eights difficult to deal with. Everything is black and white. It is all surface impressions. Their speech sounds like the rhetoric of political campaigns: "The Republicans are throwing children into poverty," or "The Democrats are just big spenders." The director who continues to work with these Eights will need to be prepared for a lot of sessions of trite, biased clichés. "I can't pray that way." "The Pope is wrong." "Spiritual direction is for sissies." The process of getting these Eights to distinguish their thoughts from their feelings is arduous. The director will hear a lot of "I think" expressed with a lot of feeling and a lot of "I feel" with a sense of deadened emotion as a result of the Eights' need to protect themselves. Such defensiveness does not mean that Conformist Eights will not break into tears. Tears could mean that they are becoming comfortable with direction as a safe place and feel free to cry, but at this level it may have more to do with their sentimental feelings.

So where can the director begin? With what these Eights consider themselves best at: righting the wrongs of the world. Having been respected for their strength, these Eights now rush in to do battle with whatever is in the way of the truth. At this stage, it is their truth, of course. But there is no question what they stand for, what they are after, and who is in the way. They are in the lead. If need be, rules will be set aside in the interest of the higher "good." If "over your dead body" is what it takes, then that is what they will do. Their attention is focused like a laser beam. It is directed to a very confined part of life, and all the energy is focused there. This is not done in some subtle, detached way, but with all the intensity of sexual passion.

Perhaps in the beginning the director cannot do much more than to get them to recognize how they pay attention. The idea is to start them on some path of refinement about themselves that will lead to a more inner-directed life. Encourage these Eights to bring all this energy and all their pet justice-oriented projects to prayer. Then suggest to them how the actions of Christ or how forms of meditation contrast in spirit with their drivenness. The idea is to introduce some dissonance into their lives, that is, dissonance between their position and that of Christianity or that of other good people. Direction on this level will be very much about finding an opening, a crack in their position, so as to introduce some nuance, something they have in short supply, if at all.

At times the director will wonder if s/he is dealing with a Three. There will be so much emphasis on outward appearances. They will make snap judgments in terms of outward behavior, and they will be overly sensitive to how they are seen by others. Group identity is very important. The difference is that the Threes want to be accepted by the group for whatever the group wants, while the Eights want to be recognized by the group for their powerful, or at least justice-oriented, positions. Obviously, the Threes are concerned about their image more than Eights are. Part of an Eight's group identification is being someone who rejects conforming to an image. At these times it would be best to devote the sessions to the search for what is really the truth that sets these people free. How can everything be so either/or? The end of the spiritual journey is a certain kind of simplicity, not division. What is really essential in life? Why do they *need* to set everything right? Why do they *need* to come on so strong? Why do they *need* to find the enemy? The director might find an opening by getting these Eights to admit to needs, needs from which they clearly operate. The Eights will want to deny them since denial is part of their defense mechanism, but being in direction presumes some openness to begin this process of admitting that they have needs.

What the director is after is to create some kind of opening whereby questions will be raised for the Eights. To move to growth and to move out of the Conformist stage these Eights need to do what Palmer suggests: "Eights grow by questioning their ideas of justice, by hearing the other side of the story, by learning to wait. You have a choice when you feel secure enough to relax your own position and can watch yourself assume control by escalating the action." And what she says about significants in the lives of Eights applies especially with the spiritual director: "Eights are helped by significants who stick to their own version of the truth, who hold ground under fire, who deal fairly, and who model the use of power in appropriate service to others."[5]

Conformists control their impulses by following the rules. To obey is to belong, and so others must obey too. In the Eights this desire that others follow the rules looks like control because that is what it is. The rules to be followed are their rules. They spend a lot of time second-guessing other people, trying to figure out what they are up to. Sixes find out the truth by locating danger. Eights do it by testing how the resistance handles itself. But in all of this there is submission to some kind of authority. It may be that others must do as Eights want, or it may be that the Eights themselves are the victims of their own narrowed attention, their own denial, and so are not free to do otherwise. The director will find it profitable to examine with the directee what authority really is, how it differs from control, and what is the nature of Christian freedom. These Eights could be helped to a deeper understanding of gospel justice, as opposed to their own, by experiencing in the liturgy a justice-oriented spirituality.[6] A gospel-directed justice has little to do with compromise, revenge, and "an eye for an eye" way of thinking.

As already noted, all persons on the Conformist level bear some resemblance to Eights. Both Conformists and Eights have a lot of "shoulds" in their lives. That is why when Eights are so focused on what they feel is unjust, they are hard on themselves as well as others as they try to equalize a seemingly unbalanced situation. The problem is not that these Eights necessarily mistake a situation of injustice; it is that they cannot perceive it comprehensively. They see everything in terms of all or nothing. To counteract this the director is advised to look for an opening to help them to expand their images of God. God is just but is a lot more than that. Closely connected with the "shoulds" in the lives of Conformists are the feelings of sexuality and aggression, which are usually viewed negatively. I suggest that in working with Conformist Eights the director deal first with aggressive feelings. Unlike others on the enneagram, these Eights see these feelings not as embarrassing but as justified, as a way to right all those wrongs. The use of the imagination in prayer to bring concrete images into play can help. These images would be those that counterbalance their own self-image or their ideas of what justice is. For instance, many New Testament images of Christ and the early community would challenge their narrowed understanding that true justice is achieved only through battle. Working with such images can help the Eights to move to that quality they need most, the quality the enneagram calls innocence. In practical terms, this means that the Eights allow some ambiguity into their lives, let themselves be a little more vulnerable. In order to move to the next level they need to introduce more possibility into their lives. They must begin the process of feeling differentiation and the admission of other worldviews.

The most obvious contradiction that will strike the director in the beginning work with the Conformist Eights is that despite their great energy in fixing a broken situation and meting out punishment where they think necessary, they actually have a very limited understanding of the social arena. They are trying to be just from a very biased position. And this is because they have little awareness of what their unconscious world is like. All that has been pushed aside in the interest of "getting the enemy." If they cannot see the whole picture on the conscious level, they will have difficulty perceiving anything below the surface. And so they do what most Conformists do: they define themselves in terms of those with whom they act, which often means those they are fighting against, with, or for. There is all this energy on the observable level and yet so very little connection with it on the unconscious level.

Directors need to hold their ground as they perceive the possibility of the Eights opening up. These Eights may be holding on to a kind of Jonathan Edwards theology — one emphasizing the "sinner in the hands of an angry God" — and so will dismiss the authority and wisdom of religious leaders, directors, and anyone else who makes them feel bound in. If the director can help them see the many contradictions in their lives and their ways of operating, most probably the real movement to health has begun.

Through the time of working with Conformist Eights, directors will learn much if they watch the directees' energy. They keep the energy coming because they are trying to stay alive. They have a lot of energy, but they cannot move it around. They cannot disperse it like Sevens, who operate from a more intellectual perspective. When the Eights become argumentative, it will help the director to see them as people who are stuck in their attention and so cannot broaden the discussion. If we recall something about the attentional style of the Sixes, it may help.

As I have already noted, Sixes pay attention through scanning the environment. Scanning means moving back and forth and from one side to the other. There is a constant searching movement, as when one is walking through a dark forest with a flash light. Imagine what it would be like if the light got stuck some place, that is, if it were not possible to move the flashlight. The light (energy) would all be concentrated in one place. As a result the rest of the forest would remain dark and, for Sixes, fearful. For Eights it means that there is no place for their hidden anger to go. It cannot be deflected into several directions. So there is more energy placed on one place (issues, people, causes) than is needed. Moving to health means moving that energy around. To help the Eight directees experience this narrowing of energy and how it influences their actions, I recommend the following meditation:

Recall a time in life when you fell in love. Try to recall a very passionate falling in love. If you cannot recall an actual time, then try to imagine what it would be like to be overwhelmingly in love. Notice how absorbing it is. It takes up all your time. It is very intense, so that just thinking of the beloved distracts you from what you are doing. It provokes a lot of feelings in you. You can think of little else accept this person. You are deeply moved, and it is a total experience. Most probably when you think of this person it will arouse you sexually, and you will become even more focused on the one loved. You find that there is more energy around this person than around anything or anyone else in your life. Notice how the attention has been so easily and so completely focused. Relive some of the things that this love has energized you to do. Now try to move your attention to God as the one with whom you are in love. Can you do it? What resistances and misgivings are you feeling? Do you think it is wrong to be in love with God this way? Do you think God can love you in this way? What are the feelings that continue to emerge?[7]

Spiritual Direction with the Conscientious Eight

While it is true for all spaces, it seems especially true for Eights that the transition into the Conscientious stage is marked by a certain tolerance for contradictions, by some acceptance that others have good and solid reasons for their actions that may be quite the opposite of the Eights' reasons, and by the dawning realization that they never seem to be able to bring about the just world for which they are working so hard. What is clear is that they are more self-aware, less dominated by their restricted style of attention. This self-awareness is seen in the claiming of personal values. For Eights that means values that have some foundation in the inner life rather than those that come only from a mere reaction to a situation. Rules have their exceptions, but now it is the rules of the Eights that have exceptions. And significantly, what is happening is that these Eights are more willing to enter into relationships that are not born out of mere confrontation. There is a widening of their feelings and so of the possibilities of commitment.

As the director notices the Eights' growth in the way they see things more comprehensively and deeply, how they open themselves up to more relationships of different kinds, how their natural honesty and goodness come through, and how they are more reflective about the way they pay attention, s/he will find the opening to enter into their inner lives. There is real depth here, although, as is to be expected, it is mainly on the conscious level. If possible, the director can encourage them to connect with others who are pursuing life in some depth, who have a sense of ultimacy about them.

It is at this level that the Eights develop the gray area of their spiritual lives. Increasingly things will be less black and white. This means they are more sophisticated in the way they view things. They find more alternatives to issues. Life becomes many-sided. They discover they have more feelings and that there are feelings about feelings. Feelings have levels. They find that they do not exist as solitary atoms in the world, that life always has a broader context. In other words, the attention is less like a laser beam and more like a floodlight. It is at this time that their strong commitment to justice moves away from their kind of justice to one that is more objective, more defined by the situation rather than by themselves.

One of the points of transition at the Conscientious level is that what was once simple and clear no longer is. This is especially problematic for these Eights. So much of their strength came from the clarity of seeing everything in terms of black and white. The director might find that they will resist moving into this kind of uncertainty. They may try to go back to the former less-complicated days. The struggle for them will be that their more open inner life will not make this easy to do. The director needs to take advantage of that. This is the process of deconstruction and relativization that all Conscientious directees must go through. The director should promote this process with whatever is at hand. For instance, with some Eights it might be easier to introduce the notion of relativity regarding their thinking about God than regarding some petty issue presently emotionally alive for them. For others, the reverse might be true.

As the Eights move through this shifting of meaning systems and perhaps experience the classic crisis of faith, it would be helpful to have them look at their anger. Why does getting angry make them feel better? It is important to point out to them the destructive effects on others of this anger. It may be more effective to have them understand that this anger is their way of trying to stay alive or, at least, awake. This may be especially critical at this time because as the simplistic worldview of the earlier stage falls away and no longer provides the basis for external response to situations, they may try to substitute anger itself as a basis. Much can be accomplished once they realize that their anger has a lot to do with their feeling dead inside. It is questionable to what degree these Eights can transform their anger into productive energy for spiritual growth since the anger dissipates so quickly.[8]

Eights at this point can reject their previous simple, fundamental principles with the same ferocity with which previously they held on to them. Moving to extremes is still characteristic of them. As usual, the director will be supportive by maintaining a strong personal position. In some sessions the director may be the only moderating experience the Eights have since in the course of an hour they can easily move from one extreme to the other. This is a time of great vulnerability for these Eights. Yet this is the precise quality they need to have to move to growth. But they will probably not be ready for a great deal of it.

They are in the process of creating their spiritual identity, and so the director can help them in two ways here. One is to assist them in finding safe places to be vulnerable such as with God or religious devotion. It is not unthinkable that Eights could have a very affectionate, warm, even sentimental relationship with some saint, with the suffering Christ, and so on. They have a warm, soft inside, and the devotional arena often is one where they need not deny it. The other way is that the director can teach them about discernment by having them look at the inner movements of the human spirit in the safe, confidential atmosphere of direction.

The positive side of the task of the director is that at this level directees are now more the author of their own lives. They are well on the way to achieving self-identity. They have their ideals, their long-term goals, and their self-respect, and they are moving away from the absolutes of the past. This is their chance to open up to life and take on new responsibilities. They now come before God with their own special gifts and talents. They are now awake and less forgetful. Palmer makes two points that are good for the director to keep mind at this stage in the spiritual journey with these Eights:

> You would think that with all the access to energy, and all that engagement with justice and truth, they would be likely to take the initiative. But Eights are far more likely to be reactive than proactive.[9]

Their self-forgetting means that they do not have their priorities clearly established. It is at this time that the director can move them to make such a reordering. Palmer notes:

> Eight's emotional needs often stem from the deeper, more submissive depths of their nature. In the interests of survival Eights can suppress their softer feelings, which makes it difficult to recognize their own needs. They find it easy to speak to an opinion, to offer protection, and to stand up for justice but difficult to remember what really matters.[10]

At the Conscientious level the director makes explicit their task of not forgetting and of moving into that part of their lives where these softer feelings are found. It is this work that will come to full flower in the next stage of adult development.

At the Conscientious level the impulse control happens through internalized standards of evaluation, discernment that is done in a

relational way, and the directees' openness to revisit past convictions about the spiritual life and their relationship with God. Also,
at this stage their interpersonal style is characterized by broadened
and deepened relationships. There is more intensity in the relationships because they are more capable of intimacy. There is both more
objectivity in the relationships in terms of understanding them free
of projection as well as more subjectivity in terms of greater emotional involvement. For these reasons this is the time for the director
to encourage these Eights to look at the place of "lust" in their lives
and what that means for their relationship with God.

The word "lust," when speaking in enneagramatic terms, refers to
excess. We note how Palmer puts it:

> Lust is craving for satisfaction.... They [Eights] are preoc-
> cupied by securing control of a source of gratification and
> forestalling potential frustration. Once the goal is set, obstacles
> seem minimal. Their task is to get what they want in the most
> expedient way possible....
>
> When an appetite for satisfaction takes off, substitutes seem
> boring. If you want something, then why not go for it? When
> desire takes hold, there's no limit until you're over the limit and
> find yourself recovering from a full-blown binge.[11]

It can be very fruitful to examine how this lust operates in the situations of security and risk. When these Eights can trust someone, they
will relax with that person. Some of the control will be lessened.
When the connection with someone is safe, often a warm relationship can develop. As they visit the Two space more regularly they
will become generous givers rather than rapacious takers of the Conformist type. The director can encourage this reaching out to others
and find here an opening into greater vulnerability and a broadening of the area between the black and white of things. Also, at this
time the director will want to guide them away from a sentimental
reaction to the people toward whom they are moving more comfort-
ably. When the Eights' relationships become sexual, there may be a
tendency to maintain control through emotional withdrawal, con-
duct seemingly at variance from the lust referred to above. They can
easily be made conscious of this at this level, and so the director can
use this as a way of having them examine their style of acting.

Along with Nines and Ones, Eights represent the angry spaces
of the enneagram. Palmer notes: "The actual sensation of anger is

pleasant, powerful, and cleansing."[12] They find that having spoken out and cleared the air, often with a lot of angry energy, they feel safer and also more open to intimacy. For this reason fighting and sex can go together. But on the Conscientious level they become increasingly uneasy with this reaction and are more open to connecting with someone with mutual interests so that they may work with them and become part of a common project. The director can proceed in a rather simple but very realistic way by encouraging these Eights to become friends with those they may have moved against in the past, more out of their fixation than out of any justifiable cause. And all this energy, all this wanting to get one's way, can be converted into being a very strong friend. They can become as manipulative as any Two, but the good director will find ways to make parallels between God's love and support of them and their love and support of their friends or fellow workers. It is at this point that the director needs to have them look at how they are caring for themselves. There is always the possibility that their Two-oriented generosity can turn into burn out.

It is true that when Conformist Eights find themselves under stress and often defenseless they will move to the Five with all its techniques of emotional withdrawal. But at this level this is less likely to happen, at least automatically. In fact, the movement to Five is something the director may want to recommend be done with some regularity. Their spiritual health depends not only on broadening their focus of attention from an either/or worldview but also on their moving into a contemplative place to enter into themselves more deeply, to become more self-aware, to let insights about their lives emerge. The Five space may be the only place where they can really do their inner spiritual work, the kind that one does on retreats, during days of recollection, and in private prayer. Here their prayer can become more affective because the privacy allows them to be more vulnerable. Here they can begin to allow themselves to own a lot of their sexual and aggressive feelings.

Usually people have a problem becoming angry with God at the Conscientious level, but these Eights may be able to do this more readily. This is the stage of growth where they can judge how generous and giving they can be. Here they can have a better sense of what they need to do to be good to themselves, not the kind of good that is equated with taking whatever they want, but the kind that easily leads them to a deeper, more comfortable relationship with God.

There is a lot of good energy here that has to do with morality, integrity, truthfulness, and altruism, and the director would be remiss not to move them in the direction of a greater social consciousness, although at this level much of this would be in the area of personal and public prayer.

Sometimes when I work with Conformist Ones and Conformist Eights I have difficulty distinguishing between them. Both are in the gut center. Both can come on strong, very critical of some situation. Both can be concerned about the areas of justice. There are often some other obvious external behaviors that are similar, but I do not base my judgment on these alone. However, when working with both on the Conscientious level, the difference becomes clearer. Ones moving to health possess an inherent way of measuring justice or the lack of it. They sense the contrast between the situation and some standard of evaluation. Eights first need to moderate their response, and then they sense the contrast in their interior response to some situation — on the one side, they feel warm and willing to be open; on the other side, they feel vulnerable, weak, and ineffective. To help feel this contrast, which is so important at this stage, I recommend the following meditation:

> Imagine that you are dancing with a partner. The two of you are dancing close together and have your arms around each other. It is the kind of dance where sometimes your partner leads and other times you do the leading. Feel what it is like when you lead and how you feel when you yield the leading to your partner. When you lead feel yourself filled with strength, power, respect, control, immediacy, dominance, excitement, determination, courage, and persistence. When your partner leads, feel yourself made up of the mild, the moderate, vulnerability, dependency, innocence, fear, boredom, tenderness, gentleness, and warmth. As you move back and forth from leading to being led, notice the different quality between the two. Notice especially what is happening in your body and not simply what you are thinking.

Spiritual Direction with the Interindividual Eight

Although the movement into the Interindividual stage may be as subtle as the movement into the Conscientious stage, the director will know when the Eights are there. They will be dealing with people who are much softer in their approach, that is, much more tolerant and more willing to accept conflict without needing to fight to resolve it. These Eights know how they have denied much about themselves and others and are now moving to an inner life where they find feelings no less strong than before, but much more differentiated. On the outside opposition is all right and can be left alone. In fact, it may be nurtured as a way of achieving greater variety in one's own experience. Certainly, the Eights will be more complex in their thinking, their way of reacting, and their desires to make connection. Long gone is that simplistic judgmental attitude that saw things only one way. This is the time of strong spiritual growth because now these Eights seek for ways to integrate by looking deeply inside for causes of their past concerns and manners of acting. Where at the Conformist stage they had dismissed psychological development as nonsense, now they pursue it intentionally. With an attention now not dominated by denial and with an energy now not moving to excess, these Eights are ready for the task of combining their inner and outer lives, their dependence and independence, their social and personal lives, and their intimacy and achievement. When these are no longer either/or considerations, they have arrived at the Interindividual stage.

The director will probably hear some heartbreaking stories, some incidents of disappointment, some real failures of ideals and the like from these Eights because it is often such things that propel them into this stage of growth. The director is now dealing with directees who are more willing to let other people be as they are. They can enter into mutual and intimate relationships from their strength without sabotaging the relationship by scaring off the other person. More intimacy is possible because the others can make their mistakes, can have their failures along their path of growth. Eights do this now in terms of a broader worldview, with a greater sense of social justice, and with an acceptance of how each of us participates in some way in the sin of the world. It is a healthy sign of being at the Interindividual level when Eights can find us all responsible for what we do, but need not punish us. Rather, they can support and love us as we are, for we are all in this together. They do not have the answer to the problems of life either, and they know it.

Whenever the inner life deepens, more intense intimacy is available. Now these Eights find that their relationships are full of feelings, especially sexual ones. But these feelings now feel differently because they are not used to provide the energy for control or simply indulged in as some kind of "This is what I want and this is what I am going to get" attitude. Feelings, especially of intimacy, are now part of a larger view of the self. Ironically, this larger view of the self does not mean that the Eights get larger in their energy. They already fill up a space when they enter it. This larger view refers more to their Five experience of reflection and movement inside. If at the Conformist stage the Eights tended to move against others in a combative fashion and if at the Conscientious stage they distinguished themselves from others while accepting the others' individuality and difference, now at this stage the Eights learn to unite with others as part of their process of self-fulfillment. Intimacy and compassion go together. As they bring their inner and outer lives together and as they tolerate more inner ambiguities, they connect with others without need to control, without setting up a battle context. They take people as they are and initiate and pursue warm, affectionate, and often intensely sexual relationships in which they are very vulnerable. With this vulnerability they bring also their strong energies and support, and sex is not so much a way of making contact as it is the result of previous contact now freed from what formerly was fear of softer emotions, lust for stimulation, need to control, intolerance of ambiguity, and manipulation.

The director will probably need to be patient during sessions with these Eights because they may easily run ahead of the director. This is now the time of the long process of what might be called "the conversion of energy." Lust for life and desire for stimulation are converted into the motivation to pursue the spiritual path. Their tendency to excess changes into the energy to support and promote others. The need to control and the dismissal of rules now are the driving forces behind their staying on the path of personal growth without getting distracted, and so they are able to reach for the "higher rules," those that lie behind the present pedestrian ones. Boredom becomes contemplation and moments of reflection. Like the Fives, these Eights need to stay present to strong emotions. The Fives need to feel the emotions in an actual experience with someone and not retreat inside. The Eights need to retreat inside so that they feel the feelings inside and do not dissipate them through a strong extroverted response.

Much of the time in the spiritual direction sessions will be spent on these Eights' freedom. We are dealing with "redeemed" freedom. It is the true freedom of the Christian. It is the biblical freedom of "the sons and daughters of God." This is the time for meditation to take as subject matter the causes of the lack of freedom or false freedom in the lives of the Eights. The director should keep in mind what this was like for the Eights at an earlier stage. Palmer's description of freedom for the Eights is helpful here:

> Eights' main concern is personal freedom....Much of their seemingly dominant behavior is in fact an effort to make sure nobody dominates them. They fear that someone in power will seize the advantage, so Eights refuse to be denied and will not be coerced into obedience. They place extreme value on independence in relationships....Rules were made to be broken. Even rules that serve their own interests are hard to obey because control feels coercive.[13]

Now the director is concerned with persons who are opening up a larger middle ground between the former black-and-white extremes; now dependency is a form of freedom and strength; now sex is the intimacy they no longer fear; now they are sensitive to the feelings of others; now the attention is broad and inclusive of the consequences of their actions. The mellow quality associated with the Interindividual stage will be more obvious with the Eights than any other enneagram space. I suggest the following meditation as a way of opening up the area of freedom for Eights:

> *Call to mind someone whom you feel comfortable naming your mentor. It may be your parents, spouse, children, or relatives, but more likely it will be a good friend, a therapist, a spiritual director, or someone with whom you do not have a strong emotional connection. Try to identify one way in which this person called you to greater freedom. Be as specific as possible regarding what was the freedom needed and what the person did or said that facilitated your movement to that freedom. What was there about this other person that made such a move possible?*
>
> *Now imagine yourself with a younger person, and he/she is the one that you are mentoring. Imagine them asking you about some area of freedom in their lives. How can you help them move to greater freedom? What is it that you do or say that makes the difference? Did you choose an area of possible freedom for this person that in fact represents for you an area where you are still in need of freedom?*

At this level these Eights see themselves from many different perspectives. Now that the unconscious life plays a more important place in their lives, the director can lead them toward the more instinctual side of themselves. A more embodied approach at this time will help them do the difficult work of reorganizing their ideals, of learning to live with the necessary limitations, and of reintegrating their past life and their lifestyle. Although there is a lot of energy in Eights, it does not necessarily mean that they are in contact with their bodies. Thus, the needed self-care for the Eights will most likely have a strong bodily component connected with their instinctual life. Out of this massive conversion of energy, the daunting task for the director is to help them discover more meaningful images of God, ones springing from their experiences of their bodies.

At this stage of development Eights are capable of considerable discernment, which for them comes through the body. Just as at one time they filled the physical and psychological spaces with themselves, now they can use that same ability to fill the spiritual space around them. Rather than concentrating on who has the power, now they can sense bodily the spiritual sensitivity and awareness of others. This could be a wonderful gift in the process of spiritual accompaniment of others. Aware of the spiritual atmosphere around them, they can detect the richness and freshness of the present moment. This is also their best way to discover where authentic justice can be found or where it may be lacking. Many of us have to use other qualities to discover what healthy Eights can do naturally in a bodily way. What Ones can do through their powers of comparison with an internal standard of perfection, Eights can do through moving beyond their skin in a spiritually perceptive way.

"Possession" and "surrender" are the words connected with the sexual Eights. These two words indicate the extremes of this subtype — on the one hand, they try to take over everything of their intimates and friends; on the other hand, they can give themselves over to intimacy when they feel safe. "Sexual subtype Eights are one of the higher energy positions on the diagram."[14]

But now possession means self-possession, and surrender means precisely that except without the guarantee of safety. More risk taking and letting go take place because these Eights find their safety in something higher, in the spiritual struggle itself. Their great power and intensity are now directed to finding God in all things. If they can have full commitment in a relationship, they can have a full commitment to God and spiritual exercises. Significantly, they can be very strong spiritual leaders. Directors might find themselves being led in direction at times. These Eights' perseverance in discovering the often inaccessible depths of spiritual experiences is admirable. Rarely will the director have experienced so much open-faced honesty.

The key terms for the social Eights are "friendship" and "social relationships." These Eights are very friendly, and it seems that many of the pleasant and enjoyable traits of the Eights come to visibility in a special way in this subtype. There is so much about friendship that makes it possible for Eights to be vulnerable that it is no surprise that in this subtype there appears to be a quieting of the usual fixations. However, the shadow side of their surrendering to and protecting their friends is the need to possess them. Often the excessiveness of the Eights comes through in the way they care for their friends.

Nevertheless, there is much about social Eights that speaks to the spiritual journey. They can be friends with their own inner world. They can be friends in an inclusive way so that they move toward those with whom they wish to be vulnerable. What better analogy is there for the total openness to God that is the goal of the spiritual life? Just as these Eights are committed to finding out the truth in a relationship, so they can see God precisely as the great truth of their lives. They strive for authentic feelings both in their relationships and in their prayer. The director can encourage them to a greater and greater transparency in their close relationships, in the public arena, and most of all in their public prayer.

The key phrase for self-preservation Eights is "satisfactory survival." This is the way Palmer describes them:

> Survival Eights exercise territorial control over space, personal belongings and a steady supply of creature comforts.... These are the survivalists: people who secure a personal bunker against invasion, who want a place that can't be gotten to and possessions that can't be touched.[15]

They seek safety through their appetite. Individually they have the same characteristics as one finds in the various survivalist groups in the United States, many of which are defending themselves against the government. These Eights can be very defensive.

But as Interindividualists, these Eights are wonderful examples of a healthy care of the self. Better than most other spaces, these Eights can help us to see what self-care that is not selfish really is. Also, there are plateaus in the spiritual journey where all that we can do is to survive. These Eights are models here. And because they are in touch with the dimensions of themselves where they can feel safe, they can help others feel safe too. These are very supportive people. The director can suggest to them situations to which they can bring these gifts. It may be that many of these Eights will be potential effective spiritual directors.

Chapter 10

The Space of Nine

Several years ago a student of mine[1] who is a Nine and who was struggling to find himself wrote a song entitled "Be Who You Are!" It is really the theme song for the Nine space since this lack of ability to say who they really are comes through in many of the usual Nine characteristics. Although not true for all, there is often a dead and heavy expression on their faces and a lack of energy that may make them appear to be "spaced out" or under the influence of drugs.[2] Much of this lack of energy is only apparent because that energy has been pushed down below the level of their consciousness. Nines shut done lest conflict arise. Sometimes this shutting down will take the form of a great deal of activity. They can seem to be very engaged in what they are doing. They will be friendly and social. But engagement for the less than healthy Nine is really a distraction. And since it is distraction and not genuine interest that motivates them, they can become engaged in anything from the most trivial, such as crossword puzzles, to the most serious, such as theories about the origin of the world. The effect is the same: distraction. If Eights look for stimulus because they are afraid they may be dead inside, Nines seek stimulus to become more dead inside.

Nines resist the journey of growth out of fear of what might emerge if they put too much attention on their inner life and become too involved with their own developmental process. They would like the world around them to be peaceful and without conflict so that their world inside can remain be the same. Because they do not attend to their emotional life, do not work through issues as they present themselves, and spend time going from place to place, person to person, or workshop to workshop to find someone who will do their inner work for them, it is difficult to engage them except at a superficial level. Serious topics that seem to have no emotional significance can frighten them. I traveled through Europe with a Nine once. It was like traveling by myself. Or, better, it was like traveling with someone who was traveling by himself. Never would he respond to a theological topic for conversation. So I resorted to menus and recipes, and that worked.

Directors must beware of doing the work of the Nines for them. They may be inclined to shift responsibility on to you, although they will not respect you if you assume that office because they will know they have tricked you. Directors could well keep in mind the words of Greg Ronning's song:

> Everybody's gone home
> But you haven't found yours,
> Don't settle for somebody else's.
> Shrug time off your mind.
> Let rocks be solid and sand.
> Listen to yourself.

Just because the Nines say insightful things about themselves in a session does not mean that much is happening. It may be the way to keep the director at bay so that the pressure is lessened. If they remember their insights the next time, then probably some transformation is going on. But the director should be prepared that the next time the Nine may be starting all over again.

Nines do not look like the angriest people on the enneagram, but they are. They are focused in the anger center. But they do not see or use the anger directly. They are experts at passive-aggressive activity. They will do anything to get you off their backs. So you hear a lot of the same phrases from them: "OK, it's all right with me. Go ahead and do it"; or "Oh, who cares about that? That doesn't make any difference." They look cooperative but are simply passive-aggressive. Their faces may show no anger because they have become expressionless. But the attention has drifted off somewhere during the middle of a conversation. They have disengaged from the world around, albeit in a friendly way.

Nines may sincerely want to move on with their lives but simply do not know how to do it. Setting priorities causes conflict. It is better to let others make the choices. Then the Nines do not need to commit themselves to a specific project. They avoid commitment like Fives — except Fives move away from commitment lest it bring up strong feelings and they will have to go out and be exposed in a fearful world. Nines avoid commitment because commitment presupposes decision and decision presupposes priorities. All of this can stir up inner conflict. And if passion is also involved, it becomes doubly problematic for the Nine.

As Nines move toward growth, the director will need to watch for backsliding, which Nines are inclined to do. They know they should be incorporating certain values in their lives, that they should act according to principles that in fact they do have, but unconsciously they are pulled back to a safe place where they can insulate themselves from involvement. But they need not lower the energy. They need not put a damper on their emotions. Suzanne Zuercher describes beautifully the world of the healthy Nine:

> Conflict, they must come to experience, can be at least worthwhile and at best enjoyable. It energizes. It infuses life with the meaning they fear does not exist. Conflict can resolve into a peace that is passionate rather than sleepy, unifying rather than boundary-creating. The environment becomes an arena where their choices declare commitment.[3]

The weakness of the Nines is that they merge with everything around them. They lose what little identity they had by handing it over to others. But this is also their great virtue, and they can do what few other spaces on the enneagram can do easily, namely, enter into union with another and with creation. As Nines move to health, the director can accompany them, not by pushing them too much or by rescuing them in their painful moments. The director can point to the means the Nines have for advancement in their spiritual life, but s/he must remember that you can only lead the horse to water. The horse must drink on its own. The last stanza of Ronning's song is good advice for Nines:

> Trust your intuition.
> Make it your call.
> You don't need no tablets of stone.
> Dare to feel.
> Cut and bleed.
> Don't try to live inside, alone.

Spiritual Direction with the Conformist Nine

Unlike working with Eights the director will find Conformist Nines to be low on energy.[4] It will be difficult not only to follow their attention, which wanders all over the terrain of both internal and external reality, but also to find out where their source of energy is. Some Nines will seem indifferent to spiritual direction. Others will seem to be in a dreamworld. Some will appear to be on drugs although they are not. Some actually fall asleep as they are talking. Such happened to me with a Nine who was struggling to tell me about feeling. There were many pauses in his monologue, and during one of them he fell asleep momentarily. Most Nines at this level are dismissive of the inner search and of the director's probing questions. Not that they are disrespectful. They will say that it is not that important. They themselves are not that important. Their inner life is not that important. The language is all about the lowering of energy. This dismissive language is a way of staying narcoticized. Palmer and other enneagram experts describe the system's most fundamental purpose as the awakening of the person. Nines, at this stage at least, are the most asleep.

Some questions that the director can possibly ask the directee, or if that is not feasible, at least have in mind, are: What is your deepest desire? How do you try to control your external world? How do you *determine* what is important for you? Nines are paradigms of the basic human problem — namely, of having lost contact with their very humanity. They represent the loss of connection with the deep self in its purest form.

Occasionally, the director will work with Nines who seem like Threes. They appear very energetic. They have hundreds of things on their agenda. They have full schedules. They are constantly on the go. Their appointment books are full. They are stretched in all directions. Where is the Nine quality here? If the director will but look, s/he will find it all over by asking a few questions of the situation (not necessarily of the Nine directee at this point): What is the principle of differentiation among all these activities? What priority of values governs the choosing of the items of this Nine's agenda? Can this Nine say why s/he has chosen these items rather than some other ones? Have these activities chosen the Nine? Is this Nine so busy because someone asked him/her to do something? The director should look for the energy in the answers (imagined or real) that the Nines give. These Nines might be racing from one item to another during the day, but what happens when they are asked what they want? Why they are doing something? Why this and not that? To ask a Three such questions motivates the person to move energetically toward the answers (usually self-referential). To ask Nines such questions might cause silence, a deadening of expression, glazed-over eyes, and most frequently, answers that give you no information whatsoever.

Palmer describes the worldview of the Nine (the Mediator) with these words: "The world won't value my efforts. Stay comfortable. Keep the peace."[5] In order to do that Nines have forgotten who they are and what are the real sources of their energies. They try to keep themselves comfortable through accommodation. To oppose someone or attempt to forge one's own personality forcefully would raise the possibility of conflict, which these Nines avoid assiduously. Merging with other people is the way to stay comfortable, to live a life without conflict, to stay asleep. Like Switzerland, they maintain their neutrality amid the opposing forces around them. In describing the Conformist stage, I earlier quoted Liebert's general description of that level of development and noted that it sounded like the unhealthy Nine. I suspect that in many of the enneagram spaces the people who need to be shocked into life initially look like unhealthy Nines. Clearly these Nines are defined by the group to which they belong. They merge psychologically and spiritually with the group and everyone in it. The director will note when it is the group speaking through the Nines and when the Nines are speaking for themselves.

Conformist Nines could be considered the paradigm of the Conformist style of thought: judging in a stereotypical fashion, basing everything on what is outside, especially other people's opinions and actions. They are as black and white in their judgments as their neighbors, the Eights. But what the latter do loudly and with the appearance of certainty, these Nines do mindlessly. That is, there does not seem to be any critical thinking going on to reach a certain conclusion. The director will look, often in vain, for some kind of opening into the inner world of the Nine. Do not expect these directees to move along by leaps and bounds. The director needs to help them discover their style of attention, but that will not be easy, and probably it cannot be approached directly. Their attention is all over the place and not anchored to anything. For the director who follows the principle "not to lead the directees but to actively follow them" (which I personally espouse), the journey will be disorganized and messy. At this stage everything seems to cause conflict, and so the directees will try to remain under the influence of their drugging while they are in a session with the director. The director needs to watch how they go unconscious through repetitive behavior.

It is not easy to give a list of reactions that describe the Nines at this level because they are inconsistent. Sometimes they act in a passive-aggressive way and sometimes not. Sometimes they are indecisive like Sixes and sometimes not. Sometimes their emotions are flat, and sometimes they are on a high. Whatever works to lower the energy is what they choose. This lowering of energy may be deliberate, as when they consciously avoid conflict, or it may not be deliberate, as when they are out of touch with themselves.

The connection with the inner life is very limited, and what is there is very fragile. Unlike Eights, Nines do not have strong personal positions. To distinguish thoughts from feelings will be a chore for them. Differentiation implies choice of some kind, and choice implies conflict. These Nines usually will not know that they are Nines and will be wandering all over the enneagram in their search for self-identity. The one thing that is clear is how ambivalent they are about themselves. One of the reasons they are called mediators is that they have the ability to see and identify with all sides of an issue. But this is not very helpful in the process of spiritual growth at this stage of development. Some decisions must be made, and they must make choices about some things. It may be that the opening will come through the director constantly pointing out their defense mechanism of falling asleep by lowering their energy and unfocusing their attention. It is not a very subtle mechanism and one that an honest Nine cannot hide from forever.

The director will be looking for ways to motivate these Nines into action. In the beginning this may be a matter of continually pointing out all their devices of resistance to the inner search: delay, numbing, inability to make decisions, keeping their conscious moments filled with the least important things in life, and letting their lives be taken over by someone else. Indolence and sloth are their fixations, the first being a mental self-forgetting and the latter an emotional laziness. Palmer describes this sloth in terms of the Nines' attention:

> You can see all sides of a question, which overwhelms your own agenda. Decisions are difficult. Conflicting opinions appear to have equal merit Attention cycles from the central issue to secondary matters. You get sidetracked to chores and backlogs of unfinished business. Your energy gets diverted from the essential tasks of the day. Your momentum slows. Without your realizing it, a holding pattern develops.[6]

The director's task is simple but hard to do: keep them paying attention. These Nines need to focus their energies on what they are doing and make decisions about what they want to do. The reason that some Nines appear so busy, so Three-like, is that they are forgetting themselves. Everyone else's agenda becomes theirs. The director can help them to take a close look at their daily schedule and have them ask which of the many things they are doing are ways of paying attention to themselves and which are ways of paying attention to the ideas and the business of others. The director should keep it simple. For each activity the director asks: "Why are you doing this?"

The overriding issue in direction at this level is to assist these Nines to begin the journey inward. Probably the more fundamental methods of prayer would be a good place to begin. They are not ready for the kind of meditation practices where they need to be self-starters. The well-known Ignatian (and not only Ignatian) methods of composition of place, of praying for what is desired, of three points for meditation, and of a final prayer embracing the emotions would be the best way to begin. The first prelude helps to focus the imagination on some scene. Asking for a specific grace combats the Nines' ambiguity about knowing what they want. The three points require the mind to focus on specific areas that are usually progressive. And the final colloquy recapitulates what is desired and prayed for. This rather methodical approach to prayer is not what Nines will enjoy at any time.[7] It is not recommended for the healthy Nines who would be able to move into the deeper forms of contemplation on their own. But on the Conformist level, where the Nines are very unfocused, it is imperative to assist them with a structured spirituality that will help them to make the movement inward.

It is possible that many Nines at this level will be visiting the Three space a great deal. The emphasis on external appearance, the importance of the opinion of the group to which they belong, and the fear of losing face — all these reinforce their tendency to merge and lose themselves in others. Directors will feel like they are trying to hold on to a rudderless boat. The Nines' attention is all over the place, and there is little connection to the true self. Who are these persons with whom the director is working? How does one get past all that trivia so the true task of spiritual direction can begin? Nines need to claim themselves, think for themselves. The problem is that they have been letting some group such as the church do all the thinking for them. The director should try to devise a way in which the Nines can watch themselves forget themselves, observe themselves merging with other people and with groups. In the direction sessions it would be good if the director could rehearse with them some "separation" exercises. They have forgotten what it is like to be separate, and unless that can become part of their experience, growth in the spiritual life will not be possible. For instance, the director can suggest that they make a written list of the groups and people they merge with. Then, they can use the list as a form of examination of conscience. I suggest the following meditation for learning how to separate:

> Recall one of your friends. You and s/he are sharing in a quiet place. You are speaking about something very important to you, and both of you are engaged in a dialogue about this issue. Imagine some issue that has a certain emotional power, such as your being sexually abused when young, your planning to have an abortion, or your being gay/lesbian. You are having a heart-to-heart talk. You and your friend can always talk freely with each other. But this time something happens, and s/he reacts negatively. Your friend refuses to listen to you anymore. How do you feel? Do you move to sharing only your thoughts rather than your feelings? Do you want to change the topic or even deny it to avoid any disruption? Do you gloss it over because you do not want to lose your connection to the friend? Who and where are you in this situation? Do you assume responsibility for yourself here, able to discontinue the discussion of this topic but also able to avoid diminishing yourself in the process?[8]

At the Conformist level Nines are as subject to rules, as obedient to authority, and as in need of approval as anyone else. But the motivation is different. For Nines following the law can be a way of being comfortable, undisturbed by the challenge of having to follow the search for the self. Palmer says: "They are attracted to familiar, known, and predictable ways of doing things, because attention is free to wander when there's no pressure."[9] They can simply wander through the day without having to handle a lot of energy. Energy only makes them uncomfortable. Part of direction at this point will, in fact, be tantamount to making these Nines feel uncomfortable. Who finds it easy to get up early in the morning if one is tired? As already noted, of all the enneagram spaces these are the ones who are most asleep. Palmer notes how good they are at energy management. The director must not equate the high-energy Nine with someone who has a focused attention or who is moving inward. It is simply the way that they fall asleep.

At the Conformist level there is a denial of negative feelings such as anger and sexual arousal. Nines will avoid these feelings because they raise conflict for them. Nines are vague about feelings in general, and they will be especially equivocal about these feelings. This does not mean that the director should ignore this reluctance to connect with these feelings. Since Nines are at the center of the anger area of the enneagram, it is especially important to have the directees begin the process of examining their anger. A good practice is for them to list their angers and the people at whom they are angry. Dealing with anger becomes increasingly important as the person grows since it is here that a lot of the energy for spiritual growth is found.

Palmer says that the Nines have difficulty shaping a personal agenda.[10] This is an important area of concern for these Nines, who must become aware of how and why they are connecting to the groups they do become engaged with. Assuming a personal agenda here can mean their becoming consciously aware that they have taken on the groups' biases, that friends are people with whom they are doing things but with whom they do not have a strong emotional connection, and that their relationship with God is still defined in terms of personal behavior, a parent to whom they are accountable.

Because the spiritual director represents authority, these Nines can readily go along with what the director recommends. This relieves their anxiety of having to try to find out the answers of life themselves. It is the easiest path to follow of the options open to them. Again, directors could deceive themselves into thinking that the cooperation of the directees represents growth of some kind. But it probably represents their way of lowering the energy for defensive purposes, or it may be a sign of their merging process with the director. In this way they still avoid responsibility for their lives and can, as it were, blame the director if the outcome is unsatisfactory.

Spiritual Direction with the Conscientious Nine

Signs of moving into the Conscientious stage of adult development are never clear. In the case of the Nines a indication would be anything that gives some evidence that they are waking up. Some recognition of the place of anger in their lives would be a good sign. A major reason for their self-deadening is the need to avoid the emergence of their inner anger. Their talking about sexuality and sexual feelings would be especially important evidence that this awakening process has begun. The one sign for which the director is hoping is increasing consciousness of the self. This is a big leap for Nines since it is precisely the self that they have forgotten. But they are becoming more introspective and learning how to separate. All people at the Conscientious stage are aware that they are not constituted by their relationships. For Nines this is particularly significant and difficult. The other spaces can employ some of their natural energy to separate, but Nines tend naturally to use their energy not to separate but to become one with. As they differentiate themselves from others, they will be able to differentiate among their feelings more readily and so create an opening for movement into the interior world.

These Nines are gradually coming to know what they want. This is shown in their ability to make decisions with greater ease. Here they need the support of the director because when they find out what they want (or when they find out they do not know what they want), the Nines' whole system can go into shock. Palmer says: "Knowing what you want can feel isolating and threatening rather than energizing. Acting for yourself is unfamiliar territory. It brings up loneliness and disinterest."[11] If the director can help the Nines to keep their energy up during times such as these, which usually require some decision making, it will be possible for the Nines to refuse to lower the energy, to move away from a totally neutral position, and to avoid playing the disinterested mediator among their own desires and wants. All this opens up the greater possibility that the external prayer of the Nines will be connected with their inner lives.

Ordinarily at the Conscientious level people are capable of more complex thinking, and their view of reality is more inclusive, especially of the social dimensions of life. Their world of feeling is wider. Nines already have the ability to see the many possible consequences and alternatives to any given situation. They have as many worlds as there are people with whom they might merge. Their world of feeling is as broad as the feeling world. How this Conscientious broadening affects the Nines at this level is that now they perceive pattern and order in their thinking rather than it being merely all over the place. Now they can distinguish among their feelings and, most importantly, their feelings about their feelings. They introduce, as it were, some kind of hierarchy in their thought and feeling worlds. In other words, setting priorities is becoming easier.

Although the movement to the Conscientious level for Nines differs somewhat from that of most of the other spaces, it is no less stressful. Whereas the others are concerned that their once stable world is now disappearing along with its certain way of proceeding, these Nines will find that this clarity that is taking place will bring with it conflict because they can no longer act from mere habit. Complexity in thinking means for most other spaces the breaking down of a rigid pattern, thus causing a sense of instability. Complexity in thinking for Nines introduces into their experience more organization but with the same distressing result. This is a key moment for Nines in spiritual direction because so much of their time should be devoted to setting priorities. This is something they need to do with someone, in this case, the director. They also need support to continue to do this. It is appropriate to set all sorts of priorities. In fact it may be more helpful to begin with the Nines by having them list in order the priorities of their ordinary daily activities, knowing that not everything can be done and so a choice must be made. Nines need to write things down, such as keeping a journal, because they tend to forget key insights. They need structure and pattern for prayer and reflection. During this time the priorities of the spiritual life must become clear or little progress beyond this stage will be possible. Their first priority should be: loving attention to the self.

As already noted, the great temptation at this time for all the spaces is to move into the unhealthy Nine space and abandon all to God, which here means "passing the buck" to God, in other words, refusing to take responsibility for their own lives. The crisis of faith for these Nines comes from the fact that they are sensing what they might want in life. This is a difficult time for the director and the directee. The directees are moving from a Conformist world where everything was given some meaning because there was no system of priorities. They merged with everything around them. They refused to focus their attention. When you forget yourself, you do not have to be concerned about yourself. Palmer notes: "Like Twos, they identify with others' needs more strongly than their own."[12]

And yet unlike Twos, these Nines go out to the other person's position rather than to the other's feelings only. Nines have such a weak personal position because they keep replacing it with the changing reactions coming from other people. They get lost in the many reactions that are coming to them. When Nines reach the Conscientious stage, they should be able to intervene in this process. Here the director can encourage them to become more spontaneous and to follow their own instinctual impulses.

As they emerge from their state of inaction or sloth, a lot is going on with these Nines. They are developing their self as opposed to all those selves with whom they have been merging. They are clearer about their goals, including long-term ones, which means they are clearer about what they want in life. They are dropping a lot of the trivia that in the past supposedly gave their lives meaning. Little of that has meaning anymore. What seems to work better now is dealing with the more significant things in life such as death, love, passion, ministry, art, and mentoring others. It would be impossible to overstress the importance that dealing with such issues has for developing the spiritual life. This does not mean that they no longer need to deal with anger. Now they are able to see their anger as a key in understanding themselves. These Nines can more readily embrace a spiritual path, choose the concrete means to pursue that path, develop frequent, even daily, patterns of prayer, and opt for one school of spirituality over another. They are now creating their own unique personal and spiritual styles. These styles will not be different, and so there will be no need for the Nines to mediate between the two sides of themselves, something that would only separate them from both their humanity and their spiritual lives.

That does not mean that there will be no resistance. That is why the director should try to establish an equal relationship with the directee. Anything that feels like dominance or submissiveness will trigger unhealthy movement on the part of Nines. The resistance will most likely be passive resistance. They tune out. They delay. They get distracted. They slow down. They get stubborn. This is done mostly through some kind of intellectualization — that is, there is a shallow emotional expression. Sometimes this will be an obvious shutting down with almost no response to anything. Sometimes it will mean an increase in activity. We must always remember that with Nines, being busy does not mean being awake, especially awake to themselves. It can just as easily be a way of falling asleep, avoiding the journey inward.

This resistance will not work as well at this stage as it did at the Conformist level because it will not be as easy to forget about the real anger that is present. This is the cue for the director. This is the time to move in on the anger in a concentrated way. The anger should be pursued through clarification so that these Nines can feel it. Directors should help these Nines find ways to express their anger, to feel the reality of it, and to look for some of its roots. I am not suggesting that this be depth analysis. I do not think progress spiritually here depends on knowing fully the sources of one's anger, but some understanding of the person's history of anger will give a focus that these Nines need to stabilize their attention. I suggest the following meditation to help the directees understand their anger:

> Picture yourself climbing a flight of stairs and entering a room. It is a pleasant room with nice appointments, rich drapes, thick carpeting, and dark, expensive-looking furniture but no frills. It is a business conference room. Seated around a table are six people. You know them all. They are co-workers. You are all part of a team beginning a special project. As you walk to your place at the table, take a look at the faces of each of your co-workers. What is your reaction to each? Do you really believe that they will be interested in your ideas? Do you feel any anger that you are here and must submit yourself to this group?
>
> As ideas for the project are bantered about, how to you react to them? Do you accept some and reject others? Do you simply consider the pros and cons of each without decision? As you favor one idea over the another, you attempt to express your opinion, but no one seems to be listening. What do you feel? Any anger over this? Let it come. How do you handle the situation? Do you simply revert to silence or do you insist on being heard? When one idea that you feel is unworkable is being espoused by several of the group and you feel you must object, how do you object? Are you angry and so critical and biting? Or do you take your anger and use the energy to listen to the group more intently and to think more clearly to come up with other ideas? Are you still a mediator when you are angry? Are you a better or worse mediator when angry?[13]

If the director were to ask Nines at the Conformist stage if they have an image of God as angry, they would probably reply in the negative. But in fact anger is very much part of their experience of God, if they would but let themselves have the experience. They are moving from an image of a God who is simply angry to a God who gets angry to achieve his/her purposes. This facilitates their movement from being persons of unacknowledged anger to people who have found the source of energy for their growth. Although in the beginning this fountain of life for them, their anger, will be very inaccessible, at this stage it can be contacted and set in motion. Palmer notes: "Nines are famous for waking up to the fact that they're angry days after the actual event.... Nines say that they need a jump start to get rolling, and that once they get into gear they're unstoppable."[14] The key is to help these Nine locate the anger, feel it, and use it. Once they are connected to their anger as well as to clearer goals about what they want in life, the director will find a real conversion taking place and the qualities of the healthy Nines will have made their appearance. The task of the director is to help them pay attention during this process. As Palmer puts it so well: "The trick for a Nine is to stay attentive while at rest and to keep paying attention when the action begins to roll."[15] An advantage for Nines here is that the pursuit of the spiritual life itself is a great source that motivates the Nines to stay attentive.

These Nines are now taking their responsibility before God. What rules they do have are internalized and give some direction for their path. Which way they are to go with their lives, how they are to relate to others and to God, is something that needs to be discerned, and so the director's presence is needed here. Like all people at the Conscientious level, Nines' evaluations of themselves, of what is right or wrong, and of other people must be done in terms of the larger social context, that is, their place in a specific community. These judgments cannot be made solipsistically. The director is the directees' connection with the larger communities, and the director needs to be their conduit to this larger reality.

Directors can feel secure that they are dealing with Conscientious Nines when those Nines are discovering insight into themselves, when their language becomes clearer, no longer covering up the fear of clarity, when they no longer try to obscure something that had been made clear earlier in a session, and when directors feel comfortable communicating their interpretation of the Nines' experience directly.

Nines' movement toward security is usually seen in terms of their using the energy of Threes. This is when the Nines become productive, efficient, goal-oriented, and concerned about their performance. The addition for Nines, as Palmer notes, is that they want to be loved for themselves.[16] The question for the director will be whether this movement — that is, making good use of their connection with the Three space — is simply the Nines' way of keeping busy so as to stay asleep or whether this is the Nines' way of truly waking up. On the Conscientious level, this Three experience would be more like what Palmer describes when she says: "Nines are in a good position to tell the difference between automatic habit and authentic choice about how to live life."[17]

Nines in security are in a place where the most continuous and consistent spiritual growth can take place. Now is the time for them to examine their habit of merging with others in order to lose themselves so that they might understand and practice what real communion with others can be for them. Since feelings are more identifiable now they can be more objective about how they feel. This brings a freedom that allows them to move into their relationships with true love. They are less likely to hand themselves over to another person because they have developed their own position based on love of themselves. They may not be ready for very intense relationships, but certainly they are capable of deep friendships in which they also take care of themselves as lovable people. These experiences and others like them can be very fulfilling for the Conscientious Nines. Palmer notes: "The beauty of Nines in security is that real satisfaction for accomplishments can take place. Nines can move to Three with a full set of feelings."[18]

Nines are in stress when there is so much to do and too little time to do it. They become paralyzed. They become aphasic, cannot comprehend what is going on, and become inarticulate. Nines have to watch their tendency to regress. New areas of stress and tension can be very difficult. Nines have a hard time accepting that the move toward health requires ongoing maintenance. If a Nine has worked on a significant and conflictual issue, often requiring great energy, attention, and use of personal resources, s/he may feel s/he deserves a "vacation" from dealing with other conflictual issues. The director must affirm the first victory but also help the Nine not to live a compartmentalized life. Unhealthy Nines do not have strong personal positions, and what little they have they can lose here. They are simply numb. When they shift the blame of their state onto others, especially authority, directors will know they are dealing with the fears of the Six. But here directors can intervene and make use of this fear for the Nines who are at the Conscientious level. The Six fear is focused, and any kind of focusing for the Nines is a plus.

This clarifying of the fear of the Six space can move Nines to assume responsibility for their lives, can help them be more reflective, can motivate them to turn inward to examine their inner lives. Often the experience of being at risk enables these Nines to reach the Conscientious stage — to become people of integrity, truth, and understanding. And best of all, now the Nines can find and own the anger that is behind this fear. This is their real source of energy, and they can use this anger now to rebuild their lives. In direction they will be rebuilding their relationship with God. They will want to redo their life of spiritual practices because these practices need to come from their own sense of self, a stronger self, and from the kind of independence they have when they know how to lead separate lives. For many Nines being in stress or at risk will be a more spiritually growthful time than being in security. It is up to the director to know where the emphasis should fall.

Spiritual Direction with the Interindividual Nine

In the early years of the enneagram in the United States, when we had a variety of notes passing through different hands, the space of Nine was often described as the place of spirituality. Perched there at the top of the enneagram circle it was the opening to the transcendent. Such claims seem to be questionable today. But I think that the director will find that the Nines as they move into the Interindividual stage are increasingly capable of deeper union with God and will readily move toward contemplative prayer. When healthy Nines' natural ability to merge is directed, it can be a powerful instrument in achieving the Christian ideal of mystical union. If they can lose themselves in others at an earlier level, they certainly can lose themselves in God at this stage.

In many ways the weaknesses of the Nines are, when turned around, the strengths of the Interindividual stage. Even unhealthy Nines can have a tolerance for self and others, can be aware of inner conflict, can live with paradox and contradiction, and can find ways to be comfortable with opposites existing together at the same time. The difference at the Interindividual level is that they do not have to forget the self in order to do these things. Now these are done from a strong personal position. These Nines can also express their feelings more clearly and their needs more urgently. Strangely, what they did before, such as admitting all sides of a case as a way of avoiding conflict or merging with both sides to avoid taking a position, they now do through their acquired powers of discrimination. What made them good mediators before is still there, only now they are good mediators because they can distinguish themselves from others and others from still others. They are no less capable of merging, but now they know the difference between their inner and outer lives, and they know how merging can lead to co-dependency. There is now a difference in the pattern of merging. At previous levels, especially the Conformist, Nines would go out and merge with another person's position and very being. Unhealthy Nines do not just want to know what it is like to be another person. They want to become that person. Healthier Nines still have the tendency to move out and merge with the other. But now they are aware of what they are doing, and they bring the other person inside themselves because they now have a stronger sense of their own selves.

All spaces at this level have a deep interest in the spiritual path, but the director will note that there is a difference here, and it has to do with some of the words that are associated with the Nines, such as "love," "union," and "participation." Those acquainted with the distinction sometimes made in Christian spirituality between meditation and contemplation will sense a movement to the more passive, receptive, less mental activity of contemplation rather than to the more methodical, intellectually directed meditation. That does not mean that the task of the director is less or is done. The deepest form of spirituality is one that approaches mystical union but is endowed with a high degree of social consciousness. As the Nines move into the Interindividual stage they may feel a call more to union than to social justice. It is the latter that will need development. They have much to learn from their Eight neighbor here. For other spaces, their social sensitivity may outrun their powers of contemplation, but this is not so for Nines.

These Nines know what they want. They step onto the world's stage with concentrated activity, with a clear position, and with the ability to be themselves while at the same time open to greater mutuality and equality. They are models of how to love. They no longer lose themselves in the other person — now they bring the other person inside themselves, caring for the other person as at the same time they are caring for themselves. They want a better, more harmonious world, and they have now so tapped into their source of energy that they are ready to contribute to making this happen. What is amazing here is how their movement to union with others and with the world as a spiritual practice is enhanced by their ability to accept complex thinking and to discern differences without this causing conflict. Whereas in the past they had to lower their energy in order to deal with two sides of an issue, with contradictory statements and situations, now they embrace this tension, and it is a source of power for them to move ahead with their lives. Rather than drug themselves in response to what seems like the overwhelming reality of social injustice, they mobilize their anger creatively to live lives of compassion in helping others without losing themselves in them.

Having achieved depth in their spiritual lives, having brought together the inner and outer parts of themselves, having expanded their view of themselves in relationships (although more in profundity than in extension), they now have more feelings available. Feelings are more easily described, and intimacy is dealt with explicitly. Intimacy for the healthy Nines is often a matter more of letting go of many of the relationships of the past than of moving into a lot of new ones. Palmer notes that "Nines find it hard to give up memories of old relationships so that new ones can develop."[19] At the Interindividual level, Nines know which relationships they wish to maintain; they put the work into them to do so; and they have the freedom to terminate the other relationships. The place of the director here is to help these Nines evaluate all these relationships in terms of the larger picture of the Christian community and their particular call to minister to other people. Many people would not recognize the healthy Nines here because they can speak directly and clearly to what they want in any relationship. The person with whom they are relating will not have to infer what they want, which is what Nines at a less healthy level would like, very similar to Fives.

As the director works with these Nines on their relationships, s/he should observe to what degree the relationships are still filled with trivia. This will be much less than before. More importantly, to what degree are the relationships still focused on doing things together? To what degree are these Nines putting their energies on common activities rather than really engaging the relationships themselves? This habit may be one of the last to go in the movement toward holiness for Nines. Work and the shared task are important ways for them to connect, and so the tendency to emphasize those will be present at all the stages. But that tendency cannot predominate at the Interindividual stage. As these Nines explore in spiritual direction the ways they merge with others, they will discover some suggestions on how to enhance their merging with God. Such union and participation in the life of God are the goals of all directees, no matter what space they are in. But Nines have a special affinity for this merging, and it would be a great loss if they did not take advantage of it.

If separation was the issue at the previous stages, now reuniting with others is the goal. This is possible because now the Nines come from a position of knowing what they want. This means that Nines, like all the other spaces, will now be reexamining their past commitments, keeping some and discarding others. The director's place is important to prevent a regression, which would be a temptation when Nines are faced with the consequences of changing a commitment. In the past they separated interiorly so that a particular relationship, for instance, no longer influenced them, but the connection appeared intact from the outside. That way the Nines avoided the loss of love and the possibility of conflict and demonstration of strong feelings. At this level the Nines can no longer play this game because they have brought together their inner and outer worlds. The director is there to help them make clean and honest separations where this is called for and to recommit themselves where this is the spiritually life-giving thing to do.

Reevaluating their priorities will also mean that the Nines will have to readjust their goals, their personal ideals. This will be possible because they now move from a strong personal position, and the task of reevaluation, in turn, will strengthen this personal position. Nines, no matter how healthy, will need to do things that will reinforce the stronger position and sense of self they have attained. For this reason alone, spiritual direction throughout their lives is recommended. This is the primary way in which Nines can take care of themselves: to move toward that strength of position that Eights have naturally.

The way they image God will make a difference in obtaining this inner concentration of attention and personal strength. This God clarifies their goals, gets them started on a path, keeps them on the same path. This is a God of decision. This God is present to every task in life. This God will not let the Nines remain sitting on the fence. This God calls them to be on their own, to be in charge of their own lives. In speaking about the Nines' inner signals Palmer says:

It's hard to find a position that's truly your own when a position and its opposite both make sense. You get caught in the middle. You see all sides of an argument and don't have a clear position yourself. You want predictability and a safe structure; to keep life comfortable and easy. You resist change.[20]

God at the Interindividual level challenges this kind of thinking, and so prayer is a time when Nines remind themselves of their priorities because God is reminding them of the same.

The sexual Nines are described by the word "union," referring in particular to their one-to-one relationships. At the earlier stages, when they are caught in their fixations, "union" refers to their handing themselves over to someone else in the sense that there is a merging into the union itself. The result is "we," not "I." But at the Interindividual level such union with another, both when the relationship is sexual and when it is not, helps the Nines to focus their attention. It gives them direction. They still merge, but now it is from strength. Connection gives them enthusiasm and courage. This is mutuality built on strength.

The director should not hesitate to suggest to these Nines the possibilities of mystical experiences. Often the desire for union moves easily into the desire to be united with the divine. God becomes the beloved. The unhealthy tendency to rid themselves of their ego-structures, which imply division and separateness, can now be transformed into union with God where the point is to lose their boundaries. This union with God can be for them the most satisfying of all experiences. They know how to love others, which includes an unconditional positive regard for others and the feeling of the feelings of others (including their conflicts) inside themselves. Qualities of their relationship to the one they love, such as stability, insights into the other's inner world, and the desire for authenticity, can all be translated to their relationship with God. I suggest the following meditation:

Imagine that you have the four following friends. Some of the suggested friends below may closely resemble your real friends. Others will not. Each friendship has a different quality. The meaning of the word "friend" changes when applied to each. One friend is your golf partner. You have known him/her for many years, and each Thursday you meet to play golf. You have even gone together to England and Scotland to play golf. A second friend is someone you have been fond of for many years, beginning in elementary school. S/he returns your friendship, although you suspect that it is stronger on your side. A third friendship is a more recent one, no more than five years old. You became friends with this person when you found that you enjoyed each other's company at your book discussion club. You suspect that this friend has stronger feelings for you than you have for him/her. A final and fourth friend is someone with whom you work in the Justice and Peace Center, where you are employed part-time. You share clear ideals with this friend, and the two of you often work together on projects that are justice-related. So warm and affectionate is the friendship that the two of you at times express your affection sexually. That part of your friendship remains a secret.

Now look at each friendship slowly and develop each one, permitting your imagination to create scenes of what each friendship would be like. Perhaps some of them can be developed from real life; others must be created out of your imagination. When you have merged with each of these four friends in different ways, ask yourself what elements of each friendship most closely resembles your relationship with God. Which qualities from each relationship would you like to have in your friendship with God?

"Social participation" is the rubric for the social Nines. Participation in group life, which was once simply a place to be inactive, is now the place of tremendous energy. Nines' participation in the church, groups in the church, or other religious-oriented groups presents them with clear agendas, real tasks to be done, ways of promoting social justice sensitivity, fuller participation in a life larger than themselves, and ways of joining in the cause of God. These Nines do not absorb the groups' energy in order to distract themselves but in order to care for others. They would be very likely to belong to groups with high ideals and a deep commitment to world improvement, groups like Bread for the World, Pax Christi, Amnesty International, the Catholic Worker, or the Christian Life Communities. Such connections energize them, and they can be fully involved, fully productive in them. Their mediating abilities, now coming from a healthy life stance, can further their work both inside these groups as well as outside. One of the reasons these Nines work well in groups, often as a stabilizing force, is that they do not have a need to have their egos massaged. They are less controlled by image than are people coming from other spaces.

The phrase "self-survival appetite" describes the subtype of the self-preservation Nines. Palmer notes that while it is true that all Nines replace essential goals with inessential ones, these Nines are voracious in their attachment to the replacement.[21] Food, television, travel, trashy novels, and the like are substitutes for the real love they are looking for. This appetite is an avoidance of the self but it has a certain amount of energy. At least something is happening. The Nine has moved in some direction.

But now self-survival does not mean that they try to drown their often unconscious feelings of anger with creature comforts. The appetite for ice cream can become the appetite for God. Merging with God feels comfortable and not conflict-producing. Their desire for the comfort that lets them muse and lets their minds wander is transformed into the comfort of being with God, which allows them to focus their attention on themselves, on caring for others, and on the changes that have to be made in their lifestyle and environment. They are far more awake because they are comfortable with the energy that wakes them. Important matters are not to be avoided but addressed because they produce the kind of energy that now moves the Nines into the comfort zone of religious experiences and spiritual practices. The director can clearly tell the difference among the self-preservation Nines who are lounging on a beach in the sunshine depending on whether they are Conformist, Conscientious, or Interindividual.

Chapter 11

The Space of One

Ones are people of shifting attention.[1] They shift by comparing. They shift between differences. They shift by evaluating. That is why they communicate a restless striving for perfection, a critical attitude toward everything. They feel compelled to perfect this imperfect world. Their attention searches out what needs to be corrected. Their first impulse is to lecture you on what demands improvement. Even their humor is often quite humorless because it is employed in the service of the high calling of the restoration of order and justice. It usually works best with fellow cynics. Since Ones seem to have been born with an internal standard of perfection, their striving for the moral thing to do can sound abstract and intellectual. In fact, they are more motivated by their anger than by some complex principle. Sixes, who obviously are operating out of fear, are, in fact, more intellectual in their looking for the good thing to do. However, Ones are not like Eights, whose objectivity in acting for a good cause can be called into question.

Ones can enjoy themselves if they can justify what they are doing. Pleasure is not an end in itself. A friend of mine who is health-conscious enjoys ice cream and permits himself that pleasure every night, but only if it is fat free. Another friend uses his day off to do good things such as exercising in the gym or praying or enjoying something culturally worthwhile. The issue is not whether these activities are appropriate for a day off — rather, it is why he has to justify his day off by doing good things, things he also does on other days of the week when there is time.

Those of us who do not live with an inner judge may easily misjudge Ones. Being criticized by a One is not quite the same as being criticized by someone who is not a One. True, when any of us criticize others, we are really criticizing ourselves, but in the case of Ones this is especially true. Ones project their self-criticisms outward, onto other people. They shift back and forth from the inside to the outside. This means not only that they criticize others but that they see others as criticizing them. Those who are not Ones but live and/or work with them can take heart by realizing that what appears to be an excessively critical nature in Ones is often balanced by their being honest and taking responsibility for their actions. When we are in a work situation, it is a relief to have someone who actually does what s/he is supposed to do.

Ones are no better in judging the nature of their responses than any other enneagram group. For instance, Sevens think they are paying you more attention than they really are, and Fours think they are more present to you than they really are. Ones think that they are more appropriate in their responses than they really are. Honest feedback is difficult enough for many people, but when all the sugar-coating is removed from the dosage, as it is with Ones, then people react angrily and think the Ones are full of uncalled-for resentment.

The difficulty with the Ones' alternating attentional style — going from the inside to the outside — is that they pick up the real or supposed expectations that others have of them. This can make Ones even more obsessive about doing the right thing. They may feel resentful that others have these expectations of them. In fact, it is not others who have such expectations but their own interior judge who is making these demands on them. Later in the chapter I shall suggest some meditations that can help Ones to confront their judge. Dealing with their judge is an inner experience for Ones, and certain kinds of meditation and spiritual practices are their resources for doing so.

Like Nines and Eights, Ones must wake up by entering deeply into themselves to touch their true source of energy. The judge will never go away, but the judge can be satisfied with a more fully integrated person. Likes the Fives on the enneagram, Ones will find integration in emotion and sensuality. Like the Sixes, they must not be afraid of pleasure. Whereas Fives flee from sensuality by diminishing the need they have for it and retreating into their mental world and Sixes barricade themselves through intellectual processing to defend themselves from strong emotion, Ones draw up a system of rules and regulations. As a result of setting up this personal legal system, the feelings of pleasure get lost or go away. Part of the direction process will be the gradual abandoning of these rules. Such is done through modeling by the director, who shows the importance of forgiving the self and who exemplifies the road to self-acceptance.

Spiritual Direction with the Conformist One

The single overriding spiritual principle at all levels of development for Ones is perfection.[2] The director working with Ones will have the opportunity to explore the subtleties of perfection in all of its aspects. Perfection runs the gamut from a form of personal destruction to a form of the highest spiritual achievement. The world will always be an imperfect place, but how the Ones respond to that world will differ as they move to health. The anger will be quite obvious at this level, whereas it will be transformed as these persons advance in their union with God and their place in the Christian community. Resentment is also obvious at this level, and it seems to have no place to go except to be expressed in all the small and large details of life. In the midst of all this criticality and judgment, the director will sense a real desire to lead a life of Christian perfection and to find peace, both spiritually and psychologically, in this pursuit. The positive side of working with Ones is that the director does not have to convince them that striving for perfection is a good thing. Individuals from some of the other spaces who buy into the so-called American Dream, at least at the Conformist level, would find such striving, which involves the virtues of hard work, honesty, and self-lessness, inimical to their more narcissistic pathway directed by the philosophy that life can get better and better and that we should be able to get more good and comfortable things for ourselves.

As is true for all spaces on the enneagram, the limitations of the personality are exacerbated at the Conformist level because Conformists do not have a well-defined sense of the self. What perfection means for these Ones is taken from the various groups to which they belong. For Christians this means that the unhealthy aspects of spiritual striving seem to find justification from some outside agency. This may be a literal interpretation of the Bible for those who are more evangelical in their leanings. One thinks of the scriptural phrase, "Be perfect as your heavenly Father is perfect," and the harm that a naive understanding of it has caused for many. Equally unhealthy would be a kind of Puritanism among both Catholic and Protestant (especially) Christians. Further, Roman Catholics can give the ideals of a school of spirituality a fundamentalistic interpretation that rivals the fervor of Protestant fundamentalists.

Ones have an internal standard of perfection by which they judge reality. The difficulty at this level is that their judgment is skewed by not being true to their inner standard of perfection and confusing it with external norms that they pick up from others, especially groups, the church being the most obvious one for Christians. Their powers of discrimination which innately are very good, are distorted because they take a black-and-white view of reality and are too rigid to qualify their judgments depending on circumstances and changing situations. We cannot use an internal standard of judgment if there is little connection with the inner life. Feelings substitute for reasoned judgment about people and situations. Ones' evaluations of what is good and what is not, their intent to improve the world around them, their desire to do the right and virtuous thing, their need to develop a sensitive and upright conscience, and their vision of the moral life are all thrown off center by a fixation on external behavior, the material world, and what is socially acceptable. What could be an almost unerring operative internal criterion is taken over by unrealistic ideals or strong sentiment.

Working with Ones the director will soon notice how important the recognition of the styles of attention is in spiritual work. Ones pay attention through constant evaluation. They have an inner judge that is always at work and that passes judgment on everything that is thought and done. Little escapes the judge, especially at this level. Ones judge themselves as they judge others. No one is exempt. The attention goes back and forth from inner to outer and back. It moves between the inner standard of perfection to what is being evaluated and back to the standard. Palmer has pointed out that the most difficult part of intervention in the attentional style of the Ones is the first step. They need to disengage the judge, to get around the judge, to get behind the judge. But when they are focused on eliminating error from the world around them, this is not easy to do. As she notes:

> If focusing on error becomes automatic, self observation stops. All you know is that you're working desperately hard, that you see loose ends everywhere, and you can't rest until it's finished. The scope of the task enlarges. More details appear. It's late. It's out of control. Your mind flogs you for being tired and helpless. It's maddening that other people don't care.[3]

The block to spiritual growth is especially clear here in the case of the Conformist Ones — namely, that it is difficult to move to the inner world when the pathway is blocked by this judge. Access to feelings, which is so important in the beginning of spiritual direction, is inhibited. Not that there are no feelings. These, especially anger and resentment, are quite on the surface and for all to see. But that is precisely the problem — they are on the surface and are being directed by the judge rather than from the inner anger that is the Ones' source of energy. As a result these Ones intellectually justify whatever anger and resentment they notice in themselves. Most of the recommendations regarding prayer at this time should probably use "baptized" mental practices directed to disengage or bypass the judge. With some success at this task, the director can then move to getting the directee to distinguish the thought world from the one of feelings.

As I have noted, there is much about the Conformist as described by Liebert that resembles the unhealthy Three. The importance of physical and social appearance, the influence of how the groups to which they belong see them, and the striving for status symbols are all signs of this. It is possible for a given director to confuse a Conformist One with a Three, but I suspect that most directors who work with both of these spaces will sense the different qualities in each. Both types are defined by the groups to which they belong, but Ones grasp group values and identity differently. If I may be permitted, I would like to use a more personal example. The religious order to which I belong is the Society of Jesus. Its founder was Ignatius of Loyola. On the enneagram I understand Ignatius to be in the space of One. He wanted to do things not just for the glory of God (a good Christian principle) but for the *greater* glory of God. Ordinary glory was not enough. The Jesuit order has taken on this spirituality in its mission to work in the *more* critical areas of need. The documents of the order are filled with this *more* and *greater* approach to the promotion of the gospel. Such striving fits well in the One space. Whereas Conformist Three Jesuits are motivated more by the public pride of belonging to such a "distinguished" group, the Conformist One Jesuits respond to that spirituality because it seems to be such a right thing to do and the order provides such an excellent place to follow such a greater goal. The feelings between the two are really very different. But it points up the particular way Ones take on group values.

Conformist Ones can mistake nonessentials for essentials, as especially revealed in their inability to discriminate among rules and norms. The smallest rubric has the same importance as a major moral principle. This is a case of the judge distracting them from any kind of inward search. Because of the importance of institutional connections at this level, it would be frustrating to have them challenge rules of the church or of other groups to which they belong. Rather, the director can explore areas where the Ones would be willing to prioritize the rules they follow. There is enough in the Christian tradition and in scripture upon which the director can draw to help these Ones see that the reduction of the spiritual life to regulations is very untraditional. Director and directee can explore together some of the reasons why authority plays such an important part in their lives and why they are so concerned that others obey the rules too. These are traits of all those at the Conformist stage, but the Ones will manifest them the most conspicuously. One way to move these Ones to distinguish thought from feelings is to have them describe how they feel when they do not receive approval from authority. They will have been thinking along a certain line that met with disapproval. There will be some dissonance here, and the director can use that as an opportunity for clarification.

Although Conformists' lives are filled with shoulds and moral imperatives, in the case of Ones this will often be connected with their inability to integrate pleasure into their lives at this time. Both Sixes and Ones have difficulty with pleasure at this level, although for different reasons. Dealing with anger and sexual feelings will be met with resistance, and probably not much deep exploration can be done at this time. But the Ones' desire to be right, clear, and honest will make it possible to look at these feelings more consciously. This may be a sign of the movement to the next stage of growth. At this point of human development the director needs to do the same thing for all the spaces, namely, to help them see that they are projecting their negative reactions to pleasure and aggression onto God. Such a God could never help them deal with these feelings effectively. These more troubling feelings are signals of the unmet needs of the Ones.

What will be interesting for the director is how social issues will be present in the world of concerns of these Ones. With the obvious exception of the Eights, other spaces may not attend to these issues until the next or even third stage of development. The Ones' approach to social justice will not be very nuanced, and it will depend upon the general way their groups deal with these matters. For them, social justice is more a matter of individual shoulds regarding others and is not seen in terms of the larger picture of systemic sin. Justice concerns are ways in which these Ones can maintain and increase their connection with a group. It is easy to see how Ones can take the social teachings of the church seriously as a way of manifesting their connection with the church community. In itself this is not wrong. But it is superficial. It may be a conscious decision, but it is insufficiently grounded on inner spiritual convictions. It is part of the way they create their identity by doing the correct thing with other people who do the correct things.

Ones in direction will need to give priority to reexamining their God if they wish to move to the next stage of development. Having projected their perfectionism on God, they are locked into a world where God is reinforcing their own fixations. Their God is too much the God of the philosophers, the God of right reason, the ethical God. This God makes them feel guilty for not living up to the standards they have created to protect themselves. This God reinforces their self-criticism. Even at this level these Ones often will sense there is something out of place with their God because they have good powers of criticism and can criticize their own criticality. Like their neighbors, the Twos, they need to find out what they need. That is the right thing to do at this time in their lives. Like their other neighbors, the Nines, they need to find out what they want. That is also the right thing to do now. But how to get around the judge? Pleasure will do it, but here the question is to get the Ones to move toward it at all. The work of the director at this time is to help them select their pleasures, ones that they can engage in without guilt, with impunity, and even with approval. And in particular this must be God's approval.

I would suggest any kind of meditation practice that helps them to notice when their anger emerges and when their attention moves to something that needs to be corrected, to error, or to something out of place. Some body work, which could include general relaxation exercises that they can continue on their own, would be good. And it might be possible to move them to focus on the pleasure of certain body work, such as massage, asking them to concentrate on the pleasure and to just have the experience without evaluating it. At those times when they stop evaluating, the judge has probably nodded off for a while. As an aid I suggest the following meditation and some reflection questions:

Quietly close your eyes, relax, and sit in a comfortable position. Imagine yourself sitting in a barber shop or a beauty parlor. As you wait for your appointment you scan the different hairstyle pictures on the wall. Do you find yourself comparing them? In what ways? What feelings emerge as you look at each picture? Do you have a desire to look like any of the people in the pictures? The stylist is running a bit late but finally calls you to be seated in the chair. Instead of attending to you immediately, the stylist makes a phone call to see if the mechanic has a car repair finished. Just as she hangs up the telephone, a distributor of supplies comes in and wants to know what your stylist needs. What feelings do you have as you wait? While sitting in the chair you notice how desperately your hair needs a cut and style. You scan the pictures on the wall again. Which one of them do you like the best? Which one would you choose if you were leaving on a long, anonymous journey tomorrow? What does your choice tell you about yourself? The stylist is ready to begin and asks: "How would you like me to cut and style your hair today?" What is your answer?[4]

After the meditation ask these questions:

1. When and how did you experience anger? Where in your body was this anger?

2. Does your preference for a certain hairstyle imply a criticism of the other styles?

3. Can you accept each style for what it is without wanting to improve on it?

4. Can you accept yourself in the same way, an imperfect creature of God and nature?

5. Gerard Manley Hopkins, S.J., opens his poem "Pied Beauty" with the line: "Glory be to God for Dappled Things." Can you accept yourself as a dappled part of creation?

Palmer interestingly refers to some different kinds of Ones found today. The director will need to know that such Ones exist. There are what she calls the New Age Ones.[5] These people have a different set of shoulds, more or less the opposite of the old shoulds. If one of the old shoulds was we should not be sexual or seek pleasure, now it is that we *should* be sexual and seek pleasure. These Ones are clearly at the Conformist stage, and the difference at the later stages of spiritual direction is that the shoulds that these Ones need to let go of will be different. The process will be the same, however.

Trap-door Ones are those who in order to release the pressure under which they usually act do the opposite of what their inner judge and value system tell them. These are the Ones who surprise everyone by going off the deep end occasionally. I know of a very religious person whose life is very ordered and who seems almost rigid in his lifestyle but who at certain times goes off and has sexual experiences that seem surprisingly out of character.[6] These persons too are at the Conformist stage, but at the later stages this behavior might provide material for reflection about the Ones' dealing with their nonadaptability.

Spiritual Direction with the Conscientious One

The signs of transition to the Conscientious stage, while true for all the spaces, are especially applicable to the Ones. When they accept that authorities disagree, that different groups demand contradictory commitments, and that they cannot meet the high standards they have set for themselves and others, then much of their world is on the way to being relativized. This is a difficult time because these Ones come to direction with lots of conflicts, and their emotional life will feel as if it is out of control. They have no choice but to accept that rules have exceptions. The evidence is against their previous intractable position about what is absolutely right or wrong. Group values remain very significant, but these Ones are forced to assume personal values also, and this inevitably causes some clash. Their relationship with their friends and the people with whom they work is changing, and these people cannot be dealt with simply through convenient categories, because they are making demands on these Ones, which means that the Ones in turn must find a self with which to respond. The Ones have reached a point where the judge cannot simplistically do what s/he did in the past: simply issue orders that had to be obeyed.

Since this is the stage when real spiritual direction can begin because the directees have learned to claim themselves and their inner authority, the director will be opening up the area of anger for the Ones in whatever ways seem possible. It is not that these Ones need to access their anger now. They are very conscious of it. It is a question of how they evaluate their anger. They need to look at the ways they are justifying their anger. They have not lived by the motto "Forgive and forget." A friend once was working with an administrator who is a One. They were dealing with an issue for which she was asked to make amends. She promptly did so. But that was not enough for him. He said: "You must be punished." He seemed incapable of considering any mitigating circumstances. He demonstrated the rigidity of the Conformist One. At the Conscientious level the director can help these Ones to see that such an attitude runs counter to the central tenets of the Christian life and following the gospel. Ones need to learn to read the signs in themselves (mind and body) that indicate that they have not let go of their anger and grudges. Often they misconstrue these signs in their attempt to justify what is for them something forbidden, namely, getting angry.

Ones tend to fantasize that they are getting approval for what they are doing from some inner source, most probably the judge. This is a way of protecting themselves. A real challenge in spiritual direction at this time is for the Ones to be able to distinguish their method of justifying their present way of operating, by which they believe that they are truly in contact with what is the correct and good thing to do, from an authentic self-appropriation. In the latter case there is a real claiming of inner authority and an acceptance of the insights into themselves. They can examine their personal needs to discover the feelings that lie beneath them. There is a willingness to look at the place of anxiety in their lives, especially the way in which they have used it to insulate themselves from unruly impulses. They no longer fear opening up the area of the unconscious so as to let possible repressed material arise.

Sexual feelings are as much under censure as their anger is. Ordinarily in direction it would be wise to begin with the anger and then move on to sexuality. What is happening here is that these Ones are becoming conscious of what they were doing at the Conformist level, that is, deceiving themselves about the nature of their anger. They had convinced themselves that their anger was righteous because they did not know how to integrate anger into their lives. There is no way to get rid of the anger. For Eights, Nines, and Ones, it is there. That is a given. What is different is that now Ones are more and more conscious that they can no longer justify their anger as they had in the past. Rather, they are claiming anger as their gift. They are very good in discriminating the good from the bad, the just from the unjust, and justifiable reactions from those that come from their own defensiveness. At the Conformist level this gift is hidden or even distorted.

These Ones are able to be in contact with their judging minds and their inner critic. They are aware of their style of attention with its constant self-criticism and judging of others. Now they are willing to call the inner judge to account. They are open to see how this constant critic has narrowed their field of experience and has made it difficult for them to have satisfying relationships. Before, things, jobs, and people were all seen in black-and-white terms. Not so now. If in the past one small mistake vitiated the entire enterprise, now on the Conscientious level they can nuance their evaluations. They can experience more feelings than mere resentment or anger in human exchanges, whether with intimates, employers, or employees. Their worlds have grown much larger, and they see more options and the consequences of these options. They are moving from the right way to do something to the many right ways of doing the same thing. Palmer notes this transition:

> You want things to be clear, to minimize gray zones. You want the answer to be either right or wrong. Ambiguity signals dead stop. You don't want to be swamped by possibilities. Ones are not comfortable with multiple options. They do not like to make quick decisions, especially in a crosscurrent of information. Once a decision is made, they do not want to reformulate and open the question again. Ones can help themselves by attending to the logic and good intentions of different points of view.[7]

Conscientious people often find themselves unanchored because of this movement into more expansive worldviews. Black and white and right and wrong made things clear. Ones will find it difficult to admit these uncertainties in their lives, and the director will have to work intensely with them on this. But this is a good time to have them examine what it is that they want, prescinding from whether it is good or not. They should be encouraged to look at all their feelings in any given situation. Perhaps their feelings lead them in the direction that they judge not to be the best, the most upright, the most ideal, the most fully approved. The question is whether that means that some particular path is not worth following at all. The director can help these Ones become comfortable with the many good things and people in their lives, none of which may be perfect. This is the time to help them to accept that their God expects less of them than they often expect of themselves. It will be a wonderful moment of insight for them when they realize that God deals more humanly with us than we do with ourselves. This is an important moment because one of the temptations of people at the Conscientious level is to deal with their world coming apart at the seams by moving into the unhealthy One space where the push toward perfection is but a form of avoidance of the inner world and of deeper values.

Surely this is a time of crisis for Ones who have spent their lives trying to be good and faithful Christians. Now they no longer believe in their God as they did; they find that they disagree with religious authority; and they are unhappy with the groups to which they belong, including family and church. This is the time for the discernment of spirits because what is going on is that these Ones are moving toward a new conscious identity. They are claiming themselves. They are judging themselves and others by a different set of criteria than they had been using. Now is the time to move them to experience some loss of control. Since this control has usually been a form of emotional control, many feelings have been suppressed, and these must be released to some degree. Forms of prayer and bodily exercises that promote a more relaxed atmosphere will help here so that feelings can be more available and less energy is poured into defending oneself against them. Palmer notes that "simple relaxation exercises are enormously helpful, especially when they are coupled with an attention practice that allows feelings to surface into awareness."[8] Here the director might suggest forms of meditation that use free association of images. The spontaneity required to follow the less logical path of image-connecting will provide freedom for more feelings to manifest themselves. I suggest the following meditation as a way of letting more feelings emerge:

Imagine that you are taking a course in weaving. You are seated in a large room with many other weavers and each of you is at your loom. It is the final day of the course and the instructor gives all of you the task of creating a small tapestry that will communicate who you are as an individual. There is one limitation that the instructor places on you, and that is that there may be no identifiable objects in the tapestry. There are to be no trees, streams, clouds, and so on. Give yourself permission to let flow whatever thoughts and images come to you as you go through the weaving process. Let whatever different feelings arise come to the fore. For instance, what do you feel and what images do you have as you do the following actions: pick the yarn, choose the color of the yarn, begin the weaving process, find yourself well into the weaving, and, finally, complete the tapestry? What texture, what design, what shades of color do you wish to have in this tapestry so that it will seem like you? Are you getting pictures in your mind that you must now translate into some kind of design in the cloth? How do you feel about the mistakes you have made in the tapestry? Errors, too, can become part of the greater design.[9]

There is now an opening up of life, a becoming conscious of who these Ones really are and most importantly what it is that they want in life. They recognize their uniqueness lies within themselves and their ability to see reality as it is, not in a critical stance toward that reality or their constant evaluation of the performance and life of others. At the same time there is a tension pulling them to be more critical of themselves because they are evaluating so much of their lives and revising significant parts of them. That energy can be directed in such a way that it is used to search for the many dimensions of their own lives where they can recognize their own weaknesses and strengths, their capacity for greater intimacy, their greater communicativeness, and their being more objective in their judgments. When Ones evaluate and judge from the head only they tend to make mistakes, but when they do it from the gut, they are very clear and very accurate.

The relaxed Ones who feel secure will seem like different people to the director. There is less judgmental thinking going on. They are enjoying life more. Pleasure is more easily admitted. The shift to the Seven space is obvious since it is such a contrast, at least with the less healthy Ones. When dealing with Conscientious Ones this movement to Seven can provide a very good time to deal with certain issues, especially that of pleasure. Palmer notes that the Ones in security when in a healthy movement know what they want: "Decisions are easily made and are based on wishes rather than shoulds. Life is simply a whole lot easier."[10] These are Ones on vacation both geographically and from the judge psychologically. Here there are more possibilities than simply the right way and the wrong way. When these Ones are in security, the director can have them look at the way they control their impulses. What are their real inner moral norms? What can cause them to feel guilty, and is this valid? How can they place their criticality in the larger context of their communities and in the Christian tradition? What will greater reliance on God rather than on a corrected world mean for them? This is also a good time to ask the directees how they nurture themselves when so much of their life has been taken up with following norms from agents who have often been unkind to them. This primarily refers to their inner judge, but it then includes parents, church, and society. The fact that these Ones will entertain these questions suggests that this is a good time to recommend that they follow a more affective form of prayer. In order to help them identify their source of energy and to develop a larger repertoire of feelings, the director can give them "permission" (something like that may be needed) to get angry with God in prayer. Once anger is expressed and felt, sexual feelings will not be far behind.

The negative side of Ones at risk resembles very much the usual descriptions of Ones that are found in the literature and are heard from speakers at workshops. These could be Conformist Ones, and Palmer well describes them:

> Ones at Four typically fear that personal flaws will lead to abandonment and grief about not measuring up to high standards of excellence. In an emotional crash, Ones can become paralyzed by depression. Ones realize, with shock, that good behavior and overexertion do not guarantee success or happiness. The One is grief-stricken.[11]

Hopefully, the director will have been able to encourage the Ones at a previous level of development to follow the anger sufficiently so that they have some idea what they want and will be able to connect with that on the Conscientious level.

The questions that Palmer poses for Ones visiting the Four space are ideal for the director to ask the directee. "What are my authentic feelings for others, rather than what I ought to feel?" "What work would inspire me, rather than what work I think I should do?" "What lifestyle would animate me rather than pacifying the inner critic?"[12] This last question is very significant for spiritual direction because much of the movement from the Conformist to the Conscientious stage will have to do with quieting the inner critic, whereas the movement into the Interindividual stage will have to do with personal animation.

Relationships can be deepened now because like the Fours these Ones are going inside and have greater contact with what is there. Certainly, they will discover their anger, but they will also find a greater capacity for intimacy and an openness to pleasure. By moving through the sadness and pain in their lives they will become more ob-

jective about themselves, and for that reason, as Palmer notes, they
will look at questions of meaning and existence. This is a necessary
condition for moving to the next stage of growth. The Conscientious
virtues as described by Liebert — inner moral standards, integrity,
truthfulness, understanding, altruism, and humor — are now all very
evident in the lives of these Ones. This is a fruitful time for spiritual
direction, a time in which the emphasis is on the search for the God
these Ones long for.

Spiritual Direction with the Interindividual One

All that had been developing at the previous stage is coming to
fruition at the Interindividual stage. The judge will be much less in
evidence or will be experienced as a judge who is tolerant, can live
with paradoxical situations, is more nuanced in judgments rendered,
and is more understanding of the dynamics of human relationships.
More importantly, these Ones have gotten behind the judge in some
way. They have learned how to make the judge work for them while
at the same time they have contacted the self that is behind the
judge. This means emotional integration as well as psychological so-
phistication. As is true for all the spaces, these Ones are reaching
a high degree of self-discernment. Because of the Ones' attentional
style, discernment is something they are good at, and when they are
healthy they are very good at it. I used to tell my students in my
courses in the enneagram and spiritual direction that when Ones discern from the head, they make mistakes, but when they discern from
the gut, they are infallible.

As Ones move into this Interindividual stage the director will need
to take their growing awareness of social issues and help them make
these issues real in their lives. It is time to put flesh on the debilitating
structures of human interaction and to give names to injustice and
marginality. They will see the connections between liturgy and social
justice, between intimacy and doing the work of the gospel. This is
the time of integrating all those elements which previously have been
held together with some tension.

The greater mutuality and intimacy that are characteristic of the
Interindividual stage are greatly promoted by these Ones' sense of
honesty and loyalty. Ones and Sixes have in common difficulties
surrounding pleasure, but they also have in common a deep sense
of commitment toward those they love and with whom they work.

Since fear is less operative for the Ones, they can move into these relationships without hesitation once they are convinced that this is the right thing to do. Ones will always want to avoid making mistakes, but at this level this attitude is softened with a sense of humor and some of the playfulness that one finds in the Six space. Also, these Ones have a great sensitivity toward others. They treat others with respect, and because they are so good at discerning the objective truth of a human situation, this respect approaches reverence for the interior world of the other. Palmer says those who live with Ones should be careful to remember details because "ones are detail conscious. They appreciate small gestures: being on time, remembering names, proper introductions." And she adds that someone in relationship with a One should "speak respectfully. Make sure no one looks foolish. Ask for permission."[13] This also implies that the healthy Ones will act toward others in that same way.

At this level the director can help the directees to get rid of any lingering self-criticism. Interindividualists are capable of living in a more complicated world, whether that be in the external world or in their mental and emotional ones. They are now ready to look at how, despite their being the critics on the enneagram, they are susceptible to criticism, often only implied, from others. For instance, on previous levels if the director would make observations such as "I like the way you are looking at other forms of prayer," or "I think it better if you avoid spending so much time on this concern," Ones would takes these comments as critical of them. They would think that the director was criticizing them for not looking at the various forms of prayer earlier or that they had missed being self-critical by overemphasizing something. Palmer describes the unhealthy Ones' reaction here in terms of their mentality of seeing criticism everywhere and a fear that their own inner judge has failed to pick up something. But at this level these are no longer the reactions of Ones. They feel comfortable with what previously they considered very ambiguous statements because they can live with ambiguity. Nevertheless, there will still be remnants of this automatic reaction, and the director can help them move away from it. A very effective way to do this is having the Ones pursue more intentionally the area of social sin and sinful structures. The complicated web of evil in which this world is caught will relativize for them their own tendencies and shortcomings.

It is always a tricky matter for the director to know when to encourage the directee to mediate directly on sin. Such meditations are part of the spiritual exercises of most Christian traditions, the *Spiritual Exercises* of Ignatius of Loyola being a preeminent example. Usually such meditations are placed at the beginning of the spiritual journey as a kind of purification process. But with Ones at this level I would recommend meditation on original sin especially as a way of broadening their experience of social justice, of contacting their unconscious world, and of advancing further their union with God. Because there is in Ones some kind of longing for an idealized state, something that resembles the longing for the lost paradise of the Garden of Eden, such meditations can move them to a profound understanding of the evil of the world over and above their personal evil. The use of such meditations can be their intentional passageway to the unconscious (to the degree that is possible) — a passageway leading to the origin of these longings. Such deepening can access for them a more significant union with God.

Also, Interindividual Ones should be able to rearticulate the concept of perfection. The classical view of perfection is something toward which we work but never really arrive at in this world. In that sense any person who strives in this way is guaranteed to fail. But a more process-oriented view of perfection is more appropriate for these Ones. In this understanding perfection means total engagement in the present moment. To be perfect means to be completely committed to the present experience, and this is not measured by some goal at the end of a process or by some abstract standard. Rather to be perfect is to give one's full existential commitment to where one is in one's present journey. It means being fully in the present tense, with an undivided heart.

Interindividual people respond to their impulses in a compassionate way. They are kind to themselves. They act from principles that have their origin deep within their interior world. This is the ideal time for the director to have these Ones look at their self-criticism as a form of the expression of their anger. "Ones criticize in self-defense, to relieve the tension of being angry at themselves. They may need reassurance but feel guilty about having to ask."[14] The anger is a sign that something is coming from the unconscious area of their lives, or at least is trying to come to consciousness. Much of this moving to consciousness will have been done at the Conscientious stage, but the areas of anger and sexuality may be delayed until this time or at least will need further development.

Despite the deeper inner life, the greater capacity for humor, and the ease at moving away from black-and-white evaluations, these Ones can still experience much pain at this time because the bringing to consciousness of the unconscious elements in their lives often calls for a reassessment of their ideals and lifestyles. The perfectionism always so characteristic of the Ones will make it difficult to question these and reconstruct them in new ways. For Ones this is the time of deep exploration of themselves as people whose basic source of energy for good and spiritual growth is their anger. And since sexual feelings and pleasure are usually close behind the feelings of anger, these will be added to their agenda of rediscovering themselves at this more advanced level of human development. We can only hope that they will have the benefit of a spiritual director at this time who can match their own powers of discernment so that they can be assisted in this process of reintegration. It is not that these Ones must jettison their ideals or change their lifestyles dramatically, although that may also happen. But they must do more than think differently about them or articulate them differently. They must feel differently about them.

This is not surprising since so much of the spiritual task on the Interindividual level is moving beyond the conscious work of the previous stage. This is the time for a greater contact with the feeling level. There is greater differentiation of feelings. This larger world of feelings also means a more comprehensive sense of the self, that is, a self seen in the larger social context. Relationships are founded on connections that have a more unconscious base, although the conscious elements of the connections still remain important. These Ones' capacity for intimacy has expanded, and so they are finding that the judge is less critical of those with whom they are relating. Sexual feelings are more prominent in their relationships, and since they no longer need to block pleasure lest it interfere with their perfectionistic agenda, they will find that their need for sexual pleasure is a salient part of their relationships. In all this the director's task is to help them find self-fulfillment with attention to the needs of others, to their personal commitments, and to how they can best care for themselves at this time.

Images of God so dominated by perfectionism in the past are now purified through the passage of the dark night, and the God who emerges is one who inspires vision and commitment but also embraces ambiguity. Perfectionism and pleasure go together in this God who is more the God who accurately discerns the life of the creatures than the one who is critical and judgmental of them. The director here need only encourage the Ones to explore a variety of images. These directees may be better at doing this than the director. What is hoped for here is a rich God who cannot be easily categorized. For me the Japanese rock garden is a wonderful example of the One mind at rest in God.

Peter Hannan, S.J., uses several images of God that are appropriate at the level of the Interindividual One. He sees God for Ones as a weaver, and this God is weaving our lives, including our weaknesses, into a tapestry of grace. God is the kind of artist who can take our sins and failures and fashion them into the features of the artwork that we are. He says:

> In this way all the good that is in us is fully appreciated and all our initiatives to realize our deepest dreams are encouraged. Because of God's desire to remold us, to make us ever anew, he is compared to the potter. He is also compared to a refiner and a teacher because of his creative efforts to bring the best out of us.[15]

A good meditation for Interindividual Ones is the kind that helps them explore themselves as fashioned by God into works of art. The following meditation is based on the images found in Tai Chi, the ancient Chinese art of movement and integration. It is not necessary to have any knowledge of Tai Chi to do this meditation. This meditation could be done through visualization only. But I recommend that one do it with body movements. It is not necessary that the movements be those that are actually used in the practice of Tai Chi. The persons meditating can make up their own movements if they want. What is important is to have some sense how our bodies correspond to the mental pictures suggested, how we physically embody these images, how the experience of the images is found within our very tissues and muscles. The hope is that then the meditator can take various images of God and so integrate them that the experience of God is embedded in the body itself. I present only three images here:

Stand in position with body straight and head held erect. Move your right arm and hand away from your body at eye level and then move your left palm toward the wrist of the right arm, the fingers of the left hand almost touching the right wrist. This is called "Grasping the Bird's Tail." Repeat this gesture until you have a bodily sense of the image of grasping the bird's tail. Now place your right palm in front of your forehead, palm turned out. Place your left arm at your left side, palm facing the floor. Keeping both hands in place, bend over at the waist half way and turn to your left until you have moved ninety degrees. This gesture is called "White Stork Flaps its Wings." Shift weight onto your left leg as you step forward on left foot. Step back on your right foot and straighten your right knee, shifting weight forward. Hold arms out in front at shoulder level with palms facing out. Now bend over at the waist and move hands down toward the floor, palms facing down. Gradually move your whole body to the right, turning left toes in and bringing right foot next to left foot. This is called "Carry Tiger to Mountain."

There are many other possible images from Tai Chi. The meditator might look at a Tai Chi manual for more images, either following the gestures of Tai Chi itself or making up some with which s/he is comfortable. The important thing is to get the body rather than the mind to create the images.[16]

"Jealousy" and "heat" are the descriptive words for the sexual Ones, those in one-to-one relationships.[17] As usual these words better depict the way the anger of the unhealthy Ones is acted out. They are angry and possessive of the other. They have earned a right to sexual pleasure and react strongly when this is threatened. They can be obsessive about the fidelity of the other. They can be jealous over things other than mates, such as the rights of others or some issue, some social cause.

At this healthy stage these Ones can be wonderful candidates to become people who will make the promotion of social justice a large part of their life's vision. They can sometimes be confused with Eights because these Ones also have a lot of energy and are single-minded in their pursuit of a goal. These Ones will be on target regarding the goal. They will have understood the issue and will have found effective ways to resolve it. They know how to support others, how to move forward in the liberation of others, and how to find ways to alleviate the suffering of others. The director can help them channel all this vibrant energy into significant areas of social work — some of which, perhaps, can be realistically done through church structures.

Social Ones are known for their nonadaptability.[18] Interestingly, these Ones at the less healthy stage are interested in social justice issues. But they do it in an unhealthy way. They are very ideological. They are uncompromising. They are not open to new ideas or information. This nonadaptability is best characterized today by the members of the Christian Right. These persons want to join and participate in something meaningful, but the problem is that they are too rigid, demanding that the other parties conform to their philosophy of life.

These Ones at the Interindividual level are very much concerned with the social arena, although they may respond in a less passionate way than the sexual Ones. Their nonadaptability is transformed into nonconformity. They take a strong stand on their own moral criteria, and at this level the chances are that they are right and their criteria are just and good. Being social people, they will be able to promote justice issues better through organizational patterns. One thinks of the community-organizing process so inspired by the work of Saul Alinsky and his followers. Justice is its own reward.

Anxiety and worry about self-survival are the keynotes of self-preservation Ones. Palmer says this anxiety is caused by the conflict between what the person wants and doing what is right. These Ones are dominated by either/or thinking. "You can either be safe or happy." "Wants are repressed." "Ones can be stingy about what they have and what they earn. . . . Love and support are therefore not freely given."[19] The worry here is the way the anger is acted out in terms of the future.

But at the Interindividual level this anxiety of the Ones has been transformed into care and concern for themselves and for others. As Ones they will be very fair in the way they care for others. Their sense of discernment makes them good people to plan for the care of others in the future. These Ones would be good directors of care programs that the community and church wish to promote. They will support and stand up for the principles on which such programs are based. Like the other Ones, they are committed to the improvement of other people and will bring to this a fine sense of how people can help themselves. They have an optimistic view of people's ability that is not romantic or unrealistic. They know when to support and when to elicit support from others. The director can well move these Ones to look for work in the community and even in the church, which so badly needs their sterling qualities.

Notes

Chapter 1: The Value of the Enneagram in Spiritual Growth

1. See Don Riso, *Personality Types* (Boston: Houghton Mifflin, 1987), 332–33. For some of the early research attempting to integrate the enneagram and Western psychology, see Helen Palmer, *The Enneagram* (San Francisco: Harper and Row, 1988), 379ff. Anyone interested in delving into the psychology of the enneagram must acquaint themselves with the work of Claudio Naranjo, M.D. See, for instance, his *Character and Neurosis: An Integrative View* (Nevada City: Gateways/IDHHB, 1994).

2. Most readers will be acquainted with the nature and nurture approaches to the origin of the enneagram. The nature approach supports the view that health is a matter of moving into the fixation rather than moving away from it. The nurture approach explains better how we can be socialized to live in certain spaces for a long period of time, such as women being socialized into the Two space or religious women and men being socialized into the space of the founder of their religious community.

3. The differences between Ichazo and other enneagram experts is reflected in the "prenote" found in Helen Palmer's *The Enneagram in Love and Work* (San Francisco: Harper, 1995), which states: "Neither Helen Palmer nor Harper-Collins Publishers is affiliated with Arica Institute, Inc., nor has this book been endorsed or authorized by Arica Institute, Inc., or by Mr. Ichazo."

4. Maria Beesing, O.P., Robert J. Nogosek, C.S.C., and Patrick H. O'Leary, S.J., *The Enneagram: A Journey of Self Discovery* (Denville, N.J.: Dimension Books, 1984). This book was clearly an important curtain-raiser in the area of the enneagram. Understandably, it has been surpassed in many ways. I find the chapter on the enneagramatic Jesus troubling. I tend to be reserved about those authors who are not theologians making Christological statements regarding the enneagram.

5. Helen Palmer, *The Enneagram* (San Francisco: Harper and Row, 1988); idem, *Enneagram in Love and Work*.

6. Richard Rohr, *Discovering the Enneagram: An Ancient Tool for a New Spiritual Journey* (New York: Crossroad, 1990); and Andreas Ebert, *Enneagram II* (New York: Crossroad, 1995).

7. See, for instance, Don Richard Riso, *Personality Types: Using the Enneagram for Self-Discovery* (Boston: Houghton Mifflin, 1987); idem, *Understanding the Enneagram: The Practical Guide to Personality Types* (Boston: Houghton Mifflin, 1990); idem, *Discovering Your Personality Type: The Enneagram Questionnaire* (Boston: Houghton Mifflin, 1992); and idem, *Enneagram Transformations* (Boston: Houghton Mifflin, 1993). These are some of Riso's works. He has developed an enneagram type-indicator that may be helpful for some, but I have found no "test" that really works to discover one's type. And

while I appreciate Riso's treatment of the enneagram along psychological lines, I am uneasy with what I perceive to be a more a priori approach, one not as closely tied to experience as Palmer's.

8. See Kathy Hurley and Ted Dobson, *What's My Type* (San Francisco: Harper, 1991); and idem, *My Best Self: Using the Enneagram to Free the Soul* (San Francisco: Harper, 1993).

9. See Claudio Naranjo, *Enneatype Structures: Self Analysis for the Seeker* (Nevada City: Gateway/IDHHB, 1990); and idem, ed., *Enneatypes in Psychotherapy* (Prescott, Ariz.: Hohm Press, 1995). I think the work of Naranjo would be most beneficial for someone who is following a spiritual path that is not the Judeo-Christian one.

10. See Margaret Frings Keyes, *Emotions and the Enneagram: Working through Your Shadow Life Script* (Muir Beach, Calif.: Molysdatur Publications, 1990).

11. Karen Webb, *The Enneagram* (London: Thorsons, 1996).

12. Published, respectively, by National Catholic Reporter Publishing Company, Inc. (Kansas City); and Enneagram Monthly, 117 Sweetmilk Creek Rd., Troy, NY. The *Enneagram Monthly* also reprints several items from other sources.

13. For *NinePoints*, write to P.O. Box 2625, Westfield, N.J. 07090-9998.

14. Some of my present efforts are to put the enneagram in conversation with the sacramental tradition of the church and specific traditions of spirituality, such as the Ignatian one.

15. Eilis Bergin and Eddie Fitzgerald, *An Enneagram Guide: A Spirituality of Love and Brokenness* (Mystic, Conn.: Twenty-Third Publications, 1993).

16. Peter Hannan, S.J., *Nine Faces of God* (Dublin: Columba Press, 1993).

17. Bernard Tickerhoof, T.O.R., *Conversion and the Enneagram* (Denville, N.J.: Dimension Books, 1993).

18. Carol Ann Gotch and David Walsh, *Soul Stuff* (Vermette, Manitoba, Canada: Inscapes Publications, 1994).

19. Barbara Metz and John Burchill, *The Enneagram and Prayer* (Denville, N.J.: Dimension Books, 1987).

20. Suzanne Zuercher, *Enneagram Spirituality* (Notre Dame, Ind.: Ave Maria Press, 1992); and idem, *Enneagram Companions* (Notre Dame, Ind.: Ave Maria Press, 1993).

21. Zuercher, *Enneagram Spirituality*, 15.

22. Suzanne Zuercher, *Merton: An Enneagram Profile* (Notre Dame, Ind.: Ave Maria Press, 1996).

23. In this section I am greatly dependent on Helen Palmer. It would be difficult to footnote every assertion I am making. In some cases I have relied on her two main books, in others, on her tapes; in others, on her intuitive training workshops; and in others, on my personal work with her. I gladly acknowledge the importance she has played in my own work with the enneagram. The mistakes are mine, which I will correct if others discover any.

24. I use the word "space" rather than "number" or "type" to describe one's place on the enneagram. Palmer, Zuercher, and others also do so. "Number" carries the overtone of being fixed and restricted, as does the word "type," whereas space has something more ample about it and so more appropriate for the development of the human being.

25. For further discussion, see chapter 2, "Attention, Intuition, and Type," in Palmer, *The Enneagram*.

26. In some of the earlier writings on the enneagram especially, the movement to health was articulated along very conscious habit-changing lines without an understanding of how the attention works or even any advertence to the fact that people pay attention in different ways. Thanks to Palmer this is now less the case.

27. Palmer describes the falling asleep of the Eight, Nine, and One center as being asleep to the very process of growth. Twos, Threes, and Fours fall asleep by falling into a false image, and Fives, Sixes, and Sevens fall asleep by falling into fear.

28. As noted, meditation is very helpful to do this. The experience of love can also make this breakthrough, although it is more complicated because of the presence of inhibitions and the fact that it is often more episodic.

29. Those acquainted with Palmer's work know that she uses the language of "inner observer." By observing one's preoccupations one can learn to intervene and correct a slanted attentional style. In this way one's fixation can become one's teacher. I do not think that it is helpful if people construe the inner observer as some kind of beam of light inside oneself. From the Christian perspective this observer is the Spirit of God working in one's discernment process. In spiritual direction it is important that the inner observers of both director and directee be at work inside each of them respectively.

30. Throughout this book there will be many psychological insights that I have learned from my work with psychiatrist Dr. Mario De Paoli, M.D. The personal nature of the relationship makes footnotes inappropriate.

31. This moving around the enneagram is particularly important for ordinary spiritual direction. Palmer's concern is to become awake by moving into altered states of consciousness. That may be relevant for spiritual direction with the highly developed person and intermittently in the usual experience of direction. But this would depend upon what one means by an "altered state."

32. I begin with Two rather than One since Two is the beginning of the heart center. Beginning with One gives the impression that the enneagram is like a pie, cut up into nine distinct pieces rather than being articulated through the three centers.

33. This summary is based on various comments from Palmer at different times.

34. This theory was found in many of the unpublished notes that were current in the 1970s. It is found in Beesing, Nogosek, and O'Leary, *The Enneagram*. Also see chapter 5 of Hurley and Dobson, *What's My Type?* It is also found in Riso, *Understanding the Enneagram*, 31.

35. Regarding this point Palmer notes that it is not that people do not go to the stress point. They definitely do, and this is verified by what people say on panels. There is, however, less energy there, but there may also be more focus such as when a Six moves to Three to get the job done.

36. Rohr, *Discovering the Enneagram*, 199.

37. Palmer, *The Enneagram*, 44.

38. I am indebted to Elizabeth Liebert for this qualification. Apparently my own past training still is influential.

39. Rohr, *Discovering the Enneagram*, 197.

40. Palmer, *The Enneagram,* 41–43.

41. For a fuller description see ibid., 49.

42. The reader can find the details of the subtypes of each of the spaces in both of Palmer's books, *The Enneagram* and *The Enneagram in Love and Work.*

43. This is really not a difference from what Palmer is saying. It might be considered a further elaboration.

44. See Hurley and Dobson, *What's My Type?* 128–29.

45. Some would want to say that there is a connection between Six and Four and that is by going through Five. Perhaps so, but that strikes me as trying to explain everything through the mechanics of the system only.

46. This seems to be the position taken in Beesing, Nogosek, O'Leary, *The Enneagram,* as well as in Rohr, *Discovering the Enneagram.* It is probably best to leave the matter of Christological statements from the point of view of the enneagram to professional theologians. I believe it worthwhile to have an ongoing dialogue between theologians and this system and, therefore, would recommend that enneagram proponents be in consultation with theologians before engaging in theological claims.

47. The *Enneagram Monthly* has carried several articles on the body and the enneagram. See the four-part series by Jerome Freedman beginning in August 1995 as well as Alan Sheets and Barbara Tovey, "Enneagram of the Body: Chi and Chakras" (January 1996); and idem, "Your Body Knows the Enneagram" (April 1996).

48. See Jon Schrieber, *Touching the Mountain: The Self-Breema Handbook: Ancient Exercises for the Modern World* (Oakland, Calif.: California Health Publications, 1989).

Chapter 2: Spiritual Direction

1. Kenneth Leech, *Soul Friend* (San Francisco: Harper and Row, 1977), 34. Leech's second chapter is devoted to the history of spiritual direction.

2. See ibid., 88 and 89.

3. Ibid., chapter 3.

4. Alan Jones, *Exploring Spiritual Direction: An Essay of Christian Friendship* (San Francisco: Harper and Row, 1982), 11ff.

5. Ibid., 29.

6. Ibid., 56.

7. Tilden Edwards, *Spiritual Friend* (New York: Paulist Press, 1980), chapter 4.

8. Ibid., 99–102.

9. Ibid., 174.

10. Joseph Allen, *Inner Way: Toward a Rebirth of Eastern Christian Spiritual Direction* (Grand Rapids: Eerdmans, 1994).

11. Ibid., 4.

12. William Barry, S.J., *Allowing the Creator to Deal with the Creature* (New York: Paulist Press, 1994).

13. Tad Dunne, *Spiritual Mentoring* (San Francisco: Harper and Row, 1991), xiv.

14. I have made some initial attempts to integrate the enneagram into the Ignatian approach.

15. Kathleen Fischer, *Women at the Well* (Mahwah, N.J.: Paulist Press, 1988).

16. Ibid., 2.

17. Elizabeth Liebert, *Changing Life Patterns: Adult Development in Spiritual Direction* (New York: Paulist Press, 1992).

18. Ibid., 1.

19. Ibid., 8.

20. Liebert has suggested that "way stations" might be a helpful way to refer to these moments.

21. In the following three sections on the stages I am totally dependent on Liebert's analysis since I have chosen her framework within which to place this treatment of the enneagram and spiritual direction. The use of her ideas as well as her text at times will be close. To footnote every sentence seems both cumbersome and unnecessary. Hopefully, it will be clear when I am editorializing, especially regarding the enneagram.

22. The descriptions of the following stages of growth may appear to the reader to be rather succinct and abstract. Hopefully, the chapters that follow, which deal with the spaces of the enneagram, will flesh out these various levels of adult development.

23. Liebert, *Changing Life Patterns*, 85.

24. It is important to note here that Liebert does not make use of the enneagram or the Palmer styles of attention in her book. Any such additions are my own.

25. Liebert suggests that it may work the other way too — that is, mistaking a Conformist for a conservative. This does seem equally as likely.

26. Liebert, *Changing Life Patterns*, 89.

27. This material is from ibid., 84–93.

28. Ibid., 99.

29. Ibid., 101. Here Liebert is relying on Mary Belenky et al., *Women's Ways of Knowing: The Development of Self, Voice, and Mind* (New York: Basic Books, 1986).

30. Liebert is of the opinion that this is true even if they lack the faith, motivation, and knowledge that are usually presumed at this level.

31. Liebert, *Chaging Life Patterns*, 103.

32. I am presuming that readers will not take these descriptive statements in an absolutistic sense. There is still another stage of growth where what is taking place here reaches further development. I am also presuming that readers understand that few people would be completely at one of the stages of development in all parts of their personhood at the same time. Hard and fast distinctions are not appropriate here.

33. Liebert, *Chaging Life Patterns*, 108.

34. This is my word, not Liebert's.

35. Liebert, *Changing Life Patterns*, 109.

36. I am not opposed to speaking to God and expressing how one feels to God. But this should not be with the expectation that one will receive some kind of answer that will dispense with the usual human ways of discovering the meaning in one's life.

37. Liebert, *Changing Life Patterns*, 111.

38. Ibid., 119.

39. Ibid., 121.

40. Ibid., 125.

41. Liebert's treatment of this stage begins on ibid., 125.

42. See ibid., 126–28, for a more lengthy description.

43. Liebert has tried to look at Etty Hillesum's life through her diaries for evidence that she could exemplify the Integrated stage. See Liebert, "The Thinking Heart: Developmental Dynamics in Etty Hillesum's *Diaries*," *Pastoral Psychology* 43, no. 6 (1994–95): 393–409.

44. For the most part I limit myself to Palmer's enneagram terminology. Usually, I refer to the different spaces by their numbers rather than by the various more descriptive terms.

45. I have chosen this approach because I find that too often when the enneagram is used in spiritual direction either it is employed simply as a form of personality typing or the people involved try to extricate a spirituality out of the structure of the enneagram itself by means of the mechanics of the enneagram, whether it be arrows, wings, centers, repressed centers, preferred centers, and the like.

Chapter 3: The Space of Two

1. For a preliminary description of some of the issues for a Two as well as the heart space as a whole see Suzanne Zuercher, *Enneagram Companions* (Notre Dame, Ind.: Ave Maria Press, 1993).

2. My thanks to Maureen H. Kelley for pointing this out to me.

3. It is important to remember that few people are completely in only one of the stages of development; most are partially in one and partially in another, or in a period of transition between stages, or in one of the many other variations of moving through adulthood. The observations made here are meant for people who are primarily in one stage or the other. Also, in this chapter on Twos, I am especially indebted to the material found in Helen Palmer, *The Enneagram in Love and Work* (San Francisco: Harper, 1995), especially 61–74. Needless to say, what refers to spiritual direction and the stages of growth is my own, with reference to Liebert. Those seeking a fuller treatment of the Two space may also wish to consult Palmer, *The Enneagram* (San Francisco: Harper and Row, 1988), chapter 7, and *NinePoints*, vols. 1, 2, 3, and 4.

4. Palmer, *The Enneagram in Love and Work*, 69.

5. The meditations I suggest in this book are a combination of some of my own thoughts, recommendations I have heard from exemplars, suggestions I have read some place, and ideas I picked up from teachers, especially Helen Palmer. Some are original; others are dependent on others.

6. Palmer, *The Enneagram in Love and Work*, 66.

7. Meditations that are based on suggestions of others are highly edited and used with permission. In some cases I have used an entire meditation, and then it is used with permission and attribution is given.

8. Palmer, *The Enneagram in Love and Work*, 70.

9. It has been several years since I knew him.

10. For an approach to the enneagram that uses chakra body stances, see Alan Sheets and Barbara Tovey, "Enneagram of the Body and the Chakras," *Enneagram Educator* 8, no. 3 (spring 1997).

11. See note 12 of chapter 4 of the present book for a note about subtypes.

12. Palmer, *Enneagram in Love and Work*, 65.

Chapter 4: The Space of Three

1. Suzanne Zuercher, *Enneagram Companions* (Notre Dame, Ind.: Ave Maria Press, 1993), 48.

2. Ibid., chapter 3.

3. Again, it should be clear that much of the enneagram material is taken from Helen Palmer's work, whether written or oral. I do not wish to claim that I always present the material as she does or that she would agree with all of my expressions of the system. I have brought my own nuances to the system. Nor would I want to ascribe to her any of the specifically Christian material.

4. For the director who wishes to read something on discernment, I suggest s/he begin with the appropriate chapters in *Eyes to See, Ears to Hear* by David Lonsdale, S.J. (Chicago: Loyola University Press, 1990), and John E. Dister, *A New Introduction to the Spiritual Exercises of St. Ignatius* (Collegeville, Minn.: Liturgical Press, 1990).

5. This meditation was stimulated from the need to experience uncertainty and emptiness that Robert Lincoln writes about in his dissertation "An Introduction to the Enneagrams of Human Personality" (Ph.D. diss., California Institute of Transpersonal Psychology, Menlo Park, Calif., 1983), 154. I am working from a manuscript copy.

6. For further discussion of the material in this section see Helen Palmer, *The Enneagram in Love and Work* (San Francisco: Harper, 1995), 92–94; and idem, *The Enneagram* (San Francisco: Harper and Row, 1988), chapter 8.

7. Palmer, *Enneagram in Love and Work*, 93.

8. See Alan Sheets and Barbara Tovey, "Enneagram of the Body and the Chakras," *Enneagram Educator* 8, no. 3 (spring 1997).

9. Palmer, *Enneagram in Love and Work*, 92.

10. Ibid., 95.

11. The material for this meditation is taken from Sallie McFague, *Models of God* (Philadelphia: Fortress Press, 1987), 128.

12. As usual, I am relying on Palmer for the basic information about the subtypes, although I have been influenced by others who have done work in this area. However, utilizing them at an advanced stage of development is my own idea.

Chapter 5: The Space of Four

1. This brief summary is dependent, for the most part, on chapter 4 of Suzanne Zuercher, *Enneagram Companions* (Notre Dame, Ind.: Ave Maria Press, 1993). See that chapter for fuller details.

2. Ibid., 53.

3. Suzanne Zuercher, *Merton: An Enneagram Profile* (Notre Dame, Ind.: Ave Maria Press, 1996), 45.

4. Ibid., 190. Several years ago I had student, Sharon Hasler, O.P., who did a paper on St. Catherine of Siena as "a unique ego-melancholy saint." She says of St. Catherine: "Catherine was very unique (as most Fours are). In the 14th century it was very unusual for a woman to travel, preach, make converts, gain

special privileges, act as a spiritual director, enter world/church politics as a mediator and to speak to authority figures in a very assertive, aggressive, challenging style." Hasler refers to Catherine's letter to Pope Gregory XI, where she tells the pope to use his power well and that if he does not, he should resign or fear the final judgment. I wonder what Catherine would say to the present pope.

5. The enneagram material is drawn from Helen Palmer's *The Enneagram in Love and Work* (San Francisco: Harper, 1995), chapter 4, pp. 107ff. For more information consult Palmer, *The Enneagram* (San Francisco: Harper and Row, 1988), chapter 9, and *NinePoints* (February/March 1996): 10.

6. If my memory serves me properly, this is an analogy used by Palmer in a lecture.

7. I cannot recall the original inspiration for this meditation. I would be happy to acknowledge such should I be so informed.

8. Palmer, *Enneagram in Love and Work,* 108.

9. Ibid., 114–15.

10. Ibid., 116.

11. Included with permission.

12. Palmer, *Enneagram in Love and Work,* 119.

13. My inspiration for this meditation comes from Robert Lincoln, "An Introduction to the Enneagrams of Human Personality" (Ph.D. diss., California Institute of Transpersonal Psychology, Menlo Park, Calif., 1983), 194.

14. For a detailed description of the unhealthy sexual Four, see Palmer, *Enneagram in Love and Word,* 110–11.

Chapter 6: The Space of Five

1. Suzanne Zuercher, *Enneagram Companions* (Notre Dame, Ind.: Ave Maria Press, 1993), chapter 7. My remarks in this introduction are based on this chapter.

2. Poem 303 in *The Complete Poems of Emily Dickinson,* ed. Thomas H. Johnson (Boston: Little, Brown and Company, 1960).

3. The enneagram material is dependent on Helen Palmer's *The Enneagram in Love and Work* (San Francisco: Harper, 1995), 127ff. See also Palmer, *The Enneagram* (San Francisco: Harper and Row, 1988), chapter 10, as well as *NinePoints* (May/June 1996): 5.

4. Thanks to Alan Scheible for this meditation.

5. See the article on detachment in Michael Downey, ed., *The New Dictionary of Christian Spirituality* (Collegeville, Minn.: Liturgical Press, 1993). Most of the writings on discernment of spirits are appropriate. Some valuable exercises are found in two books by Anthony de Mello, S.J., *Sadhana: A Way to God* (St. Louis: Institute of Jesuit Resources, 1978) and *Wellsprings: A Book of Spiritual Exercises* (Garden City, N.Y.: Doubleday, 1985).

6. Palmer, *Enneagram in Love and Work,* 135.

7. Ibid., 134; emphasis added.

8. I cannot recall the original inspiration for this meditation. I would be happy to acknowledge such should I be so informed.

9. Palmer, *Enneagram in Love and Work,* 138.

10. Ibid.

11. This shows the inadequacy of the usual approach to the arrows, where the Five is to move to Eight but not to Seven. Both Eight and Five can move to each other with profit.

12. Some writers maintain that a large number of monks are Fives.

13. Palmer, *Enneagram in Love and Work*, 140.

14. Ibid., 138.

15. Ibid., 131.

Chapter 7: The Space of Six

1. These summary remarks are built on Zuercher's description of the Six directee in *Enneagram Companions* (Notre Dame, Ind.: Ave Maria Press, 1993).

2. The enneagram material in this chapter is dependent on Helen Palmer's *The Enneagram in Love and Work* (San Francisco: Harper, 1995), 151ff. See also Palmer, *The Enneagram* (San Francisco: Harper and Row, 1988), chapter 12, as well as *NinePoints* (May/June 1996): 9.

3. Palmer, *Enneagram in Love and Work*, 152.

4. When my therapist asked me what would happen if I did something about which I was fearful, that question was followed by others: "Would the sky fall in?" "Would the world come to an end?" Usually I had no answer. But the questions are a way of introducing a sense of reality in a world full of doubt as well as developing trust in ourselves.

5. I cannot recall the original inspiration for this meditation. I would be happy to acknowledge such should I be so informed. I have made several changes to the original.

6. Palmer, *Enneagram in Love and Work*, 160.

7. A personal note: when I was first learning the intricacies of the computer, I had a friend and former student help me. He remarked that I treated the computer as a Six (which I am), in that I was always trying to figure out what was hidden behind the screen rather than simply taking the mechanism as it is. While I was not so unhealthy as to think that the computer was out to get me, I was always preoccupied with getting explanations for why I was to press one key or another.

8. Palmer, *Enneagram in Love and Work*, 159.

9. Ibid., 164.

10. Although there is much in Christian spirituality that can be considered vague, as a whole the goal of this spirituality is much more specific than the concept of "essence" in the enneagram. In the two thousand years of Christianity, the central Christological concerns and spirituality have been constantly refined in terms of human experience. It would strike me as arrogant to claim that the enneagram can be placed as a school of spirituality alongside those many schools of spirituality that have developed in Christianity whether monastic, mendicant (such as the Franciscan), or more active (such as the Ignatian). In fact, many enneagram experts seem to find little that is spiritual about the enneagram at all.

11. The idea for this meditation emerged from some ideas in Peter Hannan, S.J., *Nine Faces of God* (Dublin: Columba Press, 1992), 189.

12. Palmer, *Enneagram in Love and Work*, 162.

13. Although this meditation is of my own making, it bears the mark of several things Helen Palmer has said, especially about projection.

14. Once when I was having a session with Laura Gans, an intuition counselor I regularly consult, I asked her if she thought I have intuitive powers that would allow me to read other people and situations. She said that I had strong intuitive powers but that I did not trust them. I knew that this was my Six space showing itself in characteristic fashion.

15. Palmer, *Enneagram in Love and Work*, 156.

16. Ibid., 154.

17. Ibid., 154–55.

Chapter 8: The Space of Seven

1. See chapter 9 of Suzanne Zuercher, *Enneagram Companions* (Notre Dame, Ind.: Ave Maria Press, 1993).

2. The enneagram material in this chapter is dependent on Helen Palmer's *The Enneagram in Love and Work* (San Francisco: Harper, 1995), 175ff. See also Palmer, *The Enneagram* (San Francisco: Harper and Row, 1988), chapter 12, as well as *NinePoints* (May/June 1996): 12.

3. In this case the name of Jesus is repeated over and over, usually in conjunction with a pattern of breathing. It is similar to a mantra.

4. Palmer, *Enneagram in Love and Work*, 184.

5. I cannot recall the original inspiration for this meditation. I would be happy to acknowledge such should I be so informed.

6. Peter Hannan, S.J., *Nine Faces of God* (Dublin: Columba Press, 1992), 230–31 and 232–33, is the inspiration for this meditation.

7. Palmer, *Enneagram in Love and Work*, 189.

8. Ibid., 186.

9. Ibid., 187.

10. See chapter 2, above, and the summary of the Conscientious level.

11. I would like to thank a former student, Elaine Wellinger, for this meditation.

12. Palmer, *Enneagram in Love and Work*, 180.

Chapter 9: The Space of Eight

1. I wish to thank Jim Uhl for this poem. Jim, a former student of mine, composed this poem when he was a merchant marine officer. Jim is an Eight, and he thought this poem spoke to the power of Eight. In fact, it is filled with Eight energy and imagery.

2. Again, I am reviewing the material on the Eight directee as presented by Suzanne Zuercher in *Enneagram Companions* (Notre Dame, Ind.: Ave Maria Press, 1993), chapter 12.

3. The enneagram material in this chapter is dependent on Helen Palmer's *The Enneagram in Love and Work* (San Francisco: Harper, 1995), 199ff. See also Palmer, *The Enneagram* (San Francisco: Harper and Row, 1988), chapter 13, as well as *NinePoints* (May/June 1996): 12.

4. Palmer, *Enneagram in Love and Work*, 199–200.

5. Ibid., 202.

6. As a help to this I recommend my own book, *The Liturgy That Does Justice* (written with Christopher Kiesling, O.P.) (Collegeville, Minn.: Liturgical Press, 1990).

7. The idea for this meditation came from Peter Hannan, S.J., *Nine Faces of God* (Dublin: Columba Press, 1992), 242, 243.

8. See Palmer, *Enneagram in Love and Work*, 206.

9. Ibid., 208.

10. Ibid.

11. Ibid., 207.

12. Ibid., 210.

13. Ibid., 212.

14. Ibid., 202.

15. Ibid., 204.

Chapter 10: The Space of Nine

1. I refer to Greg Ronning, who is campus minister at Texas Lutheran University.

2. Much of this will be a summary of points Suzanne Zuercher makes in *Enneagram Companions* (Notre Dame, Ind.: Ave Maria Press, 1993), chapter 13.

3. Ibid., 155.

4. The enneagram material in this chapter is dependent on Helen Palmer's *The Enneagram in Love and Work* (San Francisco: Harper, 1995), 223ff. See also Palmer, *The Enneagram* (San Francisco: Harper and Row, 1988), chapter 14, as well as *NinePoints* (February/March 1996): 14.

5. Palmer, *Enneagram in Love and Work*, 223.

6. Ibid., 225.

7. Those directors who desire a deeper understanding of the Ignatian approach to the spiritual life might find the following books helpful: David Lonsdale, S.J., *Eyes to See, Ears to Hear: An Introduction to Ignatian Spirituality* (Chicago: Loyola University Press, 1990), and John E. Dister, S.J., *A New Introduction to the Spiritual Exercises of St. Ignatius* (Collegeville, Minn.: Liturgical Press, 1993). Needless to say, the director should be acquainted with the *Exercises* themselves and some commentaries.

8. This meditation is based on ideas taken from Peter Hannan, S.J., *Nine Faces of God* (Dublin: Columba Press, 1992), 274–75.

9. Palmer, *Enneagram in Love and Work*, 228.

10. Ibid.

11. Ibid., 229.

12. Ibid., 230.

13. Much of this meditation I owe to John J. Martin.

14. Palmer, *Enneagram in Love and Work*, 231.

15. Ibid., 232.

16. Ibid., 234.

17. Ibid.

18. Ibid.

19. Ibid., 235.

20. Ibid., 240.

21. Ibid., 227.

Chapter 11: The Space of One

1. See chapter 14 of Suzanne Zuercher, *Enneagram Companions* (Notre Dame, Ind.: Ave Maria Press, 1993).

2. The enneagram material in this chapter is dependent on Helen Palmer's *The Enneagram in Love and Work* (San Francisco: Harper, 1995), 33. See also Palmer, *The Enneagram* (San Francisco: Harper and Row, 1988), chapter 6, as well as *NinePoints* (February/March 1996): 14.

3. Palmer, *Enneagram in Love and Work*, 35.

4. I am indebted to Bernadette Helfert, SCL, for this meditation.

5. Palmer, *Enneagram in Love and Work*, 43.

6. Ibid.

7. Ibid., 41.

8. Ibid., 39.

9. The idea for this meditation came from Peter Hannan, S.J., *Nine Faces of God* (Dublin: Columba Press, 1992), 42–43.

10. Palmer, *Enneagram in Love and Work*, 46.

11. Ibid., 47.

12. Ibid., 47–48.

13. Ibid., 48.

14. Ibid., 50.

15. Hannan, *Nine Faces of God*, 39.

16. For further consultation in the matter of Tai Chi, I recommend Sophia Delza, *Tai Chi Chuan: Body and Mind in Harmony* (Albany: State University of New York Press, 1985). This volume contains the full set of movements for the Wu style of Tai Chi. It also has excellent articles on the history and principles of Tai Chi.

17. See Palmer, *Enneagram in Love and Work*, 36–37.

18. Ibid., 37.

19. See ibid., 37 and 38.

Select Bibliography

- An introduction to the enneagram:
  Richard Rohr and Andreas Ebert, *Discovering the Enneagram* (New York: Crossroad, 1990)

- A more advanced presentation of the enneagram:
  Helen Palmer, *The Enneagram* (San Francisco: Harper and Row, (1988).

- On the enneagram and human relationships:
  Helen Palmer, *The Enneagram in Love and Work* (San Francisco: Harper, 1995).

- On the enneagram and Jungian psychology:
  Margaret Frings Keyes, *Emotions and the Enneagram* (Muir Beach, Calif.: Molysdatur Publications, 1990).

- On the broad spectrum of the various fields in which the enneagram can have influence:
  A. G. E. Blake, *The Intelligent Enneagram* (Boston: Shambhala, 1996).

- On the enneagram and Christian spirituality:
  Suzanne Zuercher, *Enneagram Spirituality* (Notre Dame, Ind.: Ave Maria Press, 1992).

- On the enneagram and biography:
  Suzanne Zuercher, *Merton: An Enneagram Profile* (Notre Dame, Ind.: Ave Maria Press, 1996).